Culture and Life

ESSAYS IN MEMORY OF
CLYDE KLUCKHOHN

Edited by

Walter W. Taylor
John L. Fischer
Evon Z. Vogt

SOUTHERN ILLINOIS UNIVERSITY PRESS
Carbondale and Edwardsville

Feffer & Simons, Inc.
London and Amsterdam

Library of Congress Cataloging in Publication Data

Main entry under title:

Culture and life.

    CONTENTS: Taylor, W. W. Clyde Kluckhohn and American archaeology.—
Parsons, T. Clyde Kluckhohn and the integration of social science.—Inkeles, A.
Clyde Kluckhohn's contribution to studies of Russia and the Soviet Union. [etc.]

    1. Kluckhohn, Clyde, 1905–1960. 2. Ethnology—Addresses, essays, lectures.
I. Kluckhohn, Clyde, 1905–1960. II. Taylor, Walter Willard, ed. III. Fischer,
John L., ed. IV. Vogt, Evon Zartman, 1918–   ed.

GN21.K54C84   301.2   70–188702

ISBN 0–8093–0582–8

Contents

Foreword

As a person, Clyde Kluckhohn was a man of extraordinary magnetism and charm who had a profound influence upon those who came in personal contact with him: colleagues, students, academic and government officials, Navaho Indians, and countless others in many walks of life in many countries of the world. On his death, the sentiment spontaneously arose among a number of these friends that a volume should be prepared commemorating his work and illuminating its significance for the development of social science. An exploratory organizational meeting was held in Chicago in November of 1960 at the time of the annual meetings of the American Anthropological Association. The present volume is the long-delayed result of that meeting and the personal feelings expressed there.

Many persons were involved in the early stages of planning, and it would be extravagant, if not impossible, to name them all here. But special recognition and thanks are due to Professor Iwao Ishino of Michigan State University for his original initiative and valuable ideas in regard to the project; it is indeed unfortunate that, because of personal reasons, he has been unable to contribute to this volume.

From the beginning, it was felt that a general call for papers from all of Kluckhohn's many associates would result in a large, unwieldy, and inevitably redundant collection with no assurance of appropriateness or even of pertinency. Therefore, it was early decided that contributions should be by invitation and that invitees would be most suitably selected from among Kluckhohn's students currently working in areas representative of his many and varied interests. Evon Z. Vogt, as Kluckhohn's closest colleague in anthropology at Harvard, undertook to solicit chapters evaluating Kluckhohn's scholarly work on a number of topics considered to be of most concern to him throughout his career as a practicing social scientist. With the assistance of Professors J. O. Brew and Talcott Parsons, both of whom had been closely associated with Kluckhohn at Harvard, Vogt chose specialists from a restricted list consisting of people who had studied extensively and directly under Kluckhohn. Many of the assignments, however, proved much more difficult than had been anticipated, and some authors repeatedly requested postponements of deadlines, while not a few eventually gave up the task entirely and advised the editors to find someone else to write their chapters. As presently constituted, therefore, the list of contributors includes several persons who were colleagues but never students of Kluckhohn's. About 1965, it became apparent that the contributors, in addition to their topical areas of assignment, needed some central, basic, "living" theme around which to orient and point up their discussions. It was John L. Fischer who suggested that this theme be "patterning in culture," one of Kluck-hohn's major interests in anthropological studies. In accepting this proposal, Vogt prevailed upon Fischer to become coeditor of the volume. At a later time, in 1970, because of editorial and logistic problems having to do with the actual production and publication of the volume, Walter W. Taylor was installed as senior editor and has been responsible for putting the manuscripts and the volume itself into final form.

But despite the revived impetus imparted by the new theme of "patterning in culture," the difficulties encountered in writing certain chapters still continued. In fact, some chapters have never been received and probably have never even been written, at least in forms satisfactory to the authors; for example, it has been impossible to obtain a suitable paper on Kluckhohn's concern with physical anthropology, and several distinguished scholars have given up the attempt to produce a chapter in the area of culture-and-personality. Furthermore, in several fields it has apparently been impossible to write, at worthwhile length, about any substantive contributions which Kluckhohn made, and the authors have resorted to an analysis of biographical material in order to define the significance and influence which, it seems to be agreed, he actually did have. We, the editors, believe these problems of authorship reflected in the published texts and in the only too glaring lacunae are indeed significant, and im-

portantly so. In their way, they are inestimable aids to an understanding of Clyde Kluckhohn and are, furthermore, insightful into what
we may term the "cultural anthropology" of a segment of American
scholarly life. We believe that, carefully examined and analyzed, they
provide unique and peculiarly valuable illumination of the status and
impact of a complex and outstanding figure in a complex and increasingly important field of American social science.

Perhaps a word should be said about the title *Culture and Life*.
This was not the first one chosen. Rather, it corresponds to the dichotomy into which the first chapters to be received were discovered to
fall. In other words, gradually but early it became apparent to the
editors that, when considering Kluckhohn's work in specific areas,
the various authors, independently but with remarkable unanimity,
found it easiest to write about Kluckhohn's contributions to the concept and theory of culture and the practical application of cultural
theory to problems of modern life. These topics were most central to
his interests in whatever substantive field he might work. Thus his
studies of values, his work with government agencies dealing with
Indians, his wartime involvement in Washington, his organization of
the Russian Research Center at Harvard all fall into place as parts of
a surprisingly integrated whole concerned with culture and life. We
believe that, had his own life been spared a few more years, his continued efforts would have followed ever more intensively just such
lines. The meaning and dynamics of culture as they impinge upon
human life today were, and would have been the more as time went
on, a major if not *the* major force in Clyde Kluckhohn's work.

Walter W. Taylor
John L. Fischer
Evon Z. Vogt

March 1972

The Contributors

DAVID F. ABERLE is Professor of Anthropology at the University of British Columbia. As an undergraduate at Harvard University, he studied under Kluckhohn and later, while a graduate student at Columbia University, returned to the Department of Social Relations at Harvard, where he studied and taught and again came in contact with Kluckhohn. He was also associated with Kluckhohn in connection with fieldwork among the Ramah Navaho and during World War II when Kluckhohn brought him to Washington to work on Japanese radio propaganda.

JOHN ADAIR is Professor of Anthropology at San Francisco State College. He was field assistant to Kluckhohn at the beginning of the Ramah Navaho Project but never studied with him in an academic situation. During other fieldwork in the Southwest, particularly that upon Navaho and Pueblo silversmithing and on Navaho and Zuni veterans, Kluckhohn was advisor and active supporter.

MUNRO S. EDMONSON is Professor of Anthropology at Tulane University. As a major in the Area of Social Sciences at Harvard University, he was in one of Kluckhohn's tutorial groups, later taking courses, doing fieldwork for the Comparative Study of Values Project, and writing his doctoral dissertation under him at Harvard.

JOHN L. FISCHER is Professor of Anthropology at Tulane University. At Harvard University, he took both undergraduate and graduate courses from Kluckhohn, who was also director of his Bachelor's honors thesis and advised him during the writing of his doctoral dissertation.

ALEX INKELES is Margaret Jacks Professor of Sociology and Education at Stanford University. He was closely associated with Kluckhohn at Harvard University, both in the Department of Social Relations and in the Russian Research Center. He is coauthor with Kluckhohn of *Strategic,*

Psychological, and Sociological Strength and Vulnerabilities of the Soviet Social System (Kluckhohn et al. 1954s) and of *How the Soviet System Works* (Bauer et al. 1956).

LOUISE LAMPHERE is Assistant Professor of Anthropology at Brown University. She took her doctorate from the Department of Social Relations at Harvard University, studying there after Kluckhohn's death; she can be said to be a "second generation Kluckhohnian," being a student of his students (Aberle and Vogt). Her fieldwork has been among the Navaho, and at Ramah she has worked with many of Kluckhohn's informants with the specific purpose of complementing and filling out his ethnographic work, particularly in the areas of kinship and social organization.

TALCOTT PARSONS is Professor of Sociology at Harvard University. As is detailed in his contribution to this volume, he was closely associated with Kluckhohn there, particularly in the first, developmental years of the Department of Social Relations. He is coauthor with Kluckhohn of *Toward a Common Language for the Area of Social Science* (Parsons et al. 1941) and "Some Fundamental Categories in the Theory of Action" (Parsons et al. 1951).

ROBERT N. RAPOPORT is Director of the Institute of Family and Environmental Research, London, and a senior staff member of the Tavistock Institute of Human Relations. As a graduate student at the University of Chicago, he did fieldwork among the Ramah Navaho and first came in contact with Kluckhohn there. He took his doctorate at Harvard University, writing his dissertation under Kluckhohn on the basis of further fieldwork at Ramah.

WALTER W. TAYLOR is Professor of Anthropology at Southern Illinois University. He had courses from Kluckhohn while a graduate student at Harvard University, where also Kluckhohn was a member of his doctoral committee.

EVON Z. VOGT is Professor of Anthropology at Harvard University. Through family connections at Ramah, New Mexico, as one of the early participants in the Ramah Navaho studies, as a director of the Comparative Study of Values Project, and as a fellow faculty member at Harvard, he had a long and close association with Kluckhohn. He is coauthor with Kluckhohn of *Navaho Means People* (McCombe et al. 1951) and of "The Son of Many Beads, 1866–1954" (Kluckhohn and Vogt 1955n).

Acknowledgments

John Adair is indebted to Florence Kluckhohn (now Mrs. George E. Taylor) and to Richard Kluckhohn and his wife Lucy for extending to him the privilege of reading the papers and files of correspondence between Clyde Kluckhohn and those to whom he wrote concerning Indian administration. Thanks are also due to Sophie Aberle, John Collier, Glenn Emmons, David De Harport, Alexander Lesser, and Walter Olson for their gracious letters in answer to the author's queries, and to Norman Littell and J. Lee Correll for their assistance in the preparation of the material on the Navaho tribal land claim. The author is grateful to Laura Thompson for reading the manuscript and for additions she made to the text.

Munro S. Edmonson expresses deep appreciation to his colleague John L. Fischer for an extremely helpful critique of an early draft of his paper.

Louise Lamphere would like to thank Grace Harris and Allan Hoben for their valuable comments and criticisms on various drafts of this article. She is also grateful to Gerald Williams for his careful attention to the linguistic details of the paper and his suggestions concerning the re-analysis of Navaho ceremonial terminology.

Walter W. Taylor wishes to acknowledge his enduring gratitude to Barbara A. Peckham (Mrs. Stewart Peckham) for her contributions to the preparation of this volume and for her unfailing good nature and willingness during a job that was not all that rewarding.

INTRODUCTION

John L. Fischer
Evon Z. Vogt

CLYDE KLUCKHOHN, professor of anthropology at Harvard University, died suddenly on July 29, 1960, in Santa Fe, New Mexico, at the age of fifty-five, after suffering a heart attack. This loss was especially tragic in that Kluckhohn had just concluded a period of intense administrative activity, had resigned from the chairmanship of the Department of Anthropology at Harvard and from other administrative positions, and was preparing to take a sabbatical year during which he planned to catch up on his reading and writing. It is likely that the work of that year would have been among his most important.

Born in Le Mars, Iowa, on January 11, 1905, Clyde Kay Maben was adopted by Katherine and George Wesley Kluckhohn. His real mother had died shortly after Clyde's birth, and he was adopted by his mother's brother to relieve his father of the burden of coping with an infant son.

Clyde Kluckhohn spent his early years in Le Mars and then prepared for college at the Lawrenceville School in New Jersey. He began his undergraduate studies at Princeton University in the fall of 1922. Ill health interrupted his studies, and an experience followed which had a profound effect on his later career. His family sent him to the Vogt Ranch, near Ramah, New Mexico, to

1

live with his adopted mother's cousins, Shirley and Evon Zartman Vogt, Sr. The nearest neighbors were Navaho Indians, and young Kluckhohn developed an immediate interest in the Navahos. He began to learn to speak Navaho and to understand their customs. He obviously had from this early age both a persistent curiosity about exotic customs and a deep sensitivity to the nuances of alien ways of life—two qualities essential for an anthropologist. He fell in love with the Southwest and its peoples, undertook a long pack trip to the Rainbow Bridge in southern Utah, and published his first book, *To the Foot of the Rainbow* (1927), when he was only twenty-two years old.

He returned to undergraduate work by enrolling at the University of Wisconsin, where he took his A.B. in 1928. In 1931–32, he studied at the University of Vienna, where he had experience with psychoanalysis, and at Oxford, where he read anthropology with R. R. Marrett as a Rhodes Scholar in 1932. In 1932, Clyde Kluckhohn married Florence Rockwood, whom he had known as a fellow student at Wisconsin, and their only child, Richard Paul Rockwood Kluckhohn, was born in 1934. From 1932 to 1934, he served as assistant professor of anthropology at the University of New Mexico. He completed his Ph.D. in anthropology at Harvard in 1936. During this decade he kept in close touch with the Navahos, making a number of pack trips to completely unexplored country on Wild Horse Mesa in southern Utah and writing his second book, *Beyond the Rainbow* (1933a), about these experiences. In 1935, Kluckhohn was appointed an instructor in anthropology at Harvard, and the rest of his academic career was spent there, where he rose to full professorship and became a stimulating teacher for several academic generations of students who have since gone on to distinguished careers in the United States and abroad.

Through all these years he seldom passed up an opportunity to visit the Southwest for fieldwork with the Navahos, for it was there among the beautiful red sandstone mesas and canyons that he was most relaxed and that his most creative intellectual work was done. Traveling on horseback or in various models of old station wagons or jeeps, he became a familiar figure as he led his many devoted students through the pinyon and juniper trees in pursuit of elusive Navaho informants or lived for weeks at a time in Navaho hogans. He took great pride in his ability to speak fluent Navaho—an extremely difficult language for a person from an Indo-European language background to learn—and in the close rapport he developed with literally hundreds of Navahos, who knew him affectionately as "Hasteen Clyde." At times he seemed to regard this close relationship to the Indians as a mark of greater accomplishment than his promotion to full professor or his election to the National Academy of Sciences. From these Navaho studies have come a number of classic monographs as well as his more popular books, *The Navaho* (Kluckhohn and Leighton 1946a), *Children of the People* (Leighton and Kluckhohn 1947), *Navaho Means People* (McCombe et al. 1951), and a large number of articles in specialized journals.

Kluckhohn's Navaho research was characterized by painstaking attention to ethnographic detail, combined with sophisticated theoretical analysis. He was clearly one of the most gifted fieldworkers in anthropology, and his continuing relationships with the Navahos permitted an understanding of their intricate patterns of life, such as is impossible in fieldwork that extends over only a few seasons of investigation. He was also a voracious reader in several languages and was able to keep abreast of current developments not only in anthropology in the United States and abroad, but also with relevant trends of thought in sociology, psychology, and philosophy. This scholarly sophistication was applied to the analysis of his Navaho data.

Between 1936 and 1948, Kluckhohn served as director of the "Ramah Project," which involved some fifteen graduate students and colleagues from Harvard and elsewhere. The project's goal was to make a long-range, intensive study of the Ramah Navaho in order to describe very precisely the patterns of Navaho culture and to analyze the processes of culture change. In his introduction to the Leightons' monograph, *Gregorio, the Hand-Trembler*, Kluckhohn wrote of his Ramah Project:

The original plan was to spend two summers (with assistance from graduate students) doing the ethnography of the group as a background for the child study. Advisors assured me that Navaho culture was already well known and that it was merely necessary to describe local variations at Ramah together with the Ramah situation. It was also pointed out that no Navaho local group had been described. In 1938 I completed the first draft of an ethnography. However, when we checked it during the 1938 field season I got a sense that we had not yet mastered the basic patterns, let alone the cultural dynamics. It was resolved, therefore, to continue ethnographic investigation simultaneously with the research upon the children. Gradually there emerged the notion that the following of a small community and its culture through time was a needed experiment in anthropology. It seemed plausible that the lack of a time dimension was primarily responsible for the flat, one-dimensional quality which acute and sensitive scholars from other disciplines had noted in even the best of anthropological monographs. In 1939 a long correspondence with Professor Donald Scott, Director Emeritus of the Peabody Museum of Harvard University, clarified my thinking. Mr. Scott stressed the significance of "continuous observation of the same persons in the same environment." He suggested that "if biologists have found it profitable to spend their lives following the events in colonies of *paramecia*, it is likely that the science of man would be rewarded by intensive, longitudinal observations of a single community. [1949j:v]

In 1949, Kluckhohn extended the Ramah fieldwork when he became the founder and member of the advisory board (along with J. O. Brew and Talcott Parsons) of the "Comparative Study of Values in Five Cultures Project," which undertook far-ranging field investigations among the Navaho, Zuni, Spanish-American, Mormon, and Texan communities located in the Ramah area. This project, sponsored by the Laboratory of Social Relations and the Peabody Museum at Harvard, financed by a six-year grant (1949–55) from the Rockefeller Foundation and directed by John M. Roberts and Evon Z. Vogt, involved thirty-seven fieldworkers from a variety of the behavioral sciences and produced a large number of theoretical and empirical monographs and papers on the five cultures under investigation (see Vogt and Albert, *People of Rimrock*, 1966).

Clyde Kluckhohn was remarkable for the time, energy, and skills he put into administrative and consulting work that extended far beyond the narrow field of anthropology. Within the academic world, his most notable administrative achievement was the major role he played in the organization of the Russian Research Center at Harvard, for which he served as director from 1947 to 1954. He was also one of the founders of the Department of Social Relations at Harvard in 1946.

In addition, he was active in key positions in governmental circles in Washington and beyond. During World War II, he served as staff member, School for Overseas Administration, 1943–44; cochief, Joint Morale Survey (Military Intelligence Service and Office of War Information), 1944–45; expert consultant to the secretary of war (attached to General MacArthur's headquarters), 1946–47. After the war, he continued to serve in important posts for the government, including consultant, Research and Development Board, Department of Defense, 1948–54; consultant, Office of Indian Affairs, Department of the Interior, 1942–60; and member, Advisory Committee, Foreign Service Institute, Department of State, 1956–60. At the time of his death, he was devoting an immense amount of time to the Navaho Tribal Council's land claims case as an expert consultant. Perhaps more than any other anthropologist of this century, Clyde Kluckhohn carried this heavy administrative and consulting load with superb skill and balanced, penetrating judgment and at the same time continued to do frontline research and to publish prodigiously.

Honors bestowed on Professor Kluckhohn included the degree of L.H.D. from the University of New Mexico (1949) and the Viking Fund Medal for General Anthropology (1950). He was a member of the National Academy of Sciences, the American Philosophical Society, the American Academy of Arts and Sciences, the American Anthropological Association, of which he served as president in 1948, and the American Association for the Advancement of Science, of which he served as vice-president (Section H) in 1950. He was also an Honorary Fellow of the Royal Anthropological Institute of Great Britain and Ireland and a Fellow at the Center for Advanced Study in the Behavioral Sciences in 1954–55.

The unfortunate delay in the production of this volume, from its inception in 1960 to the present date, has not been without certain compensations. While we deeply regret this lag, the added

time has provided opportunity to see more clearly where Kluckhohn's greatest intellectual contributions lie. We now feel more
than ever that these center on the development of the theory of
culture and its applications to problems of contemporary life.
Specifically, Kluckhohn was concerned with such questions as the
tendency of cultures to become integrated around a set of central
values, the tension between the individual and his culture, the
tension between universal human values and the values of specific
cultures, the conservatism or inertia of culture, the discovery of
the covert or implicit aspects of culture, the use of linguistic theory
as a model for general cultural theory.

Kluckhohn's increasing interest in culture as the central concept of anthropology deserves some stress, especially for those
who are not themselves anthropologists and for those anthropologists who claim a primary interest in social structure. While anthropology is often classed with the behavioral sciences, the main
concern of the discipline in Kluckhohn's view was culture, not
behavior as such. Culture he regarded as socially shared "patterns
for and of behavior," a phrase he was fond of using. These patterns
would be manifested in overt behavior at times, but they could also
be present as information in other forms: as learning in the neural
systems of participants in the cultures, as writing in books in
literate cultures, and more ephemerally as speech in all cultures,
and to some extent in the artifacts and man-modified environment
in which behavior takes place.

Kluckhohn recognized clearly that factors other than culture
affected the concrete behavior of individuals. Indeed, his participation in the founding of the Harvard Department of Social Relations
bears witness to his interest in developing a general science of
human behavior. But it may have been in part his association with
representatives of other social sciences in the Department of Social
Relations, which more and more led him by contrast to emphasize
the study of culture as the particular contribution of anthropology
and to lay special stress on the behavior of individuals which most
clearly and directly typified their culture with little interference
from idiosyncratic or social pressures. And so Kluckhohn was not
ready to limit anthropology to the science of culture, narrowly

conceived. Two of his major heroes, Franz Boas and A. L. Kroeber, were general anthropologists who had made contributions in physical anthropology, linguistics, material culture, folklore, as well as in other fields. Physical anthropology, at any rate, is not primarily a cultural science, and linguistics is a rather specialized and autonomous branch of cultural science. A third major hero, Edward Sapir, was first and foremost a linguist.

While Kluckhohn tended to see other branches of anthropology in terms of effects from or on culture and was fascinated with the search for meaning and consistency in culture, he was more aware than many cultural anthropologists of the limitations of the concept of culture as the sole explanation of all human behavior. He saw deviance as a source of culture change and saw biological and material factors as sources of deviance. In spite of his reiteration of the importance of the concept of culture and of anthropologists as the interpreters of culture, Kluckhohn retained a certain reserve about the human value of many specific items of culture as well as about certain whole culture patterns. Like most anthropologists, Kluckhohn was widely tolerant of diverse cultural arrangements. He strongly admired Ruth Benedict's work and on the whole supported her advocacy of the cultural relativity of values. At the same time, on this issue as on many others, Kluckhohn avoided sticking to any single oversimplified position. He recognized that if cultures provided values for people, individuals at times could also oppose any of these values because of their idiosyncratic experience or biologically based temperament. His own personal life was sufficiently unconventional in some respects, so that he could hardly advocate the position of some anthropologists who see culture as the sole source and ultimate judge of values. He was not greatly disturbed by a mere act of deviance from cultural norms as long as it did not involve serious, unprovoked aggression. One of the values of American culture and, even more, of Navaho culture, of which he most strongly approved, was respect for individuality. This has certainly to be regarded as a rather paradoxical cultural value or perhaps even as an antivalue. Individuality carried to the extreme would seem to imply that each individual should magnify anything which sets him off from anyone else. This would lead to the breakdown of cultural values, characterized, as they are, by the presence of some kind of group consensus behind them. But Kluckhohn valued life more than culture, fascinated though he was with culture. Life he regarded as essentially disorderly and chaotic. Culture involved order imposed on life and, for the human species, was necessary for life to continue. But Kluckhohn was not a naïve functionalist, especially in his later years. He conceived of culture as being at times functional for life but often enough going off on internally or socially determined tangents which were in opposition to life. It was clear enough to him that not all individuals are made healthy and happy by their cultures, that in the long run not all societies are insured growth or survival by their cultures, and that successful societies do not indefinitely preserve their cultures intact but must change them.

Kluckhohn's advocacy of cultural relativity did not prevent him from personally evaluating the cultures which he studied or with which he came in contact. It is clear from personal remarks, for instance, that he admired the freedom of classical Greek civilization and strongly preferred U.S. culture to Russian on the grounds of greater tolerance and individual freedom. Likewise among Southwest Indians, he preferred Navaho culture to Zuni and other Pueblo cultures on similar grounds. It is not clear how much he attempted to understand the current differences between these cultures in terms of ecology and history: Would it make sense, for instance, to have Navaho individualism (developed historically among a group of wandering hunters and sheepherders) in a densely settled, agricultural Pueblo village? For one fond of life and chaos, it seems a little surprising that Kluckhohn expressed a great fondness for Japanese culture, which is notable for its extreme orderliness. Apparently Kluckhohn felt that a culture achieved satisfactory balance with individualism by being complex enough, so that a determined individual could with a little search find the proper circumstances for whatever he wanted to do.

It is popular nowadays to say that culture is always changing or that change is of the essence of culture. We suggest that Kluckhohn's view of culture was the opposite of this: that stability is of the essence of culture while change is of the essence of life.

The concept of culture as a community consensus implies at least that culture is much more stable than individual personality. If one man changes his mind about a customary practice or belief, this hardly affects the community consensus, and he himself is likely to know that the consensus is unchanged and that he is a deviant.

In his work on values, Clyde Kluckhohn paid little attention to the conception of alternative value orientations as a substitute for the concept of deviance. Florence Kluckhohn had developed this conception in part to handle cultural change: How and when does a society suddenly leap from one set of values to another? Obviously, a substantial number of individuals in any society does not give full adherence to all the dominant values and, where dominant values change, they generally do so gradually rather than by some formal vote or proclamation. Nevertheless, Clyde Kluckhohn saw fit to limit himself to considering only dominant values in his last articles on the subject. This was probably because he was developing the notion of a continuum between cultural and idiosyncratic behavior: The most cultural behavior is the behavior which meets the widest agreement, and ideally it and its interpretation or meaning should be uniform throughout the community. If there are several fairly common alternatives, the alternative which is the most cultural is the one which has the majority or plurality of adherents.

We touch here upon Kluckhohn's attitude toward binary opposition and multivalued logic. There was a period before World War II when Kluckhohn was greatly interested in semantics, including the work of Ogden and Richards, Alfred Korzybski, and Korzybski's followers. One of the main points of the general semantics school was that reality, i.e., life experience, is more complex than the linguistic forms which we use to talk about it, that language tends to make us think in "either-or" terms, in terms of binary or Aristotelian logic, when more often we should be thinking in terms of a multivalued logic to approximate reality more closely. Kluckhohn related this point to the language-and-culture views of Whorf and Sapir, both of whom he knew personally and greatly admired. Different languages, Kluckhohn would say, "sliced up" reality in different ways. Language itself was a crucial and pervasive part of culture; so it would be fair to say that different cultures simplified the chaotic flux of experience in different ways.

Nevertheless, at a somewhat later point Kluckhohn became fascinated with the usefulness of binary oppositions in linguistic and mythological analysis as practiced by Roman Jakobson and Claude Lévi-Strauss, among others. It might be thought that this later interest in binary logic contradicted his earlier interest in the multivalued logic of the general semanticists, but perhaps it did not necessarily. His conclusion, which is perhaps only implied but implied quite definitely, seems to have been that the most accurate reflection of reality requires a multivalued logic with infinitely divisible scales between opposites but that for all human beings it was easier to operate with a binary logic, that in many situations this was sufficient for action: What one mainly needs to know is whether or not a threshold has been reached. For instance, when boiling an egg one normally asks merely, "Is the water boiling yet, or not?" It is possible to measure the temperature of the water on a continuous scale, but for purposes of action a more precise measurement is irrelevant. We suggest that Kluckhohn saw at least two virtues in the application of binary logic to cultural materials. First, it provided a standard method of analyzing and comparing different cultures. Second, it implied a generalization about the operation of human culture and probably the human nervous system as well.

Kluckhohn was greatly concerned with establishing the scientific claims of anthropology. He did not want to claim that anthropology was nothing but a science, but he did believe that anthropology had a scientific aspect which required development. He believed in statistical handling of data as an aid in the establishment of objective and responsible generalizations in cultural description but, since anthropology was the science of culture and not of behavior alone, he did not give the same weight to the counting of acts or responses of subjects as would many sociologists, social psychologists, or political scientists. He was excited by the use of statistical tests of cross-cultural generalizations as exemplified by Murdock, but he stressed that scientific rigor for anthropology would be achieved most importantly to the extent to which a logical analysis of cultural materials became possible.

As we have noted above, Kluckhohn was impressed with the principle of binary logic and was not an extreme cultural relativist. If anthropology were indeed the science of culture, it should be able to make generalizations valid for all cultures, not limit itself to a cataloguing of unique details. Linguistics, Kluckhohn thought, had begun to achieve such generalizations. Roman Jakobson exemplified this in his assertion that the phonemic system of any known language could be described in terms of a relatively small number of binary variables whose values constituted the phonetically distinctive features of the phonemes. Linguistics also constituted an example of rigorous logical analysis without recourse to statistics, providing a model of what cultural analysis generally should aspire to. Since Kluckhohn's death, there has been a vigorous development of a rigorous sociolinguistics making sophisticated use of statistics, e.g., the work of William Labov. However, there still remain many "proper" linguists whose primary interest is the grammatical analysis of the idiolect of a representative speaker in a standard situation. The problems in this latter kind of study are complex and have by no means been fully solved yet. The work of Noam Chomsky and his colleagues at the Massachusetts Institute of Technology exemplifies this kind of work in its concern with linguistic competence rather than performance. Kluckhohn's emphasis on culture rather than behavior as the proper subject of study for the anthropologist parallels the Chomskyan emphasis on linguistic competence.

While Kluckhohn advocated the development of rigorous methods in anthropology, especially in the analysis of cultural data, he felt that relatively little had been accomplished along these lines so far and that anthropologists had other important tasks to do. The most important task of anthropology was the naturalistic observation of culture, the recording of enough detail over a long period of time to identify the central trends of the culture in question and to have adequate data for eventual formulation and testing of cultural hypotheses. In the collection of data, Kluckhohn emphasized the primacy of rapport with a few selected informants over extensive methods of survey using questionnaires or standard interviews. In this respect, Kluckhohn felt that anthropology had closer ties with psychiatry and clinical psychology than with other more statistically oriented social sciences.

Kluckhohn specifically encouraged his students to write down hunches and impressions as part of their field notes, even when they could not document them with observations. Like a clinician, he did not want to exclude any material which might later provide some key to interpretation. Field notes he regarded as sacred: "Never destroy your original field notes" was a repeated warning; retyping could introduce error which might later be challenged.

Kluckhohn was concerned with his own personal relationships with his informants as a possible source of distortion in his data and stressed the need for anthropological investigators to understand themselves and their biases which might affect their reporting of data. He felt it was important for the cultural anthropologist to know something of psychiatry and preferably to undergo psychoanalysis himself. This was to help him improve his understanding of the informant-ethnographer relationship and to help him to become aware of his personal reasons for asking certain questions, avoiding others, jumping to quick conclusions on some points, and delaying decisions on others. Ideally, in the publication of an ethnography, the ethnographer should identify his goals, prejudices, and biases so that the reader could take these into account in evaluating the data reported.

These precautions with the recording of ethnographic data may seem extreme to many of us, but they are undoubtedly addressed to real and serious problems which are raised when human beings study other human beings. Kluckhohn saw that long field research was not in itself a sufficient answer to the problems of bias, although desirable on other grounds. The successful anthropologist in long stretches of fieldwork tends to shed some of his own values, but this is likely to involve taking on the values of the people whom he is studying and with whom he is living. Early field notes may therefore contain a clearer statement of certain flaws in a culture than later ones, after the anthropologist has become acculturated.

In this introduction, we have tried to cover some of Clyde Kluckhohn's views which are not so apparent in his published writings but which have influenced various of his students and colleagues. This has been a difficult task, since one of Kluckhohn's characteristics as a teacher was to try to get students to develop their own views and to avoid smothering them with his views before they had time to think things through themselves. Perhaps there was also some concern with the student reaction to his opinions, some of which were currently unpopular; and very probably he considered it well to avoid asserting unpopular views on topics where he was not expert. Nevertheless, one of Kluckhohn's greatest accomplishments was his teaching. We will consider this volume an appropriate memorial if it conveys something of Kluckhohn's passionate conviction that the study of man is a most exciting and important activity for men to engage in and that it is to be advanced by tact, engagement, and hard work.

CLYDE KLUCKHOHN
AND AMERICAN ARCHAEOLOGY

Walter W. Taylor

OW does one analyze a friend? How does one reduce a radical? How is it possible to specify the influence of a person with whom one has passed hundreds of informal hours in the exercise of mind and in the unrecorded interchange of fact and fancy? How do I make "an appraisal of Clyde Kluckhohn's contributions and influence in American archaeology" or even of his influence upon myself? And if not upon myself, then how to gauge his mark upon the others?

I have tried the obvious: detailed analysis of publications, interrogation of a considerable number of professional archaeologists who studied and took their doctorates at Harvard between 1936 and 1960 (twenty-two in all, from whom twelve responses were received), and a good deal of personal introspection. The results have not been negative, but the nature of Kluckhohn's influence and the ways in which he impressed himself upon American archaeology are by no means obvious or easily defined. In fact, the conclusions which I have been more or less forced to accept may come as something of a surprise. They certainly did to me. However, I believe them to be true in essence and to be significant, not only for an appraisal of Clyde Kluckhohn's role in archaeology, but also revealing of the implications and potentialities of the teacher-pupil or, more accurately perhaps, the tutor-friend relationship which is sometimes possible in American academic and scholarly situations.

But above all and in view of his own anthropological interests, one discovery stands clear and apt: the very obvious patterning that obtained in Clyde Kluckhohn's behavior vis-à-vis both students and colleagues and the effect which cultural context had upon that patterned behavior. What I shall have to say will reveal certain facets of "the anthropology of anthropology," certain insights into the culture of anthropology, which, it seems to me, would have appealed to his sometimes wry sense of propriety and which certainly coincide with one of the anthropological emphases around which Kluckhohn's own work was oriented.

Only superficial analysis is necessary to show that the contributions of Kluckhohn's strictly archaeological publications do not fully, or even closely, account for the influence which he seems actually to have had—or which he has been credited with having. In the first place they are very few, numbering (aside from reviews and obituaries of archaeologists) only four, and only one of these of any length: "A Note on the Sources of the Drawings in the Del Rio Volume on Palenque" (1935a), his part of the report on the excavations of Bc 50–51 in Chaco Canyon (Kluckhohn and Reiter 1939a), "The Conceptual Structure in Middle American Studies" (1940c), and a very small part (approximately seven of its thirty-two pages) of the chapter "Potsherds" in *Mirror for Man* (1949a). In the second place, two of them (the Del Rio paper and "Potsherds") seem to have had little or no impact upon professionals and will not be dealt with here. Thus, only the remaining two, the Chaco report and the Maya paper, may be considered influential —but perhaps not in the way many anthropologists have come to believe.

My own analysis of the Chaco report leads me to conclude that in it Kluckhohn left an important archaeological legacy. But it seems to me that much of this bequest has been misunderstood and relatively little of it has been intellectually banked and made to pay interest to American archaeology. He himself declares its purpose to be: (1) the supplement to an earlier publication, i.e., Brand et al. 1937, and (2) the making and interpretation of distribution studies of archaeological objects not usually so studied. In the latter regard, he expresses the hope that, when others have done the same for other materials, Southwestern archaeologists might "be better able to guard against the dangers of inference from a limited number of criteria . . . and thus to reveal far more securely and distinctly the cultural history of the Southwest and the processual dynamics of that history" (Kluckhohn and Reiter 1939a:9). With aims so clearly stated, it is ironic that the report has largely been viewed by American archaeologists as a critique: For example, Woodbury says that the most "important contribution" of this report is the "Discussion," i.e., the critical section (1961:408). What I consider to be the equally, if not more, important contributions of other sections have been all but completely ignored: the distribution studies, his analysis of the cultural and chronological position of Bc 50–51 as a substantive problem, his innovative techniques such as weighing potsherds instead of counting them and the use of "wall sherds" as close-dating criteria, the use of chi-square tests, the use of pottery complexes rather than single types for relative dating. It is perhaps expectable that a chapter, given to critical evaluation which ruffles the waters of the archaeological pond, will be more often singled out for remark than other chapters that treat of less titillating subjects. But I believe it is certainly a depreciation of Kluckhohn's real contribution that his suggestions in regard to theory and method have not been more fully examined (and embraced) by American archaeology. I believe it is even more so that his goals of writing better cultural history and investigating processual dynamics have, until recently, been accepted so little in our discipline.

It has also been said that Kluckhohn's critique of the Pecos Classification "stimulated many archaeologists to examine more carefully the bases on which their chronological schemes were built" (Woodbury 1961:408). This statement sounds as if Kluckhohn found fault with the Pecos Classification on the grounds of some chronological shortcoming. A careful reading of his words will show that this was not the principle of his complaint. He himself was aware that the Pecos Classification originally had no temporal connotation (Kluckhohn and Reiter 1939a:153); he specifically says: "the real difficulty is that the [cultural and chronological] criteria are not used consistently" (1939a:153). In other words, his stated intent was not to expose the dubiousness of any chronological scheme, but to dispel the inconsistency in the definition and use of categorical referents within the Pecos Classification. He reinforces this position when he says,

Probably the single fact of greatest general import which has emerged thus far from the Bc 50–51 excavations is that the various [cultural] stages recognized by the Pecos Classification (and very commonly referred to as "periods") do not, necessarily, represent separate and clear-cut time periods, *even in the same geographical locality.* [1939a:159]

It is symptomatic of the general misapplicaton of Kluckhohn's critique that Woodbury uses this very same quotation as an example of what he (Woodbury) claims led the archaeologists to examine their chronological schemes (1961:408). The truth of the matter is that if the archaeologists, after reading the "Discussion," did indeed examine only their chronological schemes or the chronological meanings which had been tacitly tacked onto the Pecos Classification, then Kluckhohn was misunderstood, and his influence, whatever it may have been, has not followed the lines of his very explicit intent and his real contribution.

Thus, it is apparent that here Kluckhohn has not had his full potential effect nor have the implications even of his critical discussion been generally understood. Of course, I realize that I have quoted from the ideas of only one archaeologist (who, I should hasten to say, has followed Kluckhohn by publishing one of the few detailed distribution studies in Southwestern archaeology), but I have done so advisedly because I feel that he typically represents what my own experience has taught me is the case within our profession as a whole. I could be wrong. I do not think I am. In any event, I feel quite certain that we cannot look to the Chaco report to find the nature or source of Kluckhohn's influence upon American archaeology. The positive contributions are obviously there, but generally they have not taken.

Before changing the subject, one further fact may be adduced in support of this point of view: Of the twelve professional archaeologists returning answers to my questions as to Kluckhohn's influence upon them, only one mentioned the Chaco report in this regard. This person said it led him to realize that Kluckhohn, otherwise an "awesome figure," was actually interested in archaeology, a discovery which led to closer association and ultimately to lasting influence.

The Maya paper presents quite another problem. Here, there was no intention of writing a substantive work: It was explicitly stated to be "a critical review of the theoretical bases of work" in Middle American studies. But its major contribution, in my opinion, was not the criticism but the presentation of a point of view and a series of explicitly defined concepts for the handling of archaeological data: in other words, positive and constructive. In fact, his criticisms were so little documented, so little supported by specifically cited examples from the Middle American field, that they might have been written about almost any field of archaeology. It has always been my contention that the Middle American archaeologists would have been eminently justified in charging Kluckhohn with an unjustified (because unsubstantiated) assault. The fact that they did not do so in print may be more an indication of their gentlemanly but unscholarly reluctance to defend their views, than due to the weight of specified, documented evidence brought against them. Let me not be misunderstood: I agree now, and I agreed then, with the points which he raised about Middle American studies, but I cannot believe that many of his readers could (or should) have been impressed with the strength of his position. The Maya paper is a humanistic *tour de force* of theory, not a scientific critique.

For myself, I must admit I was much influenced by the Maya paper—but certainly not vis-à-vis Middle American studies: I was not substantively or substantially involved in that area. What impressed me was the manner of Kluckhohn's thinking, the utility of the theoretical concepts he defined, and his intellectual defense of my personally held view that archaeology could be more than description and taxonomy. On the other hand, I must also admit that another paper published a year earlier, "The Place of Theory in Anthropological Studies" (1939c), influenced me more because I thought it to be a better piece of work, without distracting overtones of topical polemics. As far as I am aware, this latter publication has

never aroused the emotional and partisan furor of the Maya paper—
and I believe this to be significant.

It is revealing that seven of the twelve professional archaeologists responding to my questionnaire named the Maya paper as
having had an influence upon them—and an eighth, a Mayanist, says
he was impressed by Kluckhohn's "reputation as a critic," which I
must interpret as a reference to this paper. Two said they first had
a contrabias because of this paper, one referring to the "attack on
the Carnegie Institution" and the other specifying the "criticisms of
Kidder and American archaeology generally." It seems that both of
these comments are indicative in giving first attention to the negative, critical, and personal aspects of the paper.

Of course, the truth of the matter is that Kluckhohn did not
adversely criticize Kidder. Nor did he criticize "American archaeology generally," except in two weak and passing jibes
(1940c:45,47). And his treatment of the Carnegie Institution can
not, with any justification whatsoever, be called an "attack." My
tabulation of what he actually said in the Maya paper is as follows:

	No. of Times Mentioned	Adversely	Favorably	No Value Judgments
Carnegie Inst.	4	2	–	2
A. V. Kidder	5	0	3	2
Other named individuals or institutions	11	0	6	5

From the above tabulation, it is seen that there are only two adverse
criticisms of specifically mentioned people or institutions. Both of
these concern the Carnegie Institution, but they occur in two se-
quential paragraphs on the same page, both criticize what is essentially a single failing, and both are the mildest sort of rebuke
which only a hypersensitive soul could find disturbing: in one
instance he says, "Even the Carnegie Institution's well-known and
justly praised [sic] scheme for a many-sided attack by specialists . . .
is but an extension of the received system," i.e., no questioning or
examining of premises, but merely accepting the traditional ones; in

the other, he merely says that the Carnegie staff is "predominantly preoccupied with answering questions of a factual order" (1940c:45). It is true that Kluckhohn is arguing against such an acceptance and against purely factual concern, but both of these arguments are implied criticisms, not direct: a lonely, gentle pair indeed to cause so much pother and so many hurt feelings.

To be sure, there are criticisms in the Maya paper—many of them and some harsh words. But not once are they directed at an individual and as quoted above only twice, gently, at the Carnegie Institution. They are directed specifically at "Middle American studies": he uses the phrases Middle American "students," "specialists," "field," "research," and "Maya archaeologists." But there were other archaeologists in the Maya and Middle American field besides Kidder and the Carnegie staff. If American archaeologists thought that Kluckhohn was criticizing Kidder and Carnegie, alone or even primarily, then either they had other evidence than that adduced in the Maya paper or here is a classic case of contagious misunderstanding and of "protesting too much."

To return to my questionnaire: Another two respondents say that Kluckhohn's greatest influence upon them came from the Maya paper; but they do not compare his with other possible influences, and so we do not know how great it actually was, either relatively or in the absolute. One person mentioned the influence of the "concepts of typology" in the Maya paper, but I find no discussion, and only one mention, of "typology"; this respondent may be indulging in a bit of unconscious projection—if so, I believe it to be significant. Finally, one individual seemed doubtful about any influence at all but said that an exception might be the "famous (or notorious, to some archaeologists)" Maya paper; and another said it showed him that Kluckhohn was indeed interested in archaeology, which later led to more contact and influence.

From the above analysis and discussion of Kluckhohn's two major archaeological publications, the evidence is plain that the constructive aspects of his criticisms and his positive contributions have been generally neglected and can hardly have had influence along the lines of his intent. The animosity originally aroused and the image created over the years by emotional interpretations of his words and by partisan defense against them have strongly colored succeeding judgments. The result has been that American archaeologists, especially those of more recent vintages, have been influenced by the animosity and the image to the point of failing to make their own analyses and judgments. Even among those who have more or less subscribed to his criticisms and who appreciate his positive contributions, the furor raised has tended to constrain discussion and to reduce his influence. On the other hand, among some archaeologists, there developed a realization that Kluckhohn was not really a monster of evil or a merciless trampler on the old school tie but was genuinely interested in certain aspects of their discipline. In very fortunate cases, such a realization led to understanding, appreciation, and influence.

However, if my sample of twelve respondents and my own impressions are valid criteria, this influence has not been very clearly visualized. Eight of the twelve say that they did not know him well at Harvard (or later), implying that personal impact was slight or absent; but three of these nevertheless say that he did have influence upon their archaeological work. Six say that they are "at a loss" to specify whether or not he had any influence, what it might have been, or how it might have come about; but four of these say that they felt he had been influential. Only two claim without qualification to have been influenced, but another two say that they could detect no influence whatever.

Also within these letters, two major points are mentioned with significant frequency and with surprising similarity of phrasing. Five respondents recall as one of Kluckhohn's greatest contributions to their thinking his continued insistence on the wholeness of anthropology: that one should be an anthropologist first and an ethnologist or archaeologist or linguist second. Four report that he went out of his way to encourage archaeologists: by claiming that one of his own two best *anthropological* works was the Chaco (*archaeological*) report, by saying that the archaeologists should not downgrade themselves and should recognize that their discipline is highly sophisticated and by no means simple or elementary, that archaeology could make some very important contributions to social science in general, that Alfred Tozzer (an *archaeologist*) was one of the

greatest American *anthropologists,* whose Landa volume was one of
the greatest scholarly works produced in this country, that the
archaeologists were the "only ones left" who took a total view of
anthropology. The respondents felt that this was a calculated but
sincere and honest attempt to shore up the archaeological ego in the
face of counter emphasis at Harvard and in American anthropology in general.

There are other impressions which he left upon my respondents,
such as his "intensity," his "overawing" or "awesome" reputation,
the impact of his course on current anthropological thought, and his
linking of archaeology and linguistics. It is surprising, perhaps, as
well as significant, that only one reply speaks of his "rigorous and
analytic way of thinking"; and in this regard it is also noteworthy
that one person who was very close to Kluckhohn says that he never
talked about archaeological theory, only about "general theory and
methodology." There is mention in one letter of his sophisticated,
eclectic, catholic, and flexible thought.

How then do we assess Clyde Kluckhohn's influence in the field
of American archaeology? Certainly there was one—and one that
still exists. But what is it, by what agents carried, and how did it
develop?

In the first place, I want to make it very explicit that, in trying
to answer these questions, I shall not be concerned with any
influence he may have had in his alleged role of "merciless critic"
(Woodbury 1961:407); this is a stereotype analytically shallow,
grotesquely false! What I do wish to concern myself with, however,
is his positive role and especially with the manner in which he played
this role, with his behavior so strongly and significantly patterned.

In the analysis above of his archaeological writings and the responses to my questionnaire, it has become apparent that, through
the channels of publication or in any formally academic way, his
influence seems to have been surprisingly small, not nearly enough
to account for his popular image. Therefore, in regard to these aspects, I believe that what can be said has already been said. However, for any real understanding of Clyde Kluckhohn and American
archaeology, there is more which must be said. It has become obvious
that his major influence has been broadly anthropological, not

specifically archaeological, emphasizing the unity of the discipline and the positive, integrated part to be played by archaeology. But its most significant and unique characteristic is that this influence was exerted, when it was exerted at all, almost entirely on a personal, individual-to-individual, nonformal basis. Failing this personalization, when any influence is felt, it seems to be amorphous, "difficult to define," often with major emphasis merely upon critical writings. There appears to have been little deep analysis of Kluckhohn's archaeological ideas on the parts of those who were not closely and personally associated with him—and only slightly more by those who were.

If his influence has indeed been so personalized, the question again arises: How are we to assess and understand it? I can see no other way than to recite personal and anecdotal history and then to examine its implications. Since I have no basis or justification for writing about his personal relationships with other archaeologists, I shall have to write about them with respect to myself. What I shall have to say will be highly subjective. I can hold forth little promise of conclusive, demonstrable results. I see no possibility of being objective, after the fashion of science, about a person whose role was subjectivity itself. When for years a large sphere of one's actions have, often unconsciously, been set against the touchstone of another person's approval, how can one depersonalize or objectify? How does one separate the influence from the man? The only way I think to solve this problem is to meet subjectivity head on and to embrace it without apology.

I do not remember when I first met Clyde Kluckhohn. It was sometime during 1935–36, when he came to New Haven to work with Edward Sapir. Our first correspondence is dated early in 1937, at which time a ring of familiarity is already apparent in the exchanges. Even at that time, there was an aura about him within the profession—and this was less than a year after he took his doctorate! His article on the *Kulturkreislehre* (1936a) had impressed many, depressed others, and startled not a few into the realization that here was someone to reckon with in anthropology. It had also placed him in many professional minds as an analyzer, a theorist, a critic. This image he often found burdensome and irritating, and he warned me many times against acquiring such a one, particularly when it became apparent that my ideas and specifically my doctoral dissertation were headed in that direction.

During the summer of 1938, he was at Moencopi on the Hopi reservation and several times came to Flagstaff, where we met and talked. In early August of that summer, we both moved to Chaco Canyon as staff members of the University of New Mexico's summer field school. It was at that time that he introduced me to the Tower Kiva in Chetro Ketl, where then and later we sat in the dirt, leaning against the ancient walls, and talked for hours and hours in an isolation and rapport all but impossible elsewhere. For three consecutive summers, while I worked at Chaco and he was in the Southwest, we went to the Tower Kiva on those occasions when he visited the summer school. There, in the midst of an anthropological world, both of us full of ideas and problems, we could become so immersed in talk that many times it was morning light when we walked back to camp and to work. On other occasions and in other surroundings, sometimes at a Navaho dance or watching a rodeo in Flagstaff or driving slowly over desert roads through mud or blowing sand, we had opportunities for talk and argument.

The point of this recital is that a pattern of personal relationship was established during those summer months in the Southwest between 1938 and 1940. It was a relationship, not strictly of teacher-pupil, but of friendship and of tutelage. He was relaxed in the Southwest, full of good humor and camaraderie, willing and eager, and with time to talk and bandy thoughts. There could not have been a more favorable or fortunate circumstance for getting to know Clyde Kluckhohn.

In the fall of 1938 on Clyde's urging, I went to Harvard. The relationship did not change: He merely added the role of patron to those of friend and tutor. However, things were significantly different at Harvard. He would not let me take any of his courses for credit—and in two and one-half academic years only two courses as auditor. He was officially my supervisor for a research project on some Mexican cave materials but, aside from reading my final paper, he had no communication with me about that job from start to finish. In other words, formally academic contact with him throughout my stay at Harvard was virtually nil—and what there was had precious little to do with archaeology or with any influence I can recognize. Around the Peabody Museum, all was business, bustle, and haste. What I call his "academic pattern" was in force.

One thing and one thing alone saved the day. This was the maintenance, away from formal academia, of our "personal pattern." Harvard at that time, as it may be still, was a fourteen-hour-a-day, six-days-a-week grind for all of us. But late Saturday afternoon something had to give. Relaxation set in, and a group of us would gather, almost always the same: the Kluckhohns, the Marshall Newmans, the William Kellys, the Harry Tschopiks, the Taylors. It was during those evenings and the recuperative brunch of Sunday, before starting the new week's work later in the Sabbath afternoon, that we talked shop and shop and more shop and made up through intensive relaxation for the cold, impersonal realities of the preceding week at Peabody Museum. Here, as in the Southwest, Clyde was easy in mind and spirit, and it was then that the influence began to flow again. Here was renewed the unique and priceless pattern, the tutor-friend relationship. But that influence was scientific, broadly anthropological, only rarely archaeological—and for good reason: There was only one archaeologist in the group and, more importantly, all of us were interested in all of anthropology, we students because (among other things) we were preparing for *general* examinations and Clyde because he was Clyde Kluckhohn. If we could have preserved all the words, smooth, medium, and rough, which were said by our group on those Saturday nights in Jake Worth's, in Wasserman's Saloon, at the Athens Olympia, the Union Oyster House, or in our several apartments, it is impossible that they could be published, but I am sure that they would provide revealing clues to the later careers of all of us.

Before pointing out what I believe to be the conclusions of this personal and anecdotal memoir, one more tale must be told. From the very first, Clyde did not want me to write the doctoral dissertation which I eventually did write. It had been the custom at Harvard (as he informed me with righteous emphasis) to write a dissertation in archaeology using a site report or survey as a starting point. My originally accepted dissertation topic was just such a one, based on fieldwork in Coahuila, Mexico. However, due to the pressures of wartime, it seemed quite impossible to process the mass of Mexican materials in time to stand for my degree before the armed forces called. So I tried to change to what Clyde only half jokingly called "an armchair thesis"—*and he was not for it.* I wanted to use the Mexican data and the ideas which I had developed while digging and studying them to make an analysis of archaeological theory and to demonstrate a new approach to archaeology. But he refused to approve the change—and for several reasons, one of which was that my dissertation would be theoretically and critically oriented as his had been, and he feared that a burdensome image might become attached to me as it had to him. However, toward the end of the spring semester of 1942, he asked me to give a series of lectures on archaeology to his advanced class in anthropological theory. This was my chance! And for those lectures, I unashamedly ignored the class and talked my archaeological ideas directly to Clyde while he sat in the back of the room without a gesture or a word and with no apparent interest in what I had to say. After the last session was over and the students had gone and I felt I had failed, he came to the desk, leering his knowing grin, and said, "Okay, Walt; go ahead and write it." But consent once given, he all but dropped the subject. In fact, from the end of the spring semester to my defense-of-dissertation in January, I had no contact with him at all. I do not remember whether he or Professor Tozzer was my formally assigned advisor, but it made no difference: Neither one of them paid any attention, except for a few questions and suggestions during the final weeks. In other words, the impersonal, academic pattern had been invoked—he was leaving me strictly alone.

I do not think more need be said on this. The model seems quite clear. After the war, meetings with him were fewer, but all of them followed the personal pattern, not the academic one. Whether in the Southwest or when our paths crossed in Washington, Chicago, Mexico, or other momentary landing place, it was the same: We managed a few days trip, an afternoon, a long evening, or perhaps just a meal or a drink, but I came away stimulated and replenished. Also our correspondence continued and increased considerably; his last letter to me was posted one-week-to-the-day before his fatal attack and, when Jo Brew phoned me on the afternoon of 29 July

1960, I had just mailed a reply, anticipating a meeting planned for August in the Southwest.

What, then, is the essence and meaning of all that has been said? For one thing, to those who have read him deeply, his archaeological publications, as few as they are, have certainly been influential and importantly so. But to those who read him less deeply, and unfortunately these seem to have been the majority, he was a critic, either of some emotionally held position and thus anathema, or of some restricted topic of little interest and thus ignored, in either case more talked about than known. Also, the aura which had clothed him from his earliest days in the profession and his reputation for breadth of anthropological taste made many archaeologists, already prone to be apologetic about their discipline, ready to accept his image as critic and to resent his criticisms which made them feel a guilt they would not own. As critic, Devil's advocate, and gadfly, he undoubtedly served a purpose, but it is my contention that his positive contributions were thus underrated, even overlooked: Middle American studies remain today much as they were before he wrote, with some notable but rare exceptions; distribution studies, minute contextual analyses, statistical manipulation of data are still not common in the Southwest; the confusion of temporal and cultural referents for taxonomic categories within the Pecos Classification still exists; and in both areas, again with notable exceptions, rigorous and explicit analysis of theory and method (to use the terms as he defined them) continues to be a stepchild, if not actually a bastard, in the archaeological family.

As I have already detailed in my discussion of the Chaco report and the Maya paper, I consider these positive contributions to be the explicit examination and more rigorous application of basic concepts and his definition of those concepts in terms, and in a context, applicable to archaeology. In each publication, his obvious aim was to urge American archaeology, in the guise of Middle American and Southwestern studies, to extend itself beyond mere time/space considerations and to write culture history to the fullest extent of the data. In the Chaco report, he gave examples of methods and techniques and of the ways in which some conceptual tools were being mishandled, were thus failing their purpose, and might be profitably modified. In the Maya paper, he blasted traditionalism, the acceptance without query of archaeological dogma, the failure to make the most of opportunity; and he precisely defined some very necessary concepts through which the conceptual structure of archaeology could be examined and strengthened.

In his academic and pedagogical capacity, his impact was varied in direction and strength. Yet here again, it is probably not what it is widely thought to have been. Even in his early days at Harvard, and increasingly so as time went on, he had little to do with students dedicated strictly to archaeology. My impression is that, unless an archaeologically inclined student had some special quality or appeal, either intellectually or as a person, Clyde was not attracted and, not attracted, was not disposed to pay much attention. On the other hand, when rapport was once established with a student, Clyde became genuinely interested and often generous, even extravagant, in his support. These were the students he influenced; these were the ones who absorbed his positive contributions.

Clyde Kluckhohn was in many ways a sentimentalist, and he both knew it and fought against it. It seems to me that he feared the lengths to which sentiment and emotion might carry him and that, because of this, he tended frequently to overcompensate, sometimes even to the point of virtual rejection. I believe this to be the root of his two patterns, the academic one rejecting sentiment, the personal one accepting it. Perhaps this is one of the reasons why he never returned permanently to the Southwest or to archaeology. Perhaps this is why he drove himself, why he continued at Harvard while complaining so much about the "rat race" and the "squirrel cage," why he could never accept to be any sort of frog in a smaller pond—when that pond might have been more emotionally satisfying but also more emotionally charged. Perhaps this is why, in the East and in more formal situations, he assumed a special role—which he shed with friends and in the Southwest that he loved. Perhaps this is why many of us whose ties were personal and/or Southwestern got virtually nothing from him during formally academic and professional contacts—and so much from him outside of them! He himself was undoubtedly rationalizing this position when he said,

I think one has to strike a middle course between giving the students the kind of emotional support they want and need and allowing them to be too submissive, to be too dependent. . . . [you] have to watch throwing too many facts at them or being too "warm.". . . there is a great fear of being overwhelmed. [1951d:169]

From Clyde Kluckhohn I did not get an archaeological education. But I believe I did absorb a great deal of anthropology and some fundamental ideas about education itself. What also came from him was a sentiment for work, for thoroughness and precision, for the value of thought and the necessity of making thought explicit. I can still hear the Tower Kiva echoing with invective as dark and blue as the starlit night, all because I had begged a question or assumed a premise—but I cannot for the life of me recall what question or premise it might have been. I remember him half asleep beneath a Navaho wagon and hear his drowsy words as if cadenced to the rhythm of the squaw-dance song, all enveloped in the smell of pinyon and boiling mutton. He comes back to me with the aroma of red Italian wine spilled on the tracings of a tablecloth idea, and I see him in the Smoking Room, burrowed in a chair, billowing smoke as he rips from his mouth a cigarette deep-seated between rigid fingers that poke an argument. For twenty-four years, by osmosis and slow filtration, his influence seeped in and sometimes out, and what is Clyde Kluckhohn and what is myself today I cannot say —more than I have already said.

CLYDE KLUCKHOHN AND THE
INTEGRATION OF SOCIAL SCIENCE

Talcott Parsons

THIS essay will try to illuminate a major aspect of Clyde Kluckhohn's career in social science by discussing two aspects of his
concern and activity. Both aspects indicate that he was not merely an
anthropologist, though he was certainly among the most eminent of
his generation in that discipline. His interest was never confined to
anthropology. Thus, his immersion in classical studies as an undergraduate evidently made an indelible impression on him, and perhaps his college experience as a principal organizer of the University
of Wisconsin Union set the pattern for his lifelong involvement in
organizational affairs, both inside and outside university circles.

My more specific concern, however, will be with Kluckhohn's
role as a statesman of interdisciplinary relations in the social sciences
and the relation of that role to certain aspects of his intellectual
position as an anthropologist. Along with his background in classics,
which was certainly eminently respectable in intellectual circles, a
more daring and early manifestation of Kluckhohn's interdisciplinary
concern was his involvement with psychoanalytic theory, beginning
when he was a student in Vienna. In his early Harvard days, when I
first knew him, he was highly ambivalent about this interest and, in
his role as anthropologist, tended to suppress it in favor of orthodox
anthropology—thus he excluded it entirely from his dissertation

though intrinsically it was very relevant. At this phase, as throughout his career, Kluckhohn was much concerned with validating his position as a professional anthropologist. This he did with an impressive range of contributions to the various subfields of his discipline. But at the same time, his psychoanalytic interests were indicative of an unwillingness to confine himself to the purely anthropological role.

Kluckhohn's Career in Interdisciplinary Organization at Harvard

My personal qualifications for discussing the organizational aspects of Kluckhohn's interdisciplinary contributions center on two contexts of association at Harvard, the Department and Laboratory of Social Relations (and their antecedents) and the Russian Research Center. Under the circumstances, perhaps I may be somewhat autobiographical in highlighting these two contexts, as I saw them, and in discussing them as areas of personal association with him. I am very much aware that these in turn related, sometimes quite intimately, to Kluckhohn's much wider nexus of relationships within the Harvard community and with groups outside it.

Background

I first met Clyde Kluckhohn and his wife Florence on an occasion when my wife and I were dinner guests of Suzanne and Robert Merton. If I remember correctly, this was during Merton's last year at Harvard. Kluckhohn was thus brought into an interdisciplinary network which, by including Merton and myself, involved the old Department of Sociology, already linked with the Department of Anthropology through the parts E. A. Hooton and A. M. Tozzer had played in founding and directing it. This linkage had been further strengthened through the activities of W. Lloyd Warner, who, however, soon departed for Chicago, leaving Kluckhohn as the principal younger social anthropologist at Harvard. The network was more broadly extended into the Harvard Business School, involving Elton Mayo and his associates in Industrial Research and backed by the powerful figure of L. H. Henderson. In addition, there developed important relationships with O. Hobart

Mowrer, who was then located in both the Department of Psychology and the Faculty of Education.

For Kluckhohn, however, by far the most important association in this multidisciplinary nexus was that with Henry A. Murray, then director of the Psychological Clinic. Gordon Allport was chairman of the Department of Psychology but, as a social psychologist, he stood in a certain state of tension with the older, primarily experimental tradition of the Department of Psychology as exemplified by Boring and later Stevens and Skinner. Kluckhohn, being both a psychologically and socially minded anthropologist, quite naturally gravitated into a central position in this complicated system of relationships.

A significant activity of this period was a kind of "shop club" called the "Levellers" in consideration of the many levels on which behavioral phenomena required consideration. The principal participants were the Kluckhohns, Murray, Mowrer, Roethlisberger, myself, and a few others. Meeting in each other's homes, we discussed a whole range of problems which eventually became constitutive of the Department of Social Relations organizational experiment. Another occasion for many of us to engage in interdisciplinary discussion on a group basis was Henderson's famous Pareto Seminar, which most of us attended.

The first organized, interdisciplinary teaching came in a new program of undergraduate concentration, the Area of Social Science, established on the recommendation of a faculty committee on Broader Programs of Study, of which I was a member. Although discussion of such a concentration had covered each of three areas, natural science, humanities, and social science, only in the last did an organized program materialize and, when this was set up by the faculty, I became chairman of its administrative committee. We set up a board of tutors which included Clyde Kluckhohn, Hobart Mowrer, O. H. Taylor, and John T. Dunlop. One of the important things this group did was to draft a kind of theoretical charter of basic social science under the title "Toward a Common Language for the Area of Social Science." This document was never published as a whole, but the other group members kindly permitted me to include its theoretical core section in the first edition of my *Essays in Sociological Theory* (1949). This venture operated for only two years before World War II dispersed the college population. One basis of its importance was that it included anthropology, psychology, and sociology (the disciplines eventually associated in the Department of Social Relations) with history, government, and economics. For a variety of reasons, these latter connections were not maintained when new attempts were made after World War II to create an interdisciplinary program. In the context of this field of concentration, I first had occasion for close organizational, as distinguished from more purely intellectual and social, association with Kluckhohn and learned to know the quality of his organizational talents and judgment. In my capacity as chairman of the committee, I came to rely on him more than on any other member.

One further early venture should be mentioned. During the war, there was a state of ferment in both the intellectual and organizational aspects of the three departments which were later most closely affected by the formation of the Department of Social Relations at Harvard. On the initiative of Gordon Allport, the same group of Allport, Kluckhohn, Murray, Mowrer, and myself addressed a letter to Paul H. Buck, then dean of the faculty of Arts and Sciences, suggesting a reorganization that would bring sociology and the social aspects of anthropology and psychology closer together. Dean Buck responded by appointing the signers of the letter as an *ad hoc* committee to develop and submit a proposal. The report, which resulted from a long series of meetings, was a first blueprint of the Department of Social Relations, though the plan actually implemented some three years later was considerably modified. Kluckhohn played a very prominent part in working out this plan. But immediately afterward, both he and Murray entered war service, and the group did not meet again for some time. By then, Hobart Mowrer had left Harvard for the University of Illinois.

The Department and Laboratory of Social Relations

It is clear from the above account that Kluckhohn played a central part in the series of steps leading to the establishment of the Department and Laboratory of Social Relations. Therefore, it was taken for granted that he would play a prominent part in that venture, if and when it was launched. As it happened, however, both he and Murray were on leave of absence when the organi-

zational problem came to a head in the fall of 1945. Hence, Gordon
Allport and I, soon joined by Samuel Stouffer and helped by a few
younger people, notably Jerome Bruner, bore the brunt of the
initial organizational job. Kluckhohn was, however, on hand for the
opening of the new department in the fall of 1946. He immediately
took his place as both the senior social anthropologist and a key
member of the inner circle which took primary responsibility, in
continual contact with Dean Buck, for the main policies of the department and laboratory. As the chairman of the department for its
first ten years, I can say that only Samuel Stouffer was Kluckhohn's
equal as a source of advice and judgment regarding the wide range
of complex problems which arose. And I am sure that Stouffer valued
his counsel in matters affecting the laboratory just as highly as I did
in those pertaining to the department.

Thus, despite his many other university responsibilities as both
a leading member of the Department of Anthropology and a very
active member of the Committee on General Education, Kluckhohn
certainly devoted himself with great energy and effectiveness to the
social relations experiment. In retrospect, he was clearly so key a
member that without him the department could neither have come
into being nor developed into a major unit of the university. There
certainly was no other anthropologist at Harvard who could have
played his crucial role, and it is difficult to conceive of anyone who
at that time could have come from the outside to do it. Among his
many contributions, besides his general organizational wisdom, perhaps two stand out. One was the extreme delicacy with which he
balanced the department's complex relations with the Department of
Anthropology and the Peabody Museum, maintaining relations
which, to a surprising degree, have been consistently friendly and
cooperative. The other was that, through his close friendship with
Henry Murray and others, Kluckhohn did as much as anyone to
strengthen the bridge between the psychological and social wings
of the department. The intellectual grounding of this role will be
discussed later.

The Russian Research Center

The second context of interdisciplinary organization in which I
was most closely associated with Kluckhohn was Harvard's Russian

Research Center. It should be remembered that the mobilization of the various social sciences in the field of area studies was both new and important during World War II. Also, the three disciplines of the social relations complex gained a new order of practical importance as compared with the history-government-economics complex.

During the war, Kluckhohn had played a leading role in one of the most important of these enterprises: the study of Japanese morale by the group which he and Alexander Leighton codirected in the Office of War Information. Very significantly, they had not been Japanese experts in the sense of centering on language and history. But, as general social scientists, they seemed able to collaborate effectively with those who were experts in that older sense. In Washington, Kluckhohn also renewed acquaintance with an old college friend, Charles Dollard, who immediately after the war became president of the Carnegie Corporation of New York and had associated with himself, as vice-president, a young psychologist, John W. Gardner. These new Carnegie officers were impressed with the practical potential of the area of social science disciplines represented in the Department of Social Relations.

After the war, it soon became clear that relations with the Soviet Union were becoming the most acute area of conflict in American foreign relations. Impressed with the importance of this field, with the general potential of the social science disciplines, with the promise of the social relations experiment, and with Kluckhohn personally, the Carnegie officers approached Harvard with a proposal to establish a program of research on Soviet society which, situated in a major university with high academic standards and private support, could enjoy a level of independence not available to governmental agencies. Kluckhohn became the first director of the center, an appointment which raised many eyebrows in academically conservative quarters because he lacked previous connection with study of Russia and Communism.

It was characteristic of Kluckhohn that he brought together harmoniously at the center a distinguished group of Russian experts representing all of the most important relevant disciplines and stimulated, as evidenced by the long list of Russian Research Center publications, the most comprehensive set of studies of Soviet society,

its antecedents and border relations, which any group in the Western
world has carried out. Also, he handled with great delicacy and
finesse the politically sensitive problems of a university organization
engaged in the study of Communist society. I have previously noted
(1960) how impressive it was that in the McCarthy era of attacks
on universities in general and Harvard in particular, the Russian
Research Center figured virtually not at all, though it might well
have been particularly vulnerable. Certainly the center ranks among
the most distinguished achievements of postwar American academic
life—and the credit for this goes overwhelmingly to Clyde Kluckhohn. However, it is perhaps indicative of a characteristic restlessness
that, after five years as director of the center, Kluckhohn felt he
had had enough and to the great regret of his associates requested
his own relief. Furthermore, he then dissociated himself entirely
from the center, even declining to serve on its executive committee.

In a sense, a similar feeling of having done his bit and of wishing
to move on applied to his activity in the Department of Social
Relations. Considering the magnitude of his involvements in the
Russian Research Center and in many other things, the time and
attention which Kluckhohn gave to the department and laboratory
were certainly extraordinary. When my own chairmanship of the
department was concluding, he was, on all sides I think, considered
the most desirable successor. But he declined even to give it serious
consideration. Of course, it can be said very reasonably that he had
already fulfilled more than his share of university administrative
responsibilities. Yet I feel that more was probably involved, that to a
degree he had begun to lose interest in an enterprise which some
years before had been one of his central concerns. Perhaps he was
disappointed that it had not made more rapid progress toward a
general synthesis in the field. Most important, probably, was Kluckhohn's desire to concentrate his efforts on his core interests in anthropology as such.

In sum, Kluckhohn was one of those academic men, particularly
common in the United States and Great Britain, who also have high
talents in practical organizational affairs. Had he established a firm
and relatively early commitment to administration, he could well
have been a most distinguished university president or foundation

executive. As it was, his organizational contributions were highly distinguished, but relatively fragmentary. One felt that he was in continual conflict on at least two fronts, first between administration and scholarship and teaching, and second among his variety of organizational involvements in anthropology, government, university administration, and interdisciplinary ventures. The latter certainly figured prominently in his interest and indeed, in a certain sense, they may have predominated.

The Interdisciplinary Aspect of Kluckhohn's Intellectual Interests

Clyde Kluckhohn's involvement in interdisciplinary ventures, as well as certain others, especially in Washington, was not only a function of his personal capacities and predilections, but also of the intellectual situation of the time. Now, I should like to outline briefly certain trends in the development of social science which tended to impel an able and imaginative social anthropologist to go beyond mastery of, and contribution to, his particular subject to a special concern with the importance of its "foreign relations" vis-à-vis neighboring disciplines. Indeed, I should suggest that a social anthropologist having Kluckhohn's broad humanistic education, intellectual ability, and imagination *could* not, in his generation, have remained a narrowly parochial anthropologist.

Background

First, it is quite significant that Kluckhohn had a humanistic education. As noted, he was a classics major in college, after which he went to Oxford as a Rhodes Scholar in the famous Greats Program and had his first contact with anthropology through the lectures and writings of R. R. Marrett. That this classics background remained crucial to him throughout his life is evidenced by one of his last major writings, his Brown University lectures on *Anthropology and the Classics* (1961a). It seems to me that it is the synthesis between this classical, humanistic tradition and the traditions of anthropology which provides the intellectual background of Kluckhohn's interdisciplinary interest.

It seems fair to say that anthropology, which in the sense familiar to most of us has been primarily an Anglo-American concern, is an offshoot of mid-nineteenth-century biology, a special impetus being given by Darwin's influence although the movement was considerably more general. The origin of its title seems understandable in these terms—it was the study of man as part of the larger world of living organisms and conceived as a parallel to, for example, ichthyology as the study of fishes or ornithology as the study of birds. This biological background probably accounts for certain persisting trends in anthropology: first, the tendency to be classified among the natural sciences (it is conceived basically as a branch of biology, for is not man a species of organism?); second, the prominence in anthropological thinking of problems concerning the relations between heredity and environment. It also helps to account for cultural and social anthropology's concentration on "primitive" systems, in that the basic focus was not only upon man as organism, but also upon his place in evolution: The problem of the origins of things specifically human was of paramount significance, with all its influence upon the religious controversies of the day. The tendency then was to treat the biological and the sociocultural problems of human evolution together and thus to emphasize the transitions between the human and the nonhuman in each respect. The relevance of these interests to the heredity-environment problem is patent.

In a sense, the religious storm provoked by Darwinism was related to the fact that man had been the object of much intellectual study long before the advent of Darwinian biology. However, there was a certain tendency to assume that, in the light of the new knowledge, it was necessary to begin again. The concentration on the "primitive" may be considered in part a compromise formula in that it placed the anthropologist in less direct competition with the great pre- and non-Darwinian traditions of the study of man. These traditions were, of course, deeply embedded in the religious history of our culture. But, in the more modern world, they also stemmed from somewhat more technical schemes grounded in the more secularized movements of philosophy. At the risk of oversimplification, these movements may be reduced to two main streams directly relevant here. The division between them originated in the basic Cartesian frame of reference. Roughly, they may be called the "empiricist" tradition, which emphasized the object world in the Cartesian sense and tended to assume the primacy of its physical aspects, and the "idealist" tradition, which departed from the viewpoint of the knowing subject but was soon forced to consider the senses in which knowing subjects are also objects of cognition.

The first great positive harvest of empirical knowledge had clearly been in physical science—Newton's being the great name. In the formative period of the tradition, however, there had also been human components, e.g., the "passions" of Hobbes and the "ideas" and "sensations" of Locke. These were to eventuate in the beginning movements of social science, the most important being the major frameworks of economic theory and the psychology which synthesized the "association of ideas" so prominent in Locke and so close to the orientations of biological science. Indeed, it was evidently the relatively late nineteenth-century rise of biology that opened the principal door to synthesizing these two major components of the empiricist tradition, the physical and the utilitarian movements. This supplied the cultural impetus for developing anthropology and extending it along the presently relevant line.

To understand the emergence of anthropology, however, it is also necessary to glance briefly at the other main stream, the idealistic tradition. While only the German idealistic philosophers greatly emphasized rationalizing the position philosophically, the assumption that the human condition was culturally sophisticated certainly rested on the traditions of humanistic learning stemming from the Renaissance and a common foundation of the Western intellectual world at the turn of the last century, particularly at Oxford University. Indeed, with T. H. Green and Bradley, idealistic philosophy had even made considerable impression upon the dominant tradition of British empiricism. The central idealistic concern was the human culture, specifically its structuring in patterns: The German philosophers introduced the term *Geist*, which in its Hegelian version, however, was never popular in the English-speaking world. But the major focus of idealism—the predominant importance of the creations of the mind in remaking the world—was never in doubt. The German philosophers, with their insistence on systematization, tended to view the special features of this humanistic complex according to an extremely typological formation, incorporating in it virtually the whole realm of things human but not organic in a physical sense. They tended, that is, to postulate a radical hiatus between the disciplines dealing with nature in the Newtonian sense and those treating the whole human cultural realm (see Parsons 1965b). This eventuated in the well-known conception of historicism, which held that human phenomena must be treated in ideographic or individuating terms and by means of empathic understanding. The entities conceived were less systems than individuals, regardless of whether they were total cultures or epochs or human personalities.

Finally, it should not be overlooked that French social thought maintained, in important respects, a middle position between the empiricist individualism of the English utilitarian tradition and the cultural collectivism of German idealism. In certain respects this French tradition, descending from the Enlightenment through Saint-Simon and Comte, remained basically Cartesian in its structure, down at least to the early Durkheim. With his contemporaries Bergson and Lévy-Bruhl, Durkheim is the central figure in this development. He provided a major point of reference for two related but considerably differing movements in anthropology. The earlier of these was the more or less sociological trend initiated in England by Radcliffe-Brown, whereas the second was the important development in France itself of a more culturally oriented treatment of social structure by Lévi-Strauss, which has had an important impact on a later generation of British anthropologists, Needham, Lienhardt, etc., and on some Americans.

Being conceived as the study of man in the broadest biological frame of reference, anthropology had somehow to penetrate this humanistic sphere. As physical anthropology, its more narrowly biological interests could be only very partial. Its most natural broad concern was with the problems of human evolution. However, the evidence in this field was so fragmentary that it could not very well occupy a major discipline to the exclusion of other interests. Similarly, the physical anthropology of contemporary human groups, e.g., systematizing our knowledge of races through cranial measurements and the like, did not make very striking headway. Therefore, a major and increasing portion of anthropologists studied fields in which environmental influences on man were of paramount significance.

This is the basic reference of the central anthropological concept, culture. Culture is that aspect or component of things human which is not attributable to genetically hereditary factors but which must be conceived, from the individual viewpoint, as learned and, from the collective viewpoint, as perpetuated in cultural tradition. As such, it is a patterning of human orientation in relation to the natural and, above all, to the social environment of the individual. Among the many complex consequences of this concept, it is of special interest here that it led anthropology directly into the central concerns of all the older disciplines which had treated the specifically human condition in other than a modern, biological frame of reference. Among these concerns, the humanistic point of view evidently occupied a special place.

As I suggested above, the predominantly British empiricist tradition dealt with a human component, generally through a frame of reference which became crystallized as utilitarian. This, like much else, was rooted in the Cartesian categories, departing from the position of the knowing subject as distinguished from the known object. This knowing subject, however, was not only cognizer, but also feeler and actor. He had sensations but also passions or wants, the satisfaction of which became the goals of purposive behavior. The most important scientific products of this development were, I suggested, economic theory and association psychology—though Austinian jurisprudence and the Bentham-Mill type of political theory also fit the framework.

The new biological orientation, however, predisposed toward a somewhat different emphasis, at least initially. Its main structure had previously been built on morphology, on conceptions of organization and form. Indeed, it may be said that the more inductive aspect of the theory of evolution emerged from the long history of work on morphological classifications, sometimes pejoratively called "mere taxonomy." The concept of pattern, so central to the anthropological theory of culture, clearly fits directly into this context. Thus, socio-

cultural patterns became the direct object of anthropological study
and analysis, whereas in the utilitarian tradition, so far as they were
recognized at all, they were merely considered resultants of the
operation of wants, interests, or ideas in the Lockean sense.

This is a more basic difference than is usually realized. Regardless of how many different kinds of patterns it may be necessary to
discriminate, such entities as grammatical or syntactic rules, legal
norms or modes, or behavioral style cannot be identified with the
wants or interests of individuals and groups as these have been
formulated in economics, much of psychology, and much of sociology. It is my view that a principal task of sociology involved
developing a theoretical synthesis between these different elements
in the determination of human social behavior and that Kluckhohn's
firm concentration on cultural patterning and fear of contaminating
it with nonpattern categories had much to do with the difficulty of
his relations with sociology as a discipline.

To be sure, anthropological interest was directed primarily toward
the "primitive," earlier stages of cultural, as anthropologists came to
distinguish it from genetic, human evolution. Thereby, anthropologists avoided a more direct confrontation with the older disciplines'
treatment of cultural matters. Nevertheless, humanism was a very
obvious model for treating this aspect of their subject matter. And
the fact that so many anthropologists were humanistically educated
makes it all the more appropriate.

In this setting, language soon assumed a special position. The
human universality of language, combined with the extreme plurality
and diversity of particular languages, made it a special field of
interest. Moreover, learning the language of a people in the field
presented special practical problems which were not solved in advance by grammars and dictionaries. Also, language had been so
central to the humanities that, for example, most German humanistic scholars habitually called themselves "philologists." It is no acci-
dent that linguistics was a main concern of Clyde Kluckhohn's scientific career and that, toward the end of his life, he increasingly drew
upon it for a general model for his analysis of culture, notably in
the field of values.

Another obviously related field was archaeology. This also overlapped physical anthropology in that skeletons were generally found together with artifacts, the study of which often helped reconstruct the past of cultures. Such artifacts were the primary reference of the concept "material culture," the study of which became a major branch of anthropology—of course for extant peoples, as well as for those whose cultures were extinct.

Thus, it is seen that a humanistic orientation to problems of culture can be intimately related to a biological approach toward man. In certain respects, this is particularly true of the Anglo-American tradition because it dichotomizes less sharply between natural and cultural disciplines than does the German tradition.

Kluckhohn's Orientation in Anthropology

It seems fair to say that, in the generation in which Clyde Kluckhohn grew up, the whole range of intellectual influences just sketched impinged on anthropology. Thus in England, Malinowski increasingly tried to ground his position in the utilitarian type of psychological doctrine of needs, but he carried his empirical interests far into the fields of culture and social structure. The other most prominent and influential British anthropologist of that generation, Radcliffe-Brown, grounded his work in Durkheim's ideas with a strong though by no means undiluted emphasis on the social system. In the United States, certainly the most prominent figure was Boas, and it is surely significant that he was German in origin and migrated to the United States only in early adulthood. He seems to have brought with him many of the themes of German idealistic historicism, with its tendencies to emphasize alternatively cultural *Gestalten,* which figured so prominently in its own tradition, and trait atomism, which figures so prominently in the work of the more empirically minded German historians, both alternatives, however, being primarily cultural in emphasis rather than either social or psychological.

The difference between the British and the American view is perhaps particularly clearly brought out by Goldenweiser's famous and extremely negative review of Durkheim's *Elementary Forms of Religious Life,* which was understood to reflect the considered opinion of the "Boas circle" at Columbia and hence of Boas himself.

Though couched in terms of the alleged fallacies of the group mind concept—and of course the evils of arm chair anthropologizing—the main theme was the danger of giving the kind of priority to the social system, which Durkheim certainly did. Indeed, it is particularly important to note that at that time, both in the work of Durkheim and that of the British anthropologists, the analytical distinction between cultural and social systems, which many of us are now accustomed to make, had not been firmly established. All of these authors assumed a degree of concrete undifferentiatedness which has proved today not to be tenable (see Parsons and Kroeber 1958:582).

However complex the intellectual relations between British and American anthropology and between anthropology and sociology may have been, it is clear that Kluckhohn's closest intellectual affiliations were with four men in American anthropology, namely Boas, Kroeber, Sapir, and Redfield, all of whom emphasized the more pattern-oriented and humanistic side of the general intellectual tradition—but with a serious attempt to adhere to and develop the canons of precise and objective science. Probably the most important of these relationships was to Sapir. There was close personal contact through Kluckhohn's participation in Sapir's seminar on the psychology of culture at Yale during the middle 1930s and a special association stemming from their common concern with Navaho language and culture. This relation particularly underlies Kluckhohn's continuing emphasis upon the importance of linguistics, a concern which became salient on a new level in his last years.

Among the other disciplines which came to be included in the social relations combination, clearly Kluckhohn's closest affinity was to clinical psychology. This too was grounded in a close personal relationship to Henry A. Murray but certainly had strong intellectual grounds as well. Clinical psychology, especially as Murray has understood and practiced it, is the other end of a culture-and-personality axis from Kluckhohn's main kind of anthropology. They shared the concern with pattern and with empathic understanding of the complex *Gestalt* which a culture or a personality presented. They also had in common a method of investigation, i.e., intimate association and understanding in a clinical setting. In each case, the empirical method was conceived to be more than a formal device for securing reliably objective information. It involved a special kind of reorientation of the investigator himself, which can perhaps be formulated as the internalization of the personality or culture of the object of study through something which might be called a process of "identification."

Psychoanalysis and Behavioristic Psychology

In this connection, it is not surprising that an anthropologist with Kluckhohn's orientation turned to another movement, in this case psychoanalysis, to supplement the incompleteness of his own discipline. Freud had begun his medical career in Vienna in a milieu which assumed that the problems of medicine were overwhelmingly biological—his first research contributions were in pharmacology. Later, he began to study the personality of the individual from a clinical point of view. In the end, working from a vast body of clinical data, he developed a theoretical scheme which, through departing from a narrower biological viewpoint, eventually involved the whole range of considerations that anthropologists came to consider. Psychoanalysis became a highly generalized focus of ferment over the whole range of the study of man. Authentically biological and rooted in natural science, it could promise notable synthesis between the biological antecedents and many of the central concerns of the study of culture.

The beginnings of a broad anthropological acceptance of psychoanalysis were slow, and resistances were formidable. But the relationship between psychoanalysis and anthropology was patently so close that it is hardly surprising that, in due course, a certain marriage occurred, resulting in the field of "culture and personality." From the viewpoint of the older Boasians, this was clearly a radical, rather dubious step—it was followed only with very restricting qualifications by Boas's most distinguished immediate follower, Alfred Kroeber, in spite of the fact that he studied and for a time actually practiced psychoanalysis. But for a while, it seemed to dominate cultural anthropology. In retrospect, it is clear that culture and personality presented a very natural focus for synthesis but, at the same time, involved certain tensions and selectivities. The main internal tension concerned the problem of genuinely synthesizing

the more biological reference of orthodox psychoanalysis, particularly
its tendency to emphasize that in the last analysis human behavior is
an outcome of instinctual drives.

Here it can be said that Kluckhohn resisted the pressures toward
biopsychological reductionism, which have operated very strongly
over the whole field of behavioral science, at least since Darwin.
Kluckhohn's strong concern with cultural problems precluded his
accepting any of the facile reductionist formulae. At the same time,
he was very much concerned with the maintenance of a positive
connection between these disciplines and, in fact, sponsored and
participated in major biological studies of the Navaho population.
His own solution of this problem lay along what many social scientists feel to be the most fruitful path. This concerns emphasis on the
plasticity of the human organism, its capacity for learning and hence
openness to cultural influence. This is the direct antithesis of instinct
theory, which tends to postulate that the main determinants of
human behavior lie in genetically given needs and other specific
motivational entities, from the understanding of which the details
of behavioral structuring allegedly can eventually be derived. This
controversy lies deep in the tradition of psychoanalysis where a
major trend has been to consider its main contribution to be the
demonstration of the dominance of instinctual need over all environmental factors in behavior, including the cultural. Kluckhohn
never accepted this interpretation nor that of the Neo-Freudians
like Fromm and Horney, who tended strongly to minimize the importance of the biological base of personality and, through it, of all
sociocultural behavior. This clarity with regard to major relations in
such an essential field was one of Kluckhohn's most important contributions to interdisciplinary relations.

Another important intellectual bridge between psychology and
anthropology was the movement in behavior psychology. This trend
became extremely influential during the 1920s and 1930s and gained
a particular ascendancy at Yale University in the latter decade. The
Institute of Human Relations at Yale was perhaps the most important center at which behavioristic psychology, psychoanalysis, and
anthropology were in intimate interaction. But it is interesting to note
that Yale's "official" sociology was entirely outside the movement,

despite the fact that a sociologist, Chicago-trained John Dollard, was prominent in the movement. Dollard was perhaps Kluckhohn's most important contact with this Yale group and its serious efforts to achieve a broad synthesis. Kluckhohn followed the effort with great sympathy but did not participate very notably in it. Nevertheless, it may be said that without its encouragement his most important contribution to the synthesis of psychoanalysis and anthropology, the monograph *Navaho Witchcraft* (1944a), would probably not have been possible.

The readiness of culturally oriented anthropologists—and indeed for psychoanalytically oriented personality psychologists—to resort to behavioristic learning psychology had an important basis in the idealistic tradition. This lay in the implications of the duality which developed in late German idealistic historicism, as has been mentioned above. One trend, the one most closely deriving from Hegel (and Marx), focused on macroscopic *Gestalten*, total epochs of history (see von Schelting 1934; Parsons 1937). For the modern anthropologist, the naturally relevant unit at this level was the total culture, which could be treated as a coherently integrated entity. This tendency emerged in American anthropology with Ruth Benedict, above all. It was also prominent in the linguistic culturology of Whorf, followed especially by Dorothy Lee. In relation to personality, such views of the holistic character of a culture tended toward a rather rigid conceptualization of the relation between central patterns and the modal personality which was a product of socialization in the culture.

The other basic trend in idealistic historicism was trait atomism, as we have noted above. This involved treating a total culture as a congeries of discrete trait elements which might be of the most varied character, e.g., elements of style which were at once technological and aesthetic, beliefs at various levels, and ways of doing things in social organization or ritual. In the German tradition, this alternative served primarily as a methodological basis for detailed historical research into many fields and received an immense impetus in the late nineteenth and early twentieth centuries. It had the great virtue of relieving the researcher of responsibility for large theoretical and philosophical generalizations, freeing him to follow his common sense at the technical level. Still, carried to its logical conclusion, as with Robert Lowie's reference to "that planless hodge-podge, that thing of shreds and patches called civilization" (1920:441), it could lead to difficulties. So far as culture and personality was concerned, the attempt was made to synthesize cultural theory and learning theory by equating the trait and the habit. In the theory of Clark Hull, the habit was the unit of completed learning which involved, on the one hand, the process of learning and its conditions and, on the other hand, a unit of meaningful content readily conceivable as a trait in the sense of the historical school of anthropology. This seemed to present a way out of the more rigid, psychoanalytically oriented versions of culture and personality theory by emphasizing learning as opposed to instinct and opening the door to combinatorial variability of habits and traits.

A notable product of this theoretical posture was the cross-cultural area files gathered at the Institute of Human Relations, Yale University. Kluckhohn was clearly very much attracted by the Yale formula. Besides participating to a limited extent himself, he consistently supported the research plans and academic careers of people prominently involved in it. My major impression, however, is that he shied away from making it his own main intellectual commitment and took a different tack. However, in common with the Yale group, he regarded with utmost seriousness the problem of relating the totality of *Gestalten*, in both cultural and personality references, to their analytical units which could somehow be related to, if not defined as, factors. In the end, he chose an intracultural solution of his problem, bringing together the microscopic interests and concerns of trait theory with the more macroscopic ones of cultural pattern, by attempting to synthesize the analysis of values with certain important developments in the science of linguistics.

The Study of Values and the Linguistic Model

It seems clear that Kluckhohn's intellectual frame of reference centered in this area. The aspect of culture upon which he focused was the holistic *Gestalt*, the culture as patterned. With respect to the determination of detailed behavior, he concentrated on the aspects of a culture which he called its values, its "conceptions of the desirable" to use his own phrase. In later years, Kluckhohn's more specifically scientific concern focused increasingly upon the theory of values as an aspect of culture.

In a somewhat earlier, German intellectual climate, he might have rested content with delineating value systems and interpreting the ways in which various other elements of behavior expressed and exemplified the central culture patterns. Although at times he seemed to favor just that, the tendency never really got the upper hand. Clyde Kluckhohn, as a scientist and as one with serious training in biology and several other disciplines, could not but feel a strong need to go beyond delineation and culturological interpretation to explanation. This required breaking down the holistically described phenomena into elements and dealing with variation in the interrelation among such elements. It was in the anthropological tradition that a relatively empirical and descriptive approach to values should be taken. In addition to his work on the Navaho, Kluckhohn relatively early developed a strong set of comparative interests, which were most fully implemented through his sponsorship and supervision of the study of values in the five cultures which lived closely together in New Mexico. He also at least twice made studies of American values (1945g, 1958a). In this connection, he strongly encouraged the efforts of Florence Kluckhohn, his wife, to systematize the value field in terms of a set of five orientation foci of the human situation. He did not, however, directly adopt and work with this scheme but, in his last work, attempted another, more linguistic approach.

Kluckhohn's general line of interest in values, however, faced the problems of analytical differentiation of systems. To myself, as a sociologist, the most conspicuous problem lay in the delineation of the special relevance of a culturally oriented analysis of values to their role in the structure of social systems. Here, for example, it was notable that in his exceedingly rich and insightful paper on the change of American values (1958a), he did not distinguish, among all values held by Americans, those which, as conceptions of the desirable type of society, were constitutive of the structure of the society itself. Hence, we are left with the ambiguity that conceptions of desirable tastes in food are treated on the same level as are valuations of occupational achievement or of the constitutional freedoms of individuals. More pertinent to Kluckhohn himself, however, was the problem of the relation of his treatment of values to the analytical distinctions between cultural and social systems. This problem in turn can be broken down into that of psychoanalytic theory, on the one hand, and behavioristic theory on the other, in spite of the connectedness of the two areas.

If I may venture an interpretation of this phase of Kluckhohn's development, it seems that he encountered on both fronts serious frustrations in his search for the most fruitful basis of analyzing cultural totalities into elements. In his attempt to integrate psychoanalytic personality theory with the anthropological theory of culture in its more holistic aspects, the decisive point was evidently that culture, being internalized despite the biological references of so many Freudian symbols, appeared too autonomous and independent an entity to be related systematically to independent variations in its personality base. The too neat correspondence, which many asserted, was unacceptable to him. Kluckhohn, if I interpret him rightly, failed to find a sufficiently generalized bridge to close this gap, though in *Navaho Witchcraft* (1944a) he had brilliant suggestions, while tending to concentrate on the cultural aspect of the problem. In his own theoretical preoccupations, he did not concern himself much with Freudian instincts. Like many in his generation, however, he was impressed with the work of the ethologists as promising a bridge.

The relation of behavioristic learning theory to trait theory seemed for a time to offer a second possibility for synthesis. However, parallel theoretical difficulty emerged on each side of this relation. In cultural terms alone, it does not seem possible to get from anything resembling Lowie's "planless hodge-podge" of fortuitously assembled traits or habits to Benedict's fully patterned culture without resort to other resources and modes of analysis. The difficulty was that the concept of empirical interdependence of elements in a system had not been adequately developed. The pattern or *Gestalt* involved only what Sorokin has called "logical-meaningful" relationships of components, and the "hodge-podge" emphasized relationships of historically fortuitous juxtaposition. The same basic difficulty is involved in relating discrete habits to a total personality structure. Habits are the products of fortuitous learning experiences, unless they are somehow synthesized in relation to a coherent contextual reference. The total culture at times seemed to fill this gap, but it was generally conceived so completely holistically that it seemed to permit only one type of modal personality in a whole culture. Therefore, it is not surprising that Kluckhohn was not satisfied with these ways of integrating the components that were ostensibly needed for complete anthropological theory. His turn from psychology to linguistics is itself significant both in terms of his personal history and, from the present point of view, as a major step in the right direction. The directness and exclusiveness of the step, however, seems to have been related not only to a positive, but also a negative, selection among the possibilities left open by the situation just sketched.

Anthropology and Sociology

Here we must return to certain intellectual problems and movements deriving from the subjective aspect of the empiricist tradition, namely the positions, wants, and ideas of Hobbes, Locke, and the economists. As noted above, the foundations of empirical economics and psychology were laid in these movements. The biologist, on the other hand, tended to identify his problems with the world of nature and dissociate himself from these concerns. Both medicine and anthropology identified above all with the biological tradition and, hence, they also tended not to be interested in these concerns. In a sense somewhat analogous to Freud's famous dictum that "where Id was, there shall Ego be," it may be said that where subjective wants were, there objects for scientific study gradually emerged. Thus the wants eventually had to be taken seriously by anyone whose concern was the study of man in the scientific context. This stimulated an initial differentiation of approaches, especially marked in the United States. On the one hand, psychologists became extremely uneasy about being identified with anything subjective and, more than a generation ago, began studying behavior as a natural science, especially emphasizing experimental method. Gradually, however, they have been freeing themselves from the consequences of a radical and narrow biologizing of their subject by introducing studies of symbolic structures and processes, particularly such entities as attitudes and cognative processes. On the other hand, a good many anthropologists turned to the study of culture taken more or less as a whole, treating the intermediate sectors between the organism and the cultural system quite equivocally. Psychoanalysis, then, appeared to be able to begin filling the gap, and the alliance with behavioristic psychology, though somewhat unstable, seems to provide a still further step. Kluckhohn participated in these tendencies with perhaps decreasing conviction as his intellectual position matured.

Unlike psychology, economics could not readily be biologized. I attribute this above all to the fact that for the economist the individual could serve only as a reference point—indeed, individual wants have been treated predominantly as a given for economic analysis. Technical economics, then, became concerned primarily with the social systems constituted by the interdependence of the economic interests and activities of the numerous individuals and organizational units in a society. In the anthropological sense, this presumed not only a society, a highly problematic concept to economists, but also a culture. I think that it is in this intermediate zone, the zone between the individual as an organism which behaves and has wants and the total culture, that sociology has emerged. In particular, sociology has been strongly influenced by the problems posed by the theoretical status of economics and its utilitarian background. This is clearly evident in the relation between the two in the work of Pareto and also in the crucial writings of Durkheim, who focused less specifically on economics than on the general utilitarian framework. In the idealistic tradition, it becomes clear with the Marxian concern about economic problems and particularly with the radical way in which Weber cut through the idealistic dilemma (see Parsons 1965a). My view is that economics as such could not be absorbed into either biological natural science or an anthropology with primarily cultural emphasis. For a long time, economics has intellectually gone it alone by sticking obstinately to postulating both the givenness of the wants of the individuals and the incomparability of the wants of different individuals. At the same time, the famous postulate of rationality has perhaps served as the main defense against a fuller biologizing, as well as cultural-izing, of economic theory. On the cultural side, when economics came to study the economy of a society, e.g., Adam Smith's *Wealth of Nations*, it had to focus on the social-system level of the inter-action of individuals and collectivities, e.g., firms, not upon either patterns or straits as Sombart's *Modern Capitalism* did. Within this intermediate area, however, I think it has been demonstrated on strictly theoretical grounds that economics cannot stand alone but must fit into a broader theory of social systems, one which includes a political theory in the sense of its empirical referents and has a main theoretical anchorage that is legitimately sociological (see Parsons and Smelser 1956).

Since sociology has been much closer to anthropology than have economics and political science, questions of the relation of this complex to anthropological problems have centered about issues of the status of sociology. In its relatively modern form, sociology may be said to have emerged by a process of convergence. From the utilitarian-empiricist side, it arose, on the one hand, through inter-actionist social psychology (George Herbert Mead being the most important figure), which connected it with psychology and, on the other hand, through Durkheim's analysis of the problem of social order, which, though oriented toward Spencer's conception of con-tractual relations, involved the whole problem of a market econ-omy's presuppositions in the field of institutional structures. From the cultural side, the most important figure was certainly Max Weber, who broke clearly and sharply with the two aspects of the German historical-cultural tradition sketched above, both the holistic one deriving more directly from Hegelian sources and the one rest-ing on trait atomism.

It is significant that this sociological movement did not simply go over from a utilitarian position to affirming the importance of an analytically defined cultural factor. Certainly, the content of the normative components of social systems—what I should now call values and norms—is cultural. But, as parts of social structures, these patterns have gained the special status of being institutional-ized. This involves the development of a special form both of integration with the motivational structures of individuals and of systematic interrelation with the functional exigencies of social systems. As I put it, institutions, the primary subject-matter of sociology, constitute a special zone of interpenetration between cultural and social systems. The existence and significance of such interpenetration does not, however, diminish the importance of the independent variability of the components. Thus it is necessary for social science to theorize about social systems—including their economic and political aspects—not as a branch of culture, as anthropology has often treated social organization, but as an authentically independent level in the organization of the components of action. A fairly good approximation to adequate analysis can be attained without these distinctions in the study of relatively undifferentiated societies, as has been the main interest of social anthropologists. But recently, particularly in this country, anthropologists, including Kluckhohn, have ventured into the study of complex modern (or modernizing) societies, and in such fields distinctions of this order have become imperative.

From my particular perspective as a sociologist, it seems to me that Kluckhohn's inability to see this theoretical necessity, and the opportunity and path to its fulfillment, was the most serious limitation upon his capacity as a generalized social scientist contributing to the full integration of the social science disciplines. As evidence, I may first note that he was notably "unmusical" with economics. It is perhaps not too much to say that the problems and status of economic theory left him completely cold as an intellectual challenge, even though he was well aware of the general importance of economics and even though "some of his best friends were economists." Also, he was notably ambivalent about the theoretical status of sociology as a discipline. This is rather clearly expressed in his dissenting note appended to the General Statement by the authors of *Toward a General Theory of Action.*

Many anthropologists (and certainly the undersigned) will agree today that there is an element in the social (i.e., interactive) process which is not culturally patterned, which is in some sense autonomous from culture. Nevertheless, one whose training, experiences, and prejudices are anthropological tends to feel that the present statement does not give full weight to the extent to which roles are culturally defined, social structure is part of the cultural map, the social system is built upon girders supplied by explicit and implicit culture. [In Parsons et al. 1951:27, fn.]

My comment would be that of course roles are culturally defined and social structure is part of the cultural map but that, as a zone of interpenetration, only special aspects of the social structure are parts of the cultural map and can be analyzed in cultural terms alone, however important the cultural component may be. Both the exigencies of interaction in social systems and the analytically defined interests of acting units, individual and collective, are analytically independent of cultural factors. They are not derivable from the pattern-configurations of the cultural component, however important the latter may be. The issue is not whether these elements are or are not culturally patterned (so far as the social system is integrated, which is empirically problematical, they must be) but whether the functioning of the system can be understood as a cultural process.

David Schneider has pointed out (in personal correspondence) that another basis of Kluckhohn's dissenting note was probably his conviction that the relevance of culture to the theory of action by no means exhausted its importance in human affairs, and I am entirely ready to accede to the justification of this view. It is questionable how far Kluckhohn really saw the necessity for the general analytical statement of social systems, an approach which cannot be brought under the traditional anthropological treatment of social organization as a branch of culture. Furthermore, his own treatment of concrete materials in the field of social anthropology can be said to have focused upon other aspects to the point of rather markedly avoiding a careful study of the problems of social structure—this may be said of the two volumes he wrote with Dorothea Leighton on the Navaho (Kluckhohn and Leighton 1946a; Leighton and Kluckhohn 1947).

Conclusions

Clyde Kluckhohn's intellectual, as well as his organizational, career is thus deeply involved with the intellectual situation of the time. He began with a strong personal engagement in the cultural point of view through his studies of the classics, but at the same time he was fully cognizant of the rooting of the whole discipline of anthropology in its biological heritage. The most critical problem areas concerned whether, as conceptions of culture became progressively more sophisticated, there could be direct articulation between the cultural and the biological poles of the frame of reference, as the early identification between the role of culture and that of environmental influence on behavior seemed to indicate. Kluckhohn's personal exploration of this intermediate territory took primarily a psychological direction, for reasons I have tried to make clear. He started from the cultural end in his venture into the complex field of culture and personality and showed the strongest affinity for the more holistic conceptions of personality as somehow matching the more holistic versions of the pattern configurations of cultures. In anthropology, he aligned himself with the traditions of Boas, Kroeber, Sapir, and Redfield but, unlike Kroeber, he was much concerned to explore the links of culture with the psychology of the individual. However, he found psychoanalytic attempts in this direction disappointing on the whole. He showed marked interest also in the behavioristic tradition which showed strong affiliations with the trait aspect of cultural theory.

At least to me as a sociologist, it seems that he rather conspicuously bypassed another main stream of the development of social science theory, namely, that which led from economics to much of current sociology. In spite of common roots, the traditions of thought out of which Darwinian biology—and psychoanalysis—came lacked direct articulation with the behaving individual and with the patterned configurations of the culture and seemed irrelevant to the culturally oriented anthropologist. It is, of course, my personal view that this irrelevance is more apparent than real and that Kluckhohn's contribution would have been substantially greater had he been able to achieve a better integration of these components of the behavioral order.

However this may be, the fact seems to be that in his last years he tended to become more of a pure anthropologist than before, as indicated not only by his intellectual work but also by his organizational interests. In so doing, he revived and developed his old interest in linguistics, which had undergone immense developments since he first worked with Sapir. Above all, perhaps, he saw in the concepts of phoneme and morpheme a path of analytical breakdown of patterned cultural systems which would avoid, on the one hand, the more idealistic type of Gestaltism and, on the other, the historical arbitrariness of the association of discrete traits. It could lead to much more authentically analytical treatment of cultural phenomena, especially the values with which he was so much concerned.

It is my view that in this last phase Kluckhohn was embarked on potentially a very fruitful path, one which, followed far enough, would greatly enhance the opportunities for integration of the theory of culture with that of social systems. Sometimes it is better, rather than pressing integration too immediately, to concentrate on the development of the parts to be integrated. I have a good deal of faith that, if Kluckhohn had lived long enough, a new phase of interdisciplinary exploration would have been entered. As it was, his contributions to the field as a whole were certainly among the most distinguished of his generation.

CLYDE KLUCKHOHN'S CONTRIBUTION
TO STUDIES OF RUSSIA
AND THE SOVIET UNION

Alex Inkeles

CLYDE KLUCKHOHN became director of the Russian Research Center, Harvard University, at its inception in February 1948, and continued until June 1954, when he left for a year at the Center for Advanced Study in the Behavioral Sciences at Palo Alto, California. He was not only the first director, but in a very real sense the founder, of a research center which as of 1964 had published almost fifty books and hundreds of articles on various aspects of Soviet and Russian life and politics. To this output, Clyde himself contributed but sparingly. Prior to assuming the center's directorship, he had not done scholarly work on Soviet or Russian culture. He was afterward so burdened by administrative responsibilities and so involved in his continuing interest in a number of his earlier research enterprises that he found insufficient time to really master the language or dominate the appropriate scientific literature to his satisfaction. For this reason, he imposed on himself a self-denying ordinance and rather consistently refused to write or even lecture on Soviet affairs. Since I often discussed Soviet issues with him at length, I know that he had arbitrarily set excessively high standards for himself. This became all the more evident when he began to submit drafts of the sections he undertook to write for the final report of the Project on the Soviet Social System. Be that as it may, we must acknowledge Kluckhohn's apparent decision to make his main contribution to Russian studies by fostering the development of interdisciplinary and behavioral approaches to an understanding of Soviet society and culture. He did, however, find time to write on both Russian national character and the nature of the Soviet system, and this work must be weighed in any assessments of his impact on Russian studies.

Developing Interdisciplinary Research on Soviet Russia

The formal elements of the style of work which Kluckhohn wished to institute at the Russian Research Center were described by him quite explicitly early in the life of the center (1949f, 1954d). The major objective of the center, he wrote, "is the study of Russian institutions and behavior in an effort to determine the mainsprings of the international actions and policy of the Soviet Union." This idea that domestic institutions and behavior could be a key to understanding international policy motivated the officers of the Rockefeller Foundation whose grant to Harvard made possible the establishment of the Russian Research Center. They realized that the Soviet Union would be an enormously important force in shaping human affairs after World War II and hoped that behavioral science research might deepen our understanding of, and our ability to deal with, the impending challenge. In his wartime service, Kluckhohn had already developed a commitment to the kind of social research which bore on public policy. He was, therefore, quite ready to head a center with so clear a mandate to conduct research which could enlighten the public and guide those charged with responsibility for formulating our national policy vis-à-vis Russia.

Its concern for the policy implications of Soviet studies did not, however, make the Harvard center distinctive. What made it so was the means by which it was expected to achieve its purpose. In describing the organization of the research program, Kluckhohn noted four principles by which he meant to guide the work of the Russian Research Center but which we may interpret more broadly as representing, with appropriate modification, his general approach to research in the social sciences.

The research of the Center is based on the following principles: a) the research is interdisciplinary in character, that is, scholars in a wide variety of social science fields work on cooperative projects to which each one brings the point of view and research methods developed in his own field of study; b) the fields of anthropology, psychology and sociology, which have hitherto played little part in Russian studies, are strongly represented; c) while initially most of the research is being carried out along lines firmly established in scholarship, the Center will also experiment in methods and approaches in an effort both to broaden the scope of Russian studies and to contribute to the methodology of the social sciences; d) the research will form a coherent whole and will be cumulative in content. [1949*f*:267]

It seems to me not only a reflection of Kluckhohn's eclecticism, but also of his sense of the appropriate and his astuteness as an administrator, that he did not attempt to impose too literally and brusquely the mandate from the Rockefeller Foundation that the Russian Research Center give a particularly prominent role to disciplines which in the past had been relatively neglected in the study of Soviet and other world powers. He invited to the executive committee of the center not only Talcott Parsons of the Department of Social Relations, but also Merle Fainsod and Wasily Leontiev as heads of programs in government and economics, respectively. In keeping with the behavioral emphasis, he stressed that the study of the Communist party "demands historical, psychological, and sociological content and method, as well as political." And he urged that "the investigation of the economy include topics such as standards of living, class stratification and income distribution—topics where sociologists must cooperate with economists." Yet it is notable that the first subjects selected for investigation at the Russian Center were the Communist party and the Soviet economy, rather than Russian culture patterns or Soviet national character.

I chided Kluckhohn about this, pointing to our mandate to give special emphasis to the newer behavioral disciplines, to fresh approaches and neglected problems. He replied that he had not forgotten the mandate but considered the timing of our effort of crucial importance. In a field in which political and economic problems bulked so large, he argued, the center could win a fair hearing for its less conventional explorations in social relations only after it had unmistakably established its *bona fides,* its right to be heard, through demonstrated competence in the more traditional branches of Soviet studies.

As a student of organization, I cannot forbear to state my impression that this strategy, although obviously wise, also had important, unintended consequences. In time, the traditional disciplines of economics and government, and later increasingly history, came to carry more and more weight in the Russian Research Center, while anthropology, psychology, and sociology did not hold a clearly dominant place. Indeed, by the time Kluckhohn resigned as director of the Russian Research Center in June 1954, it no longer had an anthropologist or psychologist on its staff, and sociology, while still represented, was at best only one in a set of equally important disciplines. The trends then merely emergent became in time more sharply defined. No other anthropologist or psychologist subsequently joined the staff. The field of Russian history gradually emerged as the one which attracted the largest number of students to the center, and the traditional methods of library research and documentary analysis prevailed almost completely unchallenged by other approaches. Almost everyone is agreed that the work done at the Russian Center in the more traditional disciplines is of the highest order, indeed in many ways magnificent. But it is not interdisciplinary, experimental, or methodologically innovative.

Because of Kluckhohn's interest not only in the Russian and Soviet field, but in regional studies in general, it is perhaps not inappropriate to consider briefly what may have accounted for the gradual and spontaneous but nonetheless substantial shift of emphasis in the Russian Research Center from a program centered on the more behavioral social sciences to one focused on more traditional social studies. Generalization from a single case is always precarious. In addition, the very nature of the problem makes it difficult to marshal anything resembling hard evidence. What follows is, therefore, very much my personal impression both as to what happened in the center and what caused it to come about.

In my view, two elements played a crucial role, one the product of a conscious policy decision, the other resulting from a more spontaneous process. The policy element to which I have already alluded was the decision to interpret the mandate of the Russian Center broadly so as to include work in history, economics, and government, and, more importantly, to co-opt to the executive committee of the center representatives of the disciplines. Such action was certainly in keeping with the center's spirit as an interdisciplinary organization. But the disciplines were not equally well organized or tooled up for work on Russian problems. In such a competition, the probability was great that the older disciplines with established techniques for dealing with immediate and obviously relevant problems might crowd out the newer approaches. An alternative strategy would have been to treat anthropology, sociology, and psychology as the equivalent of new industries requiring the equivalent of protection by special tariff walls, tax exemption, and a market monopoly, in order to enable them to survive the trials of the initial period of experimentation. As Philip Selznik showed so vividly in his study of the Tennessee Valley Authority (1949), to co-opt the powerful forces in one's environment may involve them in one's organization and gain it local support. But those co-opted will not necessarily work to advance the original goals of the organization which invites their participation. On the contrary, they will more likely carry their own aspirations into the new organization and redirect it to achieve their own goals, rather than the original objectives of the organization they have joined.

The other impetus to the drift away from the more behavioral approach in the Russian Research Center lay in the nature of the disciplines themselves and in Soviet society as an object of study. Of the social sciences, only history is organized almost exclusively on a territorial or regional basis. At the other end of the continuum, psychology is almost exclusively problem centered. There is no clear place, indeed one might almost say there is no legitimate role, within the structure of contemporary American *academic* psychology for the man whose chief concern is psychology *in* Russia or the psychology *of* Russians. Between these two extremes each of the other social science disciplines follows a slightly different pattern. In the United States, at least, political science and to a lesser degree economics give a legitimate role both to the comparativist and to the regional or areal specialist. Sociology, unfortunately, is very provincial in its almost exclusive focus on American society. Within those limits, furthermore, American sociology is intensely problem-oriented. This is reflected in its division into subspecialities such as deviance, stratification, the family, and the like.

Anthropology is to some degree organized on a regional basis, although the laurels generally go not to those who know most about a given people or region, but rather to those who contribute most to research on more discrete topics such as kinship or the study of personality in culture. In the case of anthropology, furthermore, we encounter most clearly a quite different impediment to bringing the behavioral disciplines to bear on the study of societies such as the Soviet Union, namely, the difficulties of doing fieldwork. Anthropologists and psychologists, and to a lesser degree sociologists, cannot work effectively without direct contact with the people they are studying. Historians, political scientists, and economists, by contrast, work mainly through documents or published sources. In the case of the Soviet Union, its character as a totalitarian political system almost completely cuts off the society and its citizens from direct access by behavioral scientists. This greatly reduced the motivation of psychologists, sociologists, and anthropologists to work in the Russian field.

If Kluckhohn did not succeed in establishing the newer social sciences and a more behavioral perspective as the dominant emphasis in the Russian Center, he nevertheless secured them a substantial place. Indeed, these disciplines played a much larger role at Harvard than at any other center of Soviet research. It was largely on his initiative that Richard Sheldon went to Finland to interview Finnish peasants who had spent long years as villagers working on collective farms under Soviet rule (see Sheldon 1952), that Demitri Shimkin developed his numerous studies of the peoples and cultures of Russia and the Soviet north (see Shimkin 1949, 1954; Shimkin and Sanjuan 1953), and Lawrence Krader his research on the Asiatic peoples (see Krader 1954). It was also at Kluckhohn's invitation that Raymond Bauer came to the center to pursue his research on the development of Soviet psychology and its conception of man (see Bauer 1952). Barrington Moore's work on ideaology and social change in Soviet society owed its inclusion in the center's work to the same initiative (see Moore 1950, 1954). And it was Kluckhohn who conceived and gave impetus to the Russian Center's major excursion in behavioral research, the Harvard Project on the Soviet Social System, which I have treated at greater length below.

In writing this review of Kluckhohn's influence on the organization of the Russian Research Center as an interdisciplinary effort, I have, as a behavioralist, perhaps unwittingly minimized his contribution by taking too narrow and parochial a view. So far as the center as a whole was concerned, it certainly embodied in marked degree the quality of open acceptance of all disciplines which could in any way contribute to our understanding of society and culture in Soviet Russia. If the center did not become truly interdisciplinary in all its work, it certainly was multidisciplinary to a degree which equaled or exceeded all other centers of regional studies. During the period in which Kluckhohn was its director, the center published many truly distinguished books and numerous important articles in political science, economics, history, and literature.

If any sins were committed at the center in the name of interdisciplinary research, they cannot be primarily laid at the door of Clyde Kluckhohn. Indeed, he was always at great pains to avoid making a cheap and sterile slogan of interdisciplinary research. He stated the case quite pointedly when he said,

The product of interdisciplinary research is not necessarily—as is sometimes carelessly assumed—a publication of which the hybrid roots are publicly validated by two or more authors who "represent" the several fields. In fact, in such instances, there is often evidence that no genuine integration has occurred. Collaboration has only advanced to the stage at which individuals with varying scholarly backgrounds have deemed it worthwhile to juxtapose their contributions within a single cover. Even less desirable are those not unfamiliar publications where no proper fusion has occurred, where the final text represents a series of compromises not fully satisfactory to any of the participants. These documents in another way lack the stamp of unity, and responsibility cannot be assigned because of the essential anonymity of the final authorship. Finally, there is the case where a single viewpoint is dominant and has reasonable internal consistency, but where there is no depth, no technical proficiency from the angle of any conventional discipline nor from that of a newly carved-out interstitial field. [1957:xiii]

Studies of Russian National Character

What Kluckhohn most hoped for the center was that it should bring the perspective of cultural anthropology to bear on an understanding of the actions of the Soviet government. Of course, he was not dealing here with a small nonliterate society, but a great—and in many ways unique—nation-state whose people were virtually completely cut off from direct contact with the outside world. Most of the techniques of anthropology were therefore not directly applicable. But he had helped fashion a new technique of anthropological analysis, which Ruth Benedict and Margaret Mead came to call "the study of culture from a distance." His chief experience with this approach came during World War II through his participation with Alexander Leighton and others at the Office of War Information in the study of Japanese morale. By using anthropological knowledge about Japanese culture as a screen for interpreting statements in the Japanese press and interview material from Japanese prisoners of war, Leighton, Kluckhohn, and their colleagues were able to interpret and predict Japanese behavior in a manner often more insightful and accurate than was possible by the usual means of political analysis (see Leighton 1949; Kluckhohn 1949a:175–78).

Kluckhohn's hope was to apply similar techniques to the understanding of Soviet behavior, which in the postwar period took on the same importance for the United States, and indeed the rest of the world, as Japan's action had during the war. Soviet behavior seemed to many to have the same qualities of strangeness and inscrutability. Of the numerous and diverse activities in historical, economic, political, and sociological analysis conducted at the center, therefore, Kluckhohn took a really strong personal interest mainly in those which bore more directly on understanding the ethos or national character of the Great Russians or the distinctive psychology of the Bolshevik elite. Of the many subjects we discussed at the center, none really fired his interest and engaged him personally so much as these. The main permanent record of his thoughts on these subjects is unfortunately limited to two modest documents, one a summary of studies of Russian national character (1955g), the other an article-length review of books on social psychology of Communist, and more specifically Bolshevik, patterns of thought and action (1955h).

Kluckhohn took great pleasure from the fact that two of the most important systematic studies on Russian national character were supported by, and in part conducted in, the Russian Research Center during his term as its director. The first grew out of an investigation by the British psychiatrist Henry Dicks (1952). Dicks's work in interviewing Soviet refugees received its prime support from other sources but, largely at Kluckhohn's initiative, it was arranged that he should spend some months in residence at the center to prepare a special report on the Russian national character as it was reflected in his interviews. The second study was part of the larger Refugee Interviewing Project of the Russian Research Center (of which more below), conducted by two Russian-speaking clinical psychologists on the center's staff, Eugenia Hanfmann and Helen Beier (Inkeles et al. 1958). Apart from these two center projects, there was a third major study of the Russian national character directed by Margaret Mead at Columbia University and the American Museum of Natural History.

Despite the substantial role he played in facilitating and stimulating the studies of Russian national character, it was only with great diffidence that Kluckhohn expressed himself publicly concerning them, claiming that at best he had only "the fairly comprehensive overview of the educated dilletante" (1955g:15). Yet in addition to a careful, systematic, and compact summary of the individual studies, he added an interesting synthesis of his own, pointing up the fact that "different analysts and observers, using different methods and data, are in excellent agreement among themselves . . . about the relatively enduring and salient personality characteristics of the Great Russian population." Among those characteristics, he noted "their passion for affiliation, for belongingness, for warmth and expressiveness in human relations . . . [and] a strong need for dependence" (1955g:15).

It is of relevance for his work on culture and personality that Kluckhohn did not insist, as did some of his anthropological colleagues, on the immutability of either Russian culture or national character. On the contrary, he suggested that social changes and other aspects of the general situation under the Soviets had acted in concert with historical tradition and child-rearing practices "to produce perceptible changes in the modal personality." But the most distinctive and personal note which he introduced into his review of these studies was in the image of a "national character drama being played out in the U.S.S.R." The Soviet elite, in his view, had undertaken "an experiment on the grand scale" in which, minority though they were, they acted "under the spell of a fierce and intolerant idealogy [to] remold a people in a direction quite contrary to the most fundamental propensities of their traditional national character." In this drama, as he saw it, the plot centered on a set of critical contrasting themes, the one side representing the more typical or modal Russian, the other the qualities of the Bolshevik elite. These contrasts included: warm, expressive expansiveness versus formality, control, and orderliness; personal loyalty, sincerity, and responsiveness versus distrust and conspiratorial mentality; strong identification with face-to-face groups versus a single, tolerated loyalty upward; being versus doing, or dependent passivity versus ceaseless instrumental "conscious activity" (1955g: 27–29).

The Harvard Project on the Soviet Social System

Of all the center's research, Kluckhohn participated most directly and fully in that with Soviet refugees. This research program, known as the Harvard Project on the Soviet Social System, rested on the testimony of former Soviet citizens who refused to return to the Soviet Union after the Second World War or later defected from the Soviet occupation forces in Germany. Kluckhohn was mainly responsible for the project's inception, and he served as its director so long as it was organized as a formal project, with myself and Raymond A. Bauer serving as director and codirector of research, respectively.

The most important materials for the Social System Project came from interviews and questionnaires, although some documen-

tary material was also collected (Bauer et al. 1956). At the core of
the research was a life history interview dealing with the informant's experiences, beliefs, and values in his family, education, work,
community, religion, politics, and other realms of daily life. These
interviews often lasted a week and frequently yielded a document of
100 or more pages based on the interviewer's notes; they were completed with 276 persons from all walks of Soviet life. The interviews were supplemented by a written questionnnaire, largely par-
alleling the themes of the interview, filled out by an additional two
thousand persons. The project also collected more than 400 interviews with informants on special topics such as factory management, the inner life of the Communist party, and the practice of
medicine in the USSR. In some cases these more specialized interviews were supplemented by written questionnaires. For example, the informant interviews with doctors and nurses were
supplemented by a questionnaire for patients soliciting their views
on the Soviet system of medical care. Finally, the project supported a
modest exploration in clinical psychology, which provided much of
the basis for its report on the Russian national character already
mentioned.

Of the center's research efforts, the Social System Project most
fully expressed Kluckhohn's aspiration to bring the behavioral sciences to bear on Soviet studies. There were at least three major
respects in which the project reflected his ideas and ideals for the
organization of research on a complex society. In the first place, it
was a decidedly interdisciplinary enterprise. Its directors were an anthropologist, a sociologist, and a psychologist, and its staff included
representatives not only from these fields but also from economics,
history, and political science. Secondly, the chief source of information came from protracted face-to-face contact between Soviet and
American citizens during the long life-history interviews which were
conducted exclusively in Russian and Ukrainian. All members of the
staff, whatever their disciplinary affiliation and specialized interest,
took part in the general interviewing program. Third, the unifying
and in many ways central theme of the project was its interest in un-
covering value and behavior patterns in which he had so strong an
interest.

Although he was extremely diffident about publishing on Soviet affairs, Kluckhohn did join in writing the project's "final report," *How the Soviet System Works* (Bauer et al. 1956). This was not so much a systematic summary of the project's findings, which was left to another and later publication (Inkeles and Bauer 1959), as an effort to use our experience with former Soviet citizens as a stimulus in formulating a fresh perspective on Soviet society. With the aid of the insights our interviews had given, we sought to throw new light on the Soviet system's past, to highlight its current and perhaps enduring characteristics, and to point out its probable lines of future development. In keeping with Kluckhohn's interests, we gave particular attention to what emerged as "repetitive patterns and recurrent themes" in our interviews. The early part of the book, for example, was devoted to a series of eight operating characteristics of the Soviet system, an awareness of which we found essential to understanding the individual's adjustment in Soviet society. These characteristics of the Soviet system included themes such as "planning and controlling," "the overcommitment of resources," and "the refusal to allow independent 'concentrations of power.'" Although the topics discussed and the language used to describe them reflect the fact that we were dealing with a large-scale industrial society, anyone familiar with Kluckhohn's approach to culture will recognize the affinity between these themes and the themes and patterns he favored for the description of nonliterate societies. The justification we offered for adopting this approach to the analysis of Soviet society reflected his stance on this issue sufficiently well to warrant reproducing it here.

Rather than focus on the conventional "institutions" (family, industry, political system, and education), according to which societies are ordinarily described, we try to depict a series of themes—or threads—that cut across the fabric of Soviet social behavior, giving it a stability or continuity or form and structure. This method will, of necessity, entail some repetition, but we have sought to give a different emphasis to the material wherever a theme recurs and to make the picture truly cumulative. We hope thus to expose central and repetitive patterns of action, a knowledge of which makes possible the forecasting of likely responses, under particular conditions, of various segments of the Soviet leadership and of the governed masses. [Bauer et al. 1956:19–20]

A Parting Note

Clyde Kluckhohn administratively shaped the Russian Research Center to foster an interdisciplinary approach to understanding Russian culture and Soviet society. He helped elaborate our image of the Russian national character and contributed substantially to our knowledge of the distinctive patterns of Soviet behavior. But I think that his greatest impact on Soviet studies in the United States was purely personal and came through the influence he exerted on the young scholars assembled at the center in its early years. The first home of the center was a small yellow frame house just outside the Harvard Yard, which looked very much like a country dacha just outside Moscow. Apart from Clyde, all the more senior members of the center staff had their offices in other buildings, but with him in that modest home the younger members of the center faculty and the graduate students spent the greater part of their time. Of course, they did a great deal to educate each other, and that was part of Clyde's plan. But the greatest impact came from his own example. He always placed ideas above disciplinary loyalties. He had a vital interest in the widest range of studies, even when they were far from his immediate concerns. Yet he was always ready, at times with heroic patience, to explain how anthropologists looked at social issues and studied culture. He was a luminous person, and the center glowed with his light. To men at the center from all fields, from literature to economics, he was a charismatic leader and a beloved person. He made vivid and real what for most is at best a vague aspiration: to combine the highest intellectual standards with the greatest humanity and compassion. I think no one of the young scholars who came in contact with him during that period was uninfluenced, uninstructed, or uninspired.

CLYDE KLUCKHOHN AND INDIAN ADMINISTRATION

John Adair

C LYDE KLUCKHOHN'S interest in pattern and configuration of culture was basic to his contribution to Indian administration. His knowledge of the integrating principles of the covert culture, "that sector of the culture of which members of the society are unaware or minimally aware," enabled him to be an effective spokesman for the Navaho since he was able to verbalize for them to the administrators these unstated premises. Further, he was able to point out where the introduction of specific programs would clash with fundamental Navaho values, using his knowledge of the covert integrating principles of Navaho culture. He wrote: "Actually, the tenacity of cultural structure, and especially of the covert structure, is one of the widest and most useful generalizations with which anthropology can provide the administrator" (1943b:219).

He was influential behind the scenes in helping to plan for action and shape decisions on the field level and on the top administrative level in Washington. Because he did this modestly, spoke but seldom about these activities in public, and wrote very little on Indian administration, this aspect of Kluckhohn's contribution as an anthropologist is relatively unknown to those who knew him as a teacher and scientist. But his dedication to the rights of the American Indian and to furthering Indian education and economic well-being was well known to the Commissioners of Indian Affairs, their field staff, the leadership in the Association on American Indian Affairs, and the Navaho tribal attorney.

Kluckhohn spent a great deal of time advising the Navaho tribal leaders at Ramah on their economic and educational problems and how to address their concerns to government officials. This was the natural outgrowth of his total involvement with the Navaho people with whom he had deep emotional ties going back to 1923, long before he became a formal student of anthropology. While it was his love for the Navaho and the Navaho country that first attracted him, such an emotional identification did not interfer with his work as a scientist but, to the contrary, was the very source and inspiration for his scientific investigations.

This same scrupulous objectivity characterized his thinking on Indian affairs. He never allowed his emotions to dominate, and he felt that any recommendations to the Office of the Commissioner of Indian Affairs or his staff should be offered only after careful and thorough field study of the people concerned, coupled with a knowledge of the literature and assessment of the total situation. One of the few articles on Indian administration written by him, "Covert Culture and Administrative Problems," which was also an essay in anthropological theory, makes just this point; he praises the Collier administration:

In no field of administration has anthropology's master concept, culture, been so basic to planning and to action.

. . . . .

If performance is often still not above criticism, this is at least as much the result of the inadequacy of the data and analytical skills which anthropology (and other social sciences) are as yet able to supply as of any administrative ineptness.

. . . . .

[and he pleads for] more systematic anthropological theory. New conceptual refinements will suggest new observations and the re-sifting of already accumulated data for illuminations which will have practical implications. [1943b:213–14]

The underlying, integrating principles, the configuration of the covert culture, must be understood by the anthropologist and communicated to the administrator. Without such understanding, the administrator falls into the trap of thinking that change in culture content (modern dress, technology, housing, etc.) is an indication of fundamental change in values. He then builds his policy for programs on such false assumptions and is brought up short when resistance sets in. As Kluckhohn says:

a program which has been carefully thought through for its possible continuities with the cultural inventory and even for its interdigitation with the first-order patterns sometimes fails to work out. This is very probably because, as Sapir says, the innovations do not "configurate correctly with the unconscious system of meanings characteristic of the given culture." [1943*b*:219]

This article and much of Kluckhohn's later writing provided just such a conceptual refinement and proved to have great practical implications. He delineated a number of configurations of the covert culture which he felt important for administrators: (1) shame as a basic sanction rather than guilt, (2) the lack of mind-body dichotomy, (3) the lack of the principle of unilateral causation. These and other aspects of the covert culture which he set forth in his later writing on Navaho values, ethics, and philosophy have had a great influence on the thinking of anthropologists, educators, physicians, and administrators concerned with planned change on the Navaho reservation.

Such a practical implication may be illustrated by the work of Cornell University College at Many Farms, Arizona (Adair 1963). There, the medical team, which included anthropologists, demonstrated that a medical service in which the physicians showed respect for the medicine men—rather than the usual indifference or open hostility expressed by many physicians and nurses—resulted in a highly successful program. In effect, this demonstrated the importance of the administrator's awareness of covert configuration: The whole organism needs treating; the personality is indivisible— you can't treat a man's "mind" without treating his "body" or vice versa. For any illness there is to be found not one but many causes.

Kluckhohn's participation as consultant, fieldworker, and analyst in the Bureau of Indian Affairs' Project in Indian Personality and

Administration was essentially directed to conveying a comprehensive understanding of Navaho culture to the administrators. The project was undertaken jointly by the Committee on Human Development at the Universtiy of Chicago and the United States Office of Indian Affairs under the overall coordination of Laura Thompson and had as its objective "to investigate, analyze, and compare the development of personality in five Indian tribes in the context of their total environment—socio-cultural, geographical, and historical —for implications in regard to Indian Service Administration" (Kluckhohn and Leighton 1946a:vii). The ultimate aim of the project was to suggest how Indian administration could be improved.

Kluckhohn participated in the project on many levels: as consultant, project designer, fieldworker in Ramah (one of the Navaho communities selected for investigation), and analyst of the field findings from the Navaho sample of communities. He was one of the anthropologists who met in the summer of 1941 in Santa Fe, along with psychologists and teachers and administrators from the bureau, for the planning and training of fieldworkers for this interdisciplinary research. Kluckhohn taught the project field staff about the dynamics of culture and personality development by means of a case study of the Navaho. With the help of Indians from neighboring pueblos, he also worked out a successful adaptation of Murray's Thematic Apperception Test for use in Indian communities. Two of his most widely read works, *The Navaho* (Kluckhohn and Leighton 1946a) and *Children of the People* (Leighton and Kluckhohn 1947), are the major published results of the findings from this project. Therein the overt aspects of the culture are well described, but it is especially the final chapters on the deeper lying patterns of language, thought, and values (essentially the covert culture) that made a contribution to understanding of the Navaho and thereby to those of the government who were concerned with their administration.

This project was inaugurated under the administration of John Collier, who had been appointed Indian commissioner in 1933. By this time, Kluckhohn was well known all through the Navaho country, not only to the Indians themselves, but to traders, missionaries, ranchers, and government men. He began to be called on for advice by the officials of this reform administration, and his contributions can best be evaluated by the administrators themselves, especially two members of Collier's field staff who were in immediate touch with the Navaho. Sophie Aberle, superintendent of the United Pueblos Agency from 1935 to 1944, recalls his role as an informal consultant to her office:

He was interested in administration because he realized that the form of the organization, its policies, decisions, statements and strategies had a profound effect upon Indian life. This insight was far ahead of his time. His advice and help strengthened my own understanding of the necessity of giving Indians plenty of information so they could know and discuss policy decisions affecting them.

His interest in administration stemmed from his understanding of the Navajo, but his interest was that of a theorist of administration. He understood, moreover, that although the form of an organization was important for accomplishing tasks undertaken, no organization pattern, however beautiful it looks on paper, could be a substitute for skill of the man at the head nor the Indians' own ability to assume responsibility.

Clyde drew upon research for his recommendations which were practical. For example, during the late thirties, three off-reservation Navajo groups who were under the Superintendent at Window Rock asked the Commissioner of Indian Affairs to have themselves transferred to the Pueblos Agency. Clyde and I discussed this transfer. He said he himself thought the off-reservation Navajos should remain with the Navajo reservation group because they had common interest, but regardless of his own judgment he thought we should follow the wishes of the group since the move was at their request. At the same time he suggested obtaining an orderly collection of information before and after the transfer for use in making further adjustments. He promised to observe the effect of the change of administration within the Ramah group himself. Soon after the administration of the Puertocito (now called Alamo), the Canoncito, and the Ramah Navajo Indians were turned over to the Pueblos Agency.

At the first meeting I had with the Ramah Indians Clyde acted as interpreter, and introduced me to many of his Ramah friends. Most of the time during that first meeting was spent listening to the Ramahs explain that they wanted more land and a school.

Clyde and I talked over the problems. Clyde had a student in Anthropology whom he thought could work with the Ramahs. He had great faith in young people, so he was not daunted by sending to Ramah a recent graduate of Radcliffe to help the Indians build their own plant, and operate the first school the Ramahs had on their own land. After that Clyde sent several students to the Pueblos Agency for special assignments. [Personal communication]

After World War II, Kluckhohn was not able to spend as much time in the Southwest as he would have liked. But he still took a very active interest in the welfare of the Navaho. Walter Olson, subagent at Zuni and responsible for bureau activities in the Ramah area, recalls his contacts with Clyde:

Clyde's initial interest in knowing me came as a result of my working with the Ramah Navajo and the Zuni Indians while stationed at Black Rock, New Mexico. Over these years Clyde made a point of coming to that area at least once a year and sometimes more often. Some years his stay was limited to a few days, while on others he stayed several weeks. He was always very interested in discussing the problems and programs for both groups of Indians. In his own inimitable way he offered a great deal of advice and information, not only to me, but to the Indian people themselves, particularly the Ramahs. From the initial getting acquainted period, our relationship developed to the frankest type of discussion in terms of subjects that affected the Indians, which of course, include my work with them. These discussions were not limited alone to Indian problems but to the broader problems of minority groups and so-called under-developed countries.

. . . . .

Clyde's interest in problems of people was catholic—education, land, medical, administrative or what have you. He saw as a total the inter-relationship and the necessity to break down problems so that they might be more easily analyzed and handled. He understood the only measure of effectiveness was accomplishment. Accomplishment to him was the establishment by the Indians of a more secure base for their own livelihood. One key to understanding such problems which he always used was the interaction of people—what people responded to and if possible why they responded. He was greatly interested, for example, in the relationship between the Indians as a group, the Texas ranchers of the Area, the Spanish American people and the earlier Mormon farmers.

. . . . .

From my own knowledge Clyde was influential behind the scenes in over-riding reluctance in the securing of more land for Indian people.

This was true just after World War II began at which time the leases held by the Bureau of Indian Affairs for land used by the Ramah Indians expired. The company owning these lands were putting them up for public sale. The government was restricted from buying such lands, the Ramah-Navajo Tribe had no money, banking institutions were unwilling to consider purchase for re-leasing and the only source was funds held by some of the North Pueblo Indians. . . . They bought the land and the government leased it for Ramah use. In later years when the Navajo Tribe had developed a fairly large treasury balance, the tribe bought such lands for Ramah-Navajo use.

The points of Clyde's involvement came as a result of a very specific and definite opposition within and without the government to such a business proposition. When Clyde learned of this he made his view known in the right places and final result was the purchase of the land.

He was most instrumental in a very quiet and unobtrusive way in battles and discussions of school policy, as for instance, [in opposing the removal of] Indians to far away places for their education. [Personal communication]

Kluckhohn's participation in Indian affairs extended beyond his involvement in Navaho matters. In 1943, he served on a Social and Economic Rehabilitation Committee of the American Association on Indian Affairs at the request of its president, Haven Emerson. The objective of this committee was to draw up a program for that organization's activities in the postwar years. In 1948, Kluckhohn was asked to serve on the board of directors of that association. In April 1948, in response to a request from the association, Kluckhohn testified before the Joint Hearings of the Indian Affairs Subcommittee on the Navaho-Hopi Rehabilitation Bill which later was enacted by Congress and enabled the building up of education, medical, welfare, and other services during the postwar period. Additionally, Kluckhohn wrote to J. C. O'Mahoney, chairman of the Senate Committee on Interior and Insular Affairs, and to Toby Morris, chairman of the same committee in the House, urging favorable action on this bill when it came to the floor in 1949.

Kluckhohn served on the board of directors of the association until March of 1957. During all but the last two years, Alexander Lesser was executive director of the association. He has written of Kluckhohn's participation in the association as follows:

He came to all the Association Board meetings he could and did something few other Board members did at all, namely, when at the Board's decision something was sent out for action by mail ballot of the entire Board, Clyde took it up in detail and at times wrote lengthy and careful analyses back. I remember this particularly in relation to proposed legislation the Association considered sponsoring—usually drawn up by Felix Cohen.

. . . . .

We should not forget that Clyde's activity with the Association was only a facet of his driving interest and concern in seeing constructive study and work advanced from an applied anthropology standpoint in the whole field of Indians and Indian affairs. . . . despite his first-hand knowledge of the Southwest and his deep interests there, this included any Indian group or area with which the Association became involved. [Personal communication]

During the Eisenhower administration, Glenn Emmons of Gallup, New Mexico, served as Indian commissioner. Emmons, who was an old friend of Kluckhohn's, called upon him for advice particularly with reference to Navaho administration. In addition, he served as a member of the board of directors of the American Indian Research Fund, organized by Emmons and a group of prominent businessmen for the purpose of attracting funds to support "complete research of certain Indian reservations to accelerate the development of their natural and human resources." This organization ceased to function actively about 1959, for lack of operating funds.

One of the very few evaluations of United States government Indian policy written by Kluckhohn (in collaboration with Robert A. Hackenberg) was "Social Science Principles and the Indian Reorganization Act" (Kluckhohn and Hackenberg 1954c). This was presented in 1953 at a symposium, "Reevaluation of the Indian Reorganization Act," sponsored by the Society for Applied Anthropology at the annual meeting of the American Anthropological Association. Kluckhohn was generous in his praise of the Indian Reorganization Act:

The IRA was a deliberate attempt to induce certain kinds of changes into Indian society and to control other changes. In its inception the authors made conscious use of the knowledge of culture change then possessed by the social sciences.

The thinking that went into the act revolves around two axioms of human behavior. First, the recognition of the importance of Indian group life and of the necessity to preserve and encourage native social controls and Indian values as the foundation upon which such changes and innovations as various Indian groups themselves decided were worth while should be made.

Second, a recognition that constructive change must not destroy psychological security and must preserve continuity in the lives of both the group and the individual so that personality integration and stability may be maintained. [Kluckhohn and Hackenberg 1954c:29]

He pointed out that the shifting of the locus of initiative for changes from the Bureau of Indian Affairs to the Indians themselves was a new departure. The Indian Reorganization Act, he said, made it possible for the tribe to plan and supervise its own economic development and to secure a charter of incorporation for business enterprises and financial assistance from a revolving loan fund provided by the federal government. Kluckhohn also made some negative observations "without substantially detracting from this impressive achievement." He went on to point out that the execution of the Indian Reorganization Act was not at the same level as the conception. The greatest failure was that, while the culture of different Indian groups was carefully considered, the culture of bureaucracy was ignored in the planning process. As a result much of the Washington planning was not put into effect "because insufficient attention was paid to the habitual ways of thinking and reacting of the group out in the field." They acted as a screen between the planners and the Indian communities.

The Indian Personality and Administrative Research Program had been established by the Collier administration "to determine the extent to which the Indian Reorganization Act had succeeded in achieving its ultimate goal, the personal security of the individual Indian." Kluckhohn pointed out that the "sweeping changes in the structure and functions of the Bureau of Indian Affairs" recommended in that program had not been acted upon. As with the Indian Reorganization Act, social science principles used in planning met with difficulty in application.

Kluckhohn concluded his address to that symposium by saying
that speaking as a citizen and friend of the Indians he felt that if the
basic principles of the Indian Reorganization Act were sound they
should be reactivated. He warned against "a premature, hasty, and
ill-considered total withdrawal of the Federal Government from Indian affairs, which might pave the way for seizure of Indian resources by the states or by local vested interests." As a member of
the board of directors of the American Association on Indian Affairs,
he was against rapid withdrawal of federal services and participated
in their fight against Public Law 280 of the Eighty-third Congress,
which granted states the right to impose civil and criminal jurisdiction on Indian communities, thereby renouncing the protection
afforded by federal jurisdiction.

In 1951, Norman M. Littell, general counsel and claims attorney for the Navaho Tribe, contacted Clyde Kluckhohn and asked
him if he would serve as an expert witness in the Navaho land claim
against the United States government to be heard before the United
States Indian Claims Commission. At that time Kluckhohn was
unable to undertake the work but did serve as a consultant to the
tribe and their attorney (without pay, at his own stipulation). In
this capacity, he made suggestions as to which research people
should be employed and the sources in the archaeological and
ethnological literature which should be covered in the prospective
research. He consulted with Richard Van Valkenburgh, the anthropologist who was selected and retained by Littell because of his extensive prior fieldwork in Navaholand, his knowledge of the Navaho
people and interpreters, and his executive capacity in supervising a
massive undertaking of fieldwork. In December 1952, Van Valkenburgh recommended employment of J. Lee Correll, who thereafter
served as his assistant. Kluckhohn conferred and worked with both
men, keeping in touch with accumulating evidence and with Littell
as to the legal significance of what the research disclosed.

The basic question which the Indian Claims Commission would
have to resolve was: What lands were wrongfully taken from the
Navahos by the United States? This involved determining the extent of Navaho occupancy and exclusive use prior to the beginning
of the territorial period in 1848 and through the time of the Navaho

return from Fort Sumner in 1868. This necessitated drawing together an enormous amount of archaeological, historical, and ethnological literature. Undoubtedly, the archaeological research in this case, concerning the location, recording, and analysis of hogans and other Navaho sites, is the most extensive ever undertaken in the Southwest.

The Navahos suffered a tragic loss when Van Valkenburgh died of a heart attack in 1957. A few months later, Kluckhohn was retained as expert witness. He worked closely with Littell in coordinating the field research which was continued under the direction of Correll, assisted by David M. Brugge. George P. Hammond, director of Bancroft Library at Berkeley, and Dale Morgan were retained by the tribe for historic research; David De Harport, at Harvard University, assisted in the gathering of ethnographic materials for the case. The plan was for Kluckhohn to bring into focus on the witness stand the massive array of data assembled by the historians, archaeologists, and ethnologists. Norman Littell writes of the part Clyde Kluckhohn played in the preparation of the case and of his appearance on the witness stand:

No words from me are needed to describe Kluckhohn's mastery of Navajo background. As Dr. Leland Wyman once said to me: "There is only one Clyde Kluckhohn in a generation."

What I can add is my comment as a lawyer in regard to his superb adaption of knowledge to the practical objectives and purposes of a law suit. This certainly lies outside the normal academic field of research and training. It is, however, the mark of a supremely intelligent mind to run the gauntlet of the lawyer's jargon as to what is material, relevant, and competent. He did so brilliantly.

Clyde was on the witness stand for four days, from January 29 to February 3, 1960, and I felt confirmed, while listening to him, in the opinion which I had expressed privately to him on more than one occasion: that the Navajo case before the Indian Claims Commission and a companion case in respect to the Navajo-Hopi boundary line, tried before a three-judge court in Arizona, represented a summation at the peak of his professional career—a final and historic service to the Navajo people whom he loved and knew so well. He and R. F. Van Valkenburgh, each in his respective walks of life, knew the Navajos as no two other

non-Navajo men of this generation have known and understood them—
in my opinion. [Personal communication]

Kluckhohn's death in the summer of 1960 prevented the completion
of his testimony. However, despite the fact that the cross-examina-
tion had not been completed, Kluckhohn's words as witness were
retained in the record by order of the commission.

It is characteristic of the man that the political action for the
American Indian in which he became engaged was highly effective
and showed the same dedication he exhibited as a scholar
and teacher.

CLYDE KLUCKHOHN'S
CONTRIBUTIONS TO
NAVAHO STUDIES

David F. Aberle

CLYDE KLUCKHOHN did fieldwork only among the Navaho, principally at Ramah, New Mexico, and (briefly) among the Hopi. Publications deriving from this work are almost entirely on the Navaho. Many of his theoretical ideas were stimulated by efforts to deal with Navaho data, while others appear in essays, the examples for which are drawn largely or entirely from Navaho materials. Certainly it was not Navaho culture alone that engendered Kluckhohn's approach, but his visits with the Navaho were a central part of his anthropological experience and of his life, and they influenced his thinking.

This essay will deal with the more general implications of his writings only as they are relevant to his Navaho work. Because of editorial problems and decisions beyond my control, I shall not be able to discuss his monograph *Navaho Witchcraft*, which, in addition to exhibiting an exemplary rigor and a great subtlety of analysis, is so crucial for our understanding of Navaho culture and which, therefore, deserves a full critical appreciation not possible to accord it here. I shall try to say what the rest of Kluckhohn's Navaho work was, why it was the way it was, and what utility it has for current fieldwork among the Navaho.

To begin with, Kluckhohn had an unabashed, romantic attach-

ment to Navaho life and the Navaho country. This can be seen in
To the Foot of the Rainbow (1927), which chronicles a trip taken
when he was less than twenty years of age, and *Beyond the Rainbow* (1933a), which tells of trips from the age of twenty-one to the
age of twenty-four. These trips through the Navaho country and
other parts of the Southwest normally began at the Vogt ranch,
near Ramah, New Mexico, where he had earlier gone for his
health. Thus, contacts with the Southwest and with the Navaho
antedated his formal training as an anthropologist and, one feels,
helped direct him toward anthropology.

In 1941, Clyde invited me to work at Ramah during the summer.
The day after I arrived I was introduced into the house of John
Chatto, married to a daughter of Bidaga, then the headman of
the Ramah Navahos, so that I might live in a Navaho household
while I did my work. That evening or the next, Clyde stopped to
visit another of Bidaga's daughters, and I went over to sit with him.
The sun gradually set over the red cliff. We sat outside with the
Navahos in the flickering firelight. One could hear soft voices and
the tinkling of sheep bells in the corral. He spoke then of his love
for the Ramah country and said, "To me it's the most beautiful
place in the whole world!" I share his attachment to the country
and the people. I think that it shaped what he wrote. In many
technical papers, he was too concerned with meticulous description to give this attitude full expression, but it appears in the two
early books mentioned above, in many evocative passages in *The
Navaho* (Kluckhohn and Leighton 1946a) and *Children of the People* (Leighton and Kluckhohn 1947), in *Navaho Means People*
(McCombe et al. 1951), in many general descriptions of the Navaho
life view, and elsewhere (e.g., 1933b, 1937, 1942b, 1945e, 1948d,
1949d, 1956c, 1960f; Kluckhohn and Vogt 1955n). Anyone who
talked with him about the Southwest recognized his love for the
land and the people, continuing from his earliest visits to the day he
died. Furthermore, the many students and members of the public
who respond to anthropology's more formal analyses by asking
"What's their life *really* like?" can find an answer in the case of the
Navaho.

A second element in his approach to the Navaho is a concern
with meticulous description. One reason for this concern, I think,

emerges directly from the nature of Navaho life. There is a very high degree of variability in Navaho behavior—from one occasion to another apparently similar one, for any given individual, and from one individual to another. On many points informants do not agree; on many others, observations are discordant with one another. One is more often than not pushed toward descriptions of central tendencies, multiple modes, or frequency distributions, rather than toward delineation of clear-cut general uniformities. Awareness of this variability has characterized the writings of ethnographers from as early as Gladys Reichard's *Social Life of the Navaho Indians* (1928) until the present time. But it was Kluckhohn and Wyman, separately and together, who first made discussion of this variability a central feature of their publications.

Two concerns emerged. The first had to do with types of behavior in which little standardization was apparent or where it was necessary to find out how much standardization—or how little— there was. Frequency counts then became the technique for describing the situation. Thus, "Participation in Ceremonials in a Navaho Community" (Kluckhohn 1938c) tells how many Ramah Navahos attended Enemy Way ceremonials for how many days during one summer, how many chants each singer performed outside the community, which sings were held how often, and so on. In "Navaho Women's Knowledge of Their Song Ceremonials" (1938b), he found out how many sings Navaho women could name, whether they could group them, and what other ones they could recognize if they were mentioned—finding an association between age and ceremonial knowledge and between close relationship to a ceremonialist and such knowledge. In "Some Personal and Social Aspects of Navaho Ceremonial Practice" (1939d), he discussed the clan and kinship connections of singers and diviners, tabulated from what kin (or non-kin) a singer learned, and what kinds of kin attended a patient's sings. These were among his earlier papers; this sort of presentation was continued in later publications.

Where behavior was more standardized, a somewhat different practice appeared, as in the work on ceremonials.

Descriptions of actual procedures, unless [designated by symbols indicating which informant(s) provided the data] . . . are based upon actual

observation by one or both of us. All other statements . . . are followed
by designations of informants if based upon information from four or
fewer Navahos. In this case, until confirmed, they must be regarded as
local or individual generalizations only. If a generalization is a matter of
general knowledge or has received independent confirmation from more
than four reliable informants it is unmarked. The attempt has been made
to check every point (except rationalizations volunteered) with at least
four informants. [Kluckhohn and Wyman 1940b:11–12]

It must be remembered that concern for sampling or frequency
counts was not common in anthropology (though certainly not unknown) when Kluckhohn began this type of presentation. He must
have felt somewhat defensive about it, since in two publications
(the revision of 1939d presented in 1962a:97; 1944a:73) he
quoted Bandelier's letter to Morgan of February 28, 1874: "An ac-
cumulation of minute details, however silly it may appear, is the only
correct means to reach the fundamental truths." And a discourse
upon the importance of frequency distributions appears in several
places (e.g., 1938b, 1938c, 1939e). If part of his concern for meticulous description of this sort was derived from the experiencing of
Navaho variability, another part stemmed from an interest in statistical approaches (see 1939e). The result was a good deal of nose-
counting, episode-counting, and so on. Yet, as will appear later, this
interest in enumerative and descriptive statistics seldom led him to
examine problems of covariation.

The concern for variability, however, may have had another
basis. Relatively early in Kluckhohn's work (although I have been
unable to locate the reference), he took the position that individual
behavioral variation corresponded to mutation as a source of biological variation and that there was selection of such variations. This
theme occurs again in his "Biological and Cultural Evolution" (in
Gerard et al. 1956). Its appearance at the beginning of his scientific
career (as I recall) and four years before its close makes me believe
that it was important to him theoretically.

Thus, in the later, coauthored paper we find:

No two speakers of the same language or dialect utter "the same" sounds
in precisely identical ways. . . . Not all of these variations, of course,
can be compared to mutations. . . . but some sound changes, like the

germinal cell mutations which do spread by inheritance, may become durably established in a population. [In Gerard et al. 1956:16]

It would appear, then, that his concern for description of variant patterns of behavior, variant beliefs, variant observed behaviors, and so on, was not only a matter of desire for precision, instead of loose generalization in description, but was an element in an approach that he adumbrated but did not implement, that of dealing with change through the examination of behavioral variation.

This approach, however, was not entirely at peace with another approach, one that suggests a "great man" element in his theory of culture change. He referred several times to the possible role of an idiosyncratic chief in creating, for example, religious changes—sometimes with, sometimes without qualifications (Kluckhohn and Kelly 1945b:86–87 and also a mimeographed, fuller version that was circulated in 1944; Kluckhohn 1949a:67).

A third element in Kluckhohn's way of dealing with Navaho materials was, of course, the search for pattern. The search for pattern in Navaho life combined with the recognition of the tremendous variability in Navaho behavior seems to create a tension in fieldworkers, and Clyde was no exception. If we examine "Some Personal and Social Aspects of Navaho Ceremonial Practice," we can see evidence of this problem.

No circumstance reflects more dramatically the interdependence of the ceremonial and social organization than the fact that if a singer or curer sings over his own wife, their future relationship is perforce governed by the rules regulating the behavior between men and women of the same clan. [Kluckhohn 1939d:57]

Compare that statement with the following conclusions about the relationship between a person learning a sing and his teacher: "Close biological-sociological relationship appears to be a determinant of the transmission of ceremonial knowledge in more than three cases out of four" (Kluckhohn 1962a:106; this is an edited version of 1939d). Compare also: "To questions of the sort, 'From whom does one learn a ceremonial?' replies follow this general pattern: 'From anyone. Usually from a relative, but it can be from anyone'" (1962a:107). Or compare that paper as a whole to "An Introduction to Navaho Chant Practice" with its classically clear break-down of the complexities of Navaho chants into "more or less dis-crete units ('ceremonies' and 'acts and procedures')" (Kluckhohn and Wyman 1940b:13). Frequencies, to be sure, form patterns but not of the sort that most delighted Clyde's heart. His conception of rigor demanded the frequency counts, but it was clear that patterns satisfied his aesthetic sense.

A fourth and final element in Kluckhohn's approach to matters Navaho—and the list could be greatly enlarged—was his humane concern with the problems facing Navahos. This appears most clearly in *The Navaho* and *Children of the People,* but also in *Navaho Means People* and other places (e.g., 1937, 1945c, 1955d). This concern was undoubtedly manifested in activities on behalf of Ramah Navahos in many unrecorded instances, but it appeared mainly in the form of writing for the public and for what he hoped were enlightened administrators or administrators capable of enlightenment (e.g., the prefaces to *The Navaho* and *Children of the People*). In such circumstances, he wrote most often with the happy assumption that, if they were enlightened by the anthropologists, the powerful would act to help the powerless. This was a natural assumption for an anthropologist who knew the New Deal and knew John Collier. It is an assumption that favored Kluckhohn's work, but one that some anthropologists would question today.

These elements combined to make Kluckhohn a magnificent ethnographer of Navaho life and an interpreter of that life to various American publics, but not, by and large, an explainer of Navaho life in the sense of showing a systematic concern with cause and effect relationships. For present purposes, by "interpreter" is meant someone who can show members of one culture how the world looks to the members of another, and it is no small accomplishment. An explanation (in the sense used here) has to go beyond this: To say that people behave in a particular way because they believe that is the way to behave is not an explanation; it is a commonplace since we seldom find people who say, "we behave one way but believe a different way"—and if they do tell us that, then they have introduced additional beliefs as their own folk explanations. Thus, for example, seldom does Kluckhohn concern himself with why Navahos have the kind of political system they have or why paternal kin appear more often at a patient's ceremonial than matrilineal kin. There are many, many minor exceptions to this statement: Scattered throughout *The Navaho* is a variety of valuable explanations, but the only major exceptions I know where systematic explanation is attempted are *Navajo Witchcraft* (1944*a*) and "Group Tensions: Analysis of a Case History" (1945*c*).

However all this may be, my task here is the assaying of his contribution to our understanding of the Navaho, and it is very great indeed. It is impossible, however, in writing about it, to separate Kluckhohn's contribution from Leland Wyman's or Dorothea Leighton's. We turn now to some of the major works.

"Navaho Classification of Their Song Ceremonials" (Wyman and Kluckhohn 1938) is the best and most compendious list of Navaho chants and is an important effort at grouping them according to native principles. There is reason to think that the classification may require revision. But any fieldworker among the Navaho will continue to rely on the chant list and to find it of great utility in discussions with informants. The larger companion volume, "An Introduction to Navaho Chant Practice" (Kluckhohn and Wyman 1940*b*), will continue to guide every fieldworker who has not become an expert of the first water in the mazes of chant performance. As for *Navaho Witchcraft*, after some eight summers of listening to witchcraft stories, I have found some information which supplements Kluckhohn's, but none that I recall that contradicts it. More important, one who knows the book is able to ask productive questions in the field and to understand hints and comments that would otherwise pass him by.

The Navaho and *Children of the People* (both with Dorothea Leighton), but particularly the former, are certainly the best existing descriptions of Navaho life for the period 1920–45; they are the best-rounded ethnography of the Navaho for any period now available; and, though written primarily for a nonprofessional audience, they contain materials on a variety of topics that make them worth repeated readings. To take a personal example, I have been working for some time on why Navaho families often have two or more dwelling places, used in alternation or rotation, and why hogans are often abandoned or torn down and new structures built near their former location. I find that much of what I now know is to be found in *The Navaho* (Kluckhohn and Leighton 1946a:46). But for me these facts are now connected with others in ways that Kluckhohn did not mention. The apparent completeness of his work, indeed, makes it necessary for me to set his work aside if I am to think of new questions, develop new implications, and attempt a different style of analysis. These four studies alone, together with the *Bibliography of the Navaho Indians* coauthored with Katherine Spencer (Kluckhohn and Spencer 1940a), will maintain their crucial value for any Navaho fieldworker for decades to come and will be of importance for an understanding of this American Indian group and for comparative studies long after Navaho culture changes almost beyond recognition.

However, this positive evaluation will not suffer if there are a few critical comments. First, although he was the author of a paper on the application of association coefficients to ethnological data (1939b), Kluckhohn by and large used distributions of single variables, not associations of two or more variables, when he quantified his data. In order to decide who teaches a Navaho ceremonialist, it is necessary to tally which kin and nonkin taught which singers in a given area. Nevertheless, sometimes the descriptive tallies are not tied to very lively problems and, thus, sometimes the demand for precision is wearying, because no end point except precision is clearly delineated.

Second, where the enumerative statistics suggest problems, these are not always seized on. Thus he notes (1939d) that men learn their ceremonials mainly from paternal kin and, in the same paper, that a dead singer's pouch is likely to be inherited by his matrilineal relatives. These differences are not brought into conjunction, nor are their implications in a matrilineal society explored. In this particular case, the reason may be Kluckhohn's often-expressed wry distaste for kinship studies—although he had the highest praise for Murdock's *Social Structure* (1949). Whereas he disliked the work of Radcliffe-Brown, he considered Murdock's work to bring to kinship studies the precision he had found in linguistics—the highest praise he could accord.

Third, even in his largest explanatory effort, *Navaho Witch-craft*, he rarely presented associational data in support of his points, even where they would have been available and relevant. Thus he says that his material confirms William Morgan's suggestion that Navaho witchcraft accusations directed at affines are commoner in patrilocal than in matrilocal units (1944*a*:57). But what follows is not a tabulation of accusations and household types but a reasonable explanation as to why this relationship should occur.

Fourth, as has been said, there is the relative paucity of explanations and the substitution of interpretation for explanation. For example, there is a beautiful description in *The Navaho* of the headman system (Kluckhohn and Leighton 1946*a*:69 ff.). It brings out the weak authority of the headman, describes the consensus procedures through which decisions are most often made, and so on. Any one who has tried afresh to study the Navaho political system in hopes of finding a clearer structure will appreciate these pages. There is the interesting comment that the headman is not likely to be wealthy and that wealthy men use behind-the-scenes pressure and seldom hold formal leadership positions. But from these and other facts about the polity, he moves to say that it is hard to describe the polity because

The People have a set of categories altogether different from that of white Western culture. . . . Authority, to their minds, extends only indefinitely and transitorily beyond the established rules of behavior between sex groups, age groups, and, especially, classes of relatives. [Kluckhohn and Leighton 1946*a*:72]

This, however, is a description of an ideology parallel with the behaviors described immediately before this passage: an interpretation, not an explanation.

Yet a sort of explanation can be supplied. Thus, if we look at Navaho technology, environment, and social organization in the period immediately prior to conquest, we can see that it is a tribal society organized into segments of like order—communities or bands subdivided into groups of clansmen (and in other ways as well). It is characteristic of such units that their headmen can have only meditating authority under most circumstances—which is pre-

cisely what we find among the Navaho. Selection of a headman,
then, is likely (though not inevitably) to be from among those with
persuasive powers, rich or poor. But in addition, a rich and influential man as a leader for a set of such segments is a contradiction in
terms: He is head of a bloc of kin, jockeying with other blocs to
get his way. The mediator, then, must be someone else. He must be,
in the sense that, if he is the head of a powerful bloc of kin, the
society is well on the way to being hierarchically ordered at the local
level. Navaho society had not made that transition; so long as it did
not, such leaders as Kluckhohn described would emerge.

This is an explanation by classification: Societies made up of
relatively equal, large, unilineal kinship blocs must in part operate
by mediation. Mediators are distinguished by persuasive, not coer-
cive abilities. It raises, of course, a further "why" question: Why
were not Navaho unilineal units hierarchically ordered? That issue
will be left aside here. But it raises the additional question: Why
did such a system survive after conquest and the domination of the
U.S. government? And why was that system superseded by the
chapter system, the vitality of which Kluckhohn underrates (Kluckhohn and Leighton 1946a:101)? To answer these would take us
into further questions of cultural adaptation. At this point, the
purpose is only to indicate that interpretation often substitutes for
explanation in Kluckhohn's work and to provide a partial explanation, in contrast to an interpretation, to illuminate the difference.

One final criticism. Whereas Kluckhohn recognized clearly that
the Navahos were deprived, suffering, and undergoing disorganiza-
tion (e.g., Kluckhohn and Leighton 1946a:passim; Kluckhohn
1944a:72, 1945c), he tended to underplay the degree of exploita-
tion and dominance of whites, government, and others. For example,
"Group Tensions" (1945c) focuses overwhelmingly on types of
anxious and aggressive responses of Navahos in a variety of frustrat-
ing circumstances but provides no systematic analysis of the reasons
why they were so repeatedly frustrated, focusing instead on the
reduction of tensions based on "unrealistic" grounds. And *The
Navaho* is clearly an offering to administrators that focuses on inter-
group understandings: "The greatest single problem faced by the
Government has been that of communication" (Kluckhohn and

Leighton 1946a:92). It is hard to pinpoint this criticism, except by reference to the analysis of Navaho-trader relationships (1946a: 79–80). Here a sort of balance sheet is drawn up to show how the trader does some good things for the Navaho and some bad things to him—but the Navaho does some bad things to the trader, too. "As always in the field of relations with whites, there is a great deal of pure misunderstanding" (1946a:80). The fact is that being a Navaho is not a profitable enterprise and being a trader is. Until this is recognized, it seems difficult to balance the equities or inequities in the situation. Once it is recognized, the reasons for mutual suspicion become clear.

But these criticisms do not affect the central evaluation given here. At its best, Kluckhohn's Navaho work was remarkably precise. Where possible, it outlined Navaho patterns with great clarity. Where there was variation, this was clearly indicated. It covered an amazing number of features of Navaho culture. It will remain as an ethnographic landmark, as a guide to fieldworkers decade after decade, and as a pleasure to read. Fortunately it still leaves room for those who came after: There are still many explanatory tasks to be completed.

CLYDE KLUCKHOHN AS
ETHNOGRAPHER AND STUDENT
OF NAVAHO CEREMONIALISM

Louise Lamphere

Evon Z. Vogt

CLYDE KLUCKHOHN'S contact with the Navaho extended over a period of nearly four decades—from his first trip to the Southwest in 1922, when he was only seventeen years of age, until his last trip when he died in Santa Fe in 1960. His first article on the Navaho, published when he was only eighteen, appeared in *El Palacio* in 1923 and was entitled "The Dance of the Hasjelti." His last articles on the Navaho were published posthumously in the *Encyclopedia Britannica* in 1961 and in the *Anthropological Papers* of the Bureau of American Ethnology in 1966. A definitive count of the months of formal fieldwork he undertook among the Navaho during this time span has not been calculated, but it runs into several years. Perhaps even more significant was his nearly fluent control of the difficult Navaho language, which he mastered early and continued at a level which has been reached by only a few, if any, of his students and by only a handful of others working among the Navaho. This knowledge of the Navaho language, combined with a genuine passion for the Navaho and their colorful land, led to sensitive and intensive fieldwork of the highest quality.

Kluckhohn pursued a variety of intellectual interests among the Navaho, from material culture to values, but his first paper on "The Dance of the Hasjelti" proved to be a premonition of his continuing major interest: religion, ceremony, and beliefs (including witchcraft). He frankly admitted that kinship bored him. Although he did fundamental work in culture and personality, especially in studies of the socialization process, and in cultural patterning and value systems, we believe his technical work on Navaho religion will be remembered the longest. We have, therefore, chosen to focus upon Kluckhohn's work on Navaho religion, especially his ethnographic studies on how the Navahos classify their own ceremonials and how the ritual system can be described by anthropologists.

An overview of his contributions along these lines reveals the significant changes which have taken place in anthropology since the late 1930s and early 1940s, when some of Kluckhohn's most important material was published. Kluckhohn himself took part in some of the changes toward the end of his life and, indeed, his Navaho work as a whole can be said to anticipate many of the developments of the 1950s and 1960s.

In the first section of this paper, originally drafted by Vogt, Kluckhohn's orientation to both description and theory will be briefly recapitulated. The influence of linguistics on Kluckhohn's Navaho work will also be described. In the second section, originally drafted by Lamphere, a reanalysis of Kluckhohn's data on Navaho ceremonial terminology and ritual will be presented. The two discoveries we made in writing this paper are: (1) the incredible ethnographic richness of the data on Navaho religion that is displayed in Kluckhohn's published work, (2) the extent to which, at the time of his death, Kluckhohn had anticipated and was moving toward the more rigorous methodological developments in ethnoscience and toward the structural anthropology of Claude Lévi-Strauss, Edmund Leach, and others.

Ethnographic Description and Theory

Kluckhohn's ethnographic approach emphasized precise recording and detailed description. His studies of ceremonial participation (1938b, 1938c, 1939d), the classification of ceremonial terminology (Wyman and Kluckhohn 1938; Kluckhohn 1960e), ritual behavior (Kluckhohn and Wyman 1940b), and witchcraft (Kluckhohn 1944a) are filled with careful reports of informant statements and accounts of observed behaviors. The importance of detail was crucial to Kluckhohn's conception of adequate ethnography as clearly indicated by the following footnote in Kluckhohn and Wyman's monograph:

We realize that . . . we have given masses of detail on variation which may seem needless and burdensome to some. But, in our opinion, only by so providing a corpus of material can both variation and interaction be studied scientifically. What may seem to the anthropologists of our generation only an odd or a meaningless variation may become deeply significant when more refined methods of analysis have been developed. But then, very probably, the original observations could no longer be made. We have, therefore, been scrupulous about even those details which today seem most trivial in the hope that our descriptions can thus always be reduced to their behavioral references and placed fairly adequately in their immediate context of situation by those who may, in the future, care to use them. [1940b:10–11, fn. 7]

Kluckhohn's ethnographic descriptions were an important advance over the writings of many previous investigators who had been content to present vague generalizations. On the other hand, Kluckhohn was not content to gather a mass of unconnected detail which constituted a list of culture traits. Rather, he was interested in specific topics such as Navaho witchcraft or ceremonial terminology. He often addressed himself to very particular questions, such as, "What ceremonials are known? How many ceremonial practitioners are there? What ceremonials have been held during a specific period of time? What ceremonials have sample individuals held during their lifetimes? What proportion of family income is devoted to ceremonial activity?"

Kluckhohn's ethnography was not only guided by specific interests but also characterized by particular data-gathering techniques. He was always careful to use a large number of informants, to note their position in the community, and to report discrepancies in their statements. Each statement of fact was cross-checked with several informants and variations were reported as well as the stable responses. Likewise, several instances of a particular behavioral sequence were observed and variations were noted. For example, in studying performances of four chants (Kluckhohn and Wyman 1940*b*) at least two performances were observed, detailed notes were taken, and similarities and differences were reported. In both detail and method, Kluckhohn's early publications on the Navaho are an excellent example of the approach used by many American anthropologists at the time.

In the past decade, however, the criteria for an adequate ethnography have changed. In addition to details, more recent writers have insisted that ethnographic description meet the criteria of (1) productivity (in terms of appropriate anticipation if not actual prediction), (2) replicability or testability, and (3) economy (Conklin 1965:26). As Frake writes:

This conception of a cultural description implies that an ethnography should be a theory of cultural behavior in a particular society, the adequacy of which is to be evaluated by the ability of a stranger to the culture (who may be the ethnographer) to use the ethnography's statements as instructions for appropriately anticipating the scenes of the society. I say "appropriately anticipate" rather than "predict" because a failure of an ethnographic statement to predict correctly does not necessarily imply descriptive inadequacy as long as the members of the described society are as surprised by the failure as is the ethnographer. [1964*b*:112]

To meet these more rigorous criteria, new data gathering techniques which are clearly influenced by linguistic analysis have been suggested. With these new eliciting procedures, a present-day ethnographer might treat some of Kluckhohn's topics in a much different manner; however, as shown in the second section of this paper, it is also possible to use the details so carefully collected by Kluckhohn to reveal new patterns in the same data.

Kluckhohn's publications on the Navaho reveal not only his fine sense for precise ethnographic recording, but also much of his most perceptive theoretical writing. In his classic monograph *Navaho Witchcraft* (1944*a*) and in many of his papers in the 1940s, especially "Myths and Rituals: A General Theory" (1942*a*), he was strongly influenced by the intellectual currents of the time, and his theory can best be described as a type of functionalism.

Even though he labels his interpretive section of *Navaho Witchcraft* as "An Essay in Structural Dynamics," he states that "A structural analysis (an investigation of 'functional dependencies') is a study in the interrelation of parts" (1944a:45) and goes on to make clear, in his interpretation of Navaho witchcraft as "providing culturally defined adaptive and adjustive responses," that his approach is functional rather than structural in Lévi-Strauss's (1963) more current sense. He differentiates between "adaptive" (responses for survival of the individual or the society) and "adjustive" (responses which remove the motivation stimulating the individual), and he introduces Merton's (1949) distinction between manifest and latent function. He also worries about the "cost" of witchcraft beliefs in increasing anxieties, etc. But in spite of these theoretical embellishments, it is clear that Kluckhohn is following the major tenets of functional theory.

Similarly, in his "Myths and Rituals," Kluckhohn concludes that

In the absence of a codified law and of an authoritarian "chief" or other father substitute, it is only through the myth-ritual system that Navahos can make a socially supported, unified response to all of these disintegrating threats. The all-pervasive configurations of word symbols (myths) and of act symbols (rituals) preserve the cohesion of the society and sustain the individual, protecting him from intolerable conflict.

. . . . .

For myth and ritual have a common psychological basis. Ritual is an obsessive repetitive activity—often a symbolic dramatization of the fundamental "needs" of the society, whether "economic," "biological," "social," or "sexual." Mythology is the rationalization of these same needs, whether they are all expressed in overt ceremonial or not. [1942a:77–78]

Significantly enough, Kluckhohn himself later recognized the limitations of functional theory, in part in his papers on values and more explicitly in his famous paper on "The Limitations of Adaptation and Adjustment as Concepts for Understanding Cultural Behavior." Here he states that:

My analysis [in *Navaho Witchcraft*] . . . was basically a functional one. I would suggest merely that the phrase "adaptive and adjustive responses" is a means for avoiding the ambiguities that have inhered in "functional," since that word has diverse connotations from physiology, mathematics, and other disciplines. (1949*b*:105)

He then goes on to express his disenchantment with functional theory in these words:

Theories based on these [functional] premises have markedly increased our ability to understand human behavior and have even led to a limited capacity to predict in certain areas. But I must confess to an increasing dissatisfaction with them as they stand.

. . . . .

Functionalism is adequate to strictly structural questions but not to those of process. . . . Even at the flat time level, the functionalist must strainfully invoke the idea of latent function and of indirect adjustive value to explain why days and even weeks are spent in polishing the nonbusiness faces of axes. Prestige symbols, yes. But why axes—in cultures where stone axes have had no manifest function for hundreds of years?

. . . . .

One of the "laws" which the earlier functionalists advanced was that those animals and plants in a people's habitat which have economic value become invested with symbolic significance. This is probably a valid statistical generalization, but after it is advanced as the "explanation" of totemism, such totems as flies, sting rays, sparrow hawks, bile, and anal sores were discovered in Australia. . . . Radcliffe-Brown and others have had to do some awkward squirming. [1949*b*:107–10]

He concludes that:

We require a way of thinking which takes account of the pull of expectancies as well as the push of tensions, that recognizes that growth and creativity come as much or more from instability as from stability, which emphasizes culturally created values as well as the immediately observable external environment. [1949*b*:112–13]

Not only did Kluckhohn come to realize the limitations of functional theory, but he also began to develop, as early as 1941 in his article for the Sapir volume on "Patterning as Exemplified in Navaho Culture," an alternative type of theory which anticipated the currently fashionable structural anthropology of Lévi-Strauss. This theoretical thread appeared again in his article on "Covert Culture and Administrative Problems" (1943*b*) and was developed still further in his three most important articles on values (1951f, 1956e, and 1959e). We suggest that, while these articles on patterns and values were moving importantly in the direction of structural theory, they were inspired failures. They seem to have misfired for different reasons. In the two articles on patterns, Kluckhohn utilized solid and specific Navaho data but tried to interpret these data with vague concepts derived from the then fashionable linguistics of Bloomfield (1933) and the psychoanalytically derived notions of Sapir (1927). In his papers on values (especially 1956e and 1959e), Kluckhohn had hold of much more productive concepts derived from the structural linguistics of Jakobson and Halle (1956) but attempted to apply them to diffuse data on values which he combed from the field-note files of the Harvard Values Study Project in the Southwest. Had Kluckhohn restricted himself to the wealth of highly specific Navaho data that he knew so well, we feel the effort would have been more successful and more enduring as one chapter in the development of structural theory. For it is worth noting that the binary oppositions so much used by Lévi-Strauss in his analysis of myths (e.g., Lévi-Strauss 1964) are present in the Kluckhohn papers as he attempts to adapt the notion of "distinctive features" (Jakobson, Fant, and Halle 1952; Jakobson and Halle 1956) to the value emphases of the five Southwestern cultures. It is also noteworthy that while Kluckhohn never once refers to Lévi-Strauss in any of these papers, we know from personal communication that Kluckhohn was a great admirer of Lévi-Strauss as a theoretician. Shortly before his death, Kluckhohn spoke at length with one of us (Vogt) about the forthcoming Lévi-Strauss volumes on what he understood would be a grammar of American Indian mythology and expressed himself as believing that they would open a whole new era of path-breaking theoretical development in anthropology.

In brief, it is clear to us that Kluckhohn came to recognize clearly the limitations of functional theory and that he was a pioneer in his attempt to adapt and utilize linguistic concepts in the analysis of cultural data. Had he lived, we feel strongly that he would not only have felt much at home with the rapidly developing interest in Lévi-Strauss and others who are cultivating structural theory, but would also have attempted to reinterpret his Navaho data along these lines.

Navaho Ceremonial Classification and Ritual Pattern

Kluckhohn's major contributions to the study of Navaho religion dealt with the topics of ceremonial classification and the description of ritual. He coauthored a monograph with Leland C. Wyman: *Navaho Classification of Their Song Ceremonials* (Wyman and Kluckhohn 1938); this and an article on "Navaho Categories" (1960e) show Kluckhohn's concern for native terminology and folk classification, two topics which have been the focus of recent publications utilizing formal semantic analysis. The general topics are similar, but the approach to data shows a sharp contrast between Kluckhohn and more recent writers. Hence, it seems relevant to discuss in detail Kluckhohn's work on ceremonial terminology and suggest how the data might be reanalyzed.

The descriptive material on Navaho ritual published in *An Introduction to Navaho Chant Practice* (Kluckhohn and Wyman 1940b) can also be used for reanalysis. By examining the various contexts in which symbolic elements and ritual action occur, it can be shown that ceremonies (1) replicate the main elements of Navaho cosmology and (2) provide for the patient's cure through transactions with the supernatural and through symbolic actions directed toward the patient.

It will be shown how these two analyses, based on two separate sets of data, converge on the same principles (the contrast between *hózhǫ́* or "pleasant conditions" and *hóchǫ́* or "ugly conditions"), thus revealing more clearly the relationship between terminology and ritual symbolism, two rather different aspects of Navaho religion. Before the specifics are presented, a brief outline of Navaho ceremonialism is necessary.

Navaho ritual consists primarily of curing ceremonies or chants conducted for a patient by a practitioner called a "chanter" or "singer." (Navaho terms for English words and phrases used in the text of this paper will be found in the Glossary at the end.) Each chant has a myth which relates how the ancestors of the

Navaho acquired the ritual procedures from the supernaturals (see Spencer 1957). The myth tells of a hero who experiences a series of misfortunes (e.g., illness, poverty, bodily destruction or transformation, abandonments in an inaccessible place, etc.). He is aided by various supernaturals and in the process learns the ceremony which is instrumental in curing his illness or restoring conditions to their normal state. On his return, he teaches the ceremony to the people. Likewise, a Navaho singer teaches his knowledge to an apprentice. A Navaho spends long hours of practice with a singer who knows the chant he wishes to learn. Through these sessions and attendance at chants given by his teacher, he learns (1) the requisite songs which accompany all ritual acts, (2) the skills for collecting ingredients, making and using various medicines and ritual paraphernalia, and (3) the myth which is the charter for the ritual and which includes a description of the ritual within the larger tale.

When illness disrupts the life of a Navaho, he will often go to a diagnostician for a diagnosis. Most diagnosticians practice hand trembling, though there are still a few who perform star gazing or listening. Very often there is consultation with one of the prospective patient's relatives or neighbors who does hand trembling; however, a patient (accompanied by several close relatives such as spouse, parents, or children) may travel 25 or 50 miles to a hand trembler he considers particularly good.

The Navaho believe that sickness is due to improper contact with those things which are dangerous including the following: (1) natural phenomena such as lightning, winds, thunder, and sometimes the earth, sun, or moon; (2) some species of animals including bear, deer, coyote, porcupine, snakes, eagle, and fish (32 kinds listed in Wyman and Kluckhohn 1938); (3) ceremonial paraphernalia or activities which are contacted at inappropriate times; (4) ghosts of either Navahos or aliens and witches (including werewolves). By performing the hand trembling, a diviner is able to discover which of the above is causing the illness, and he suggests the chant appropriate for dealing with that particular etiological factor. The relations between physical symptoms, etiology, and chant are not fully worked out, but etiology is of prime importance in the selection. This can be seen from figure *1*, which shows a list of several chants, the etiological factors, and the symptoms associated with each. Note for instance that Shooting Chants are given for sickness caused by lightning, arrows, or snakes, but snakes are also an etiological factor connected with Beauty Way and Navaho Wind Way. In turn, physical symptoms such as "itching all over" may be associated with eagles or with cactus, making Eagle Way appropriate in the former case and Navaho Wind Way appropriate in the latter case.

A hand trembler or other diagnostician need not be consulted, as the patient and his family in discussing the recent experiences of the patient may decide upon an obvious cause, such as contact with a lightning-struck tree a few days before onset of the illness. A close relative of the patient (parent, sibling, spouse, or child) is dispatched to a singer in the area who knows the appropriate chant. This intermediary negotiates with the singer concerning the length of the ceremony and various supplementary ceremonies. Within this framework, the singer may decide upon sandpaintings or medicines to accord with the disease. A time is set for the singer's arrival and the beginning of the ceremony.

Navaho chants are two, five, or nine nights (a "night" is counted from one sunset to the next) and composed of component ceremonies. Though the content of these component ceremonies, i.e., the specific songs, medicines, paraphernalia, and sandpaintings, differ from ceremony to ceremony, the structure is similar. Many chants include a bath, a sandpainting ritual, a sweat and emetic ceremony, and an all-night sing the last night. Each component ceremony is composed of ritual acts which are directed against the etiological factor causing the illness.

An early problem in describing Navaho ceremonies was "the need for an ordered presentation of Navaho systematizations of the relationships of their complex body of ceremonials" (Wyman and Kluckhohn 1938:3). *Navaho Classification of Their Song Ceremonials* was published to provide a more complete list of Navaho ceremonies and to show how the Navaho's own categories are organized. The authors originally collected forty-nine distinct names of ceremonies including several kinds of Blessing Way and three

1. RELATIONS BETWEEN PHYSICAL SYMPTOMS, ETIOLOGY, AND CHANT

	Chants or Ways	Etiological Factors	Symptoms
IIA 1.	Hail Way	injury by water	frozen feet, muscle soreness, tiredness, lameness, paralysis
2.	Water Way	injury by water	resuscitation from drowning, deafness
3.	Shooting Ways	lightning, arrows, snakes	colds, fevers, paralysis, abdominal pain
4.	Red Ant Way	ants or horned toads	
IIB 1.	Mountain Top Way	porcupine sickness, bear sickness, weasels	constipation, anuria, internal pain, gall bladder, mental disease
2.	Excess Way		mania or promiscuity, all kinds of excesses
3.	Beauty Way	snakes, horned toads	snake bite, rheumatism, sore throat, stomach pain; kidney, bladder, abdominal pain
IIC 1.	Night Way	supernaturals	head and eye ailments, arthritis
2.	Big God Way		blindness and stiffness
3.	Plume Way	deer infection	rheumatism
4.	Dog Way		
5.	Coyote Way		promiscuity, mania, rabies, sore throat, stomach trouble
IID 1.	Navaho Wind Way	wind infection, snakes, cactus, sun, moon, earth	heart and lung trouble, stomach trouble, itching all over, eye trouble
2.	Apache Wind Way	winds	heart and head
IIE 1.	Hand Trembling Way	hand trembling sickness	nervousness, mental distress
IIF 1.	Eagle Way	eagle infection	head diseases, boils, sores, sore throat, legs swollen, "itching all over"

From Wyman and Kluckhohn 1938; Kluckhohn and Wyman 1940b.

War Ceremonies which are not considered chants. The data are based on names compiled from published accounts which were carefully amplified and cross-checked using informants (mostly singers) on several parts of the reservation. They attempted to collect all the native terminology relevant to ceremonies, a method which contrasts with the eliciting procedure suggested by Frake (1964a) and Metzger and Williams (1966). The difference is critical for the reanalysis presented later in this paper.

Wyman later pointed out that the original list could be greatly simplified if only the most frequently performed chants are considered. He said:

After subtracting duplications due to the occurrence of male and female branches and to performances according to various rituals [i.e., Evil Way, Life Way], we are left with twenty-six names for distinct ceremonial complexes. Nine of these are surely extinct or obsolescent and seven others are uncommon or very rarely performed. Only ten are well known and often seen. [1957:13]

In spite of this potential simplification, it is the structure of the classification which is of the greatest interest. Wyman and Kluckhohn (1938) presented the ceremonials within a taxonomy of four groups which are divided into subgroups. Thus, the domain of Navaho ceremonies can be seen as a taxonomy with the format illustrated in figure 2. They argue that these four groups are ac-

2. WYMAN AND KLUCKHOHN DATA VIEWED AS A TAXONOMY

	I	II							III	IV	
Group	Blessing Way	Holy Way							Life Way	Evil Way	
Subgroup	A	A	B	C	D	E	F	G	A	A	B
Ceremonial	1	1	1	1	1	1	1	1	1	1	1
	2	2	2	2	2	2	2	2	2	2	2
	3	3	3	3					3	3	3
	4	4	4	4					4	4	
		5	5	5					5	5	
		6	6						6	6	
		7								7	
		8									
		9									
		10									
		11									

curate supercategories since there are Navaho terms for each group
and Navaho informants were able to name ceremonies for each
term. There are also significant differences in the rituals performed
under each group. Only in Holy Way Chants, for example, does
the singer use a gourd or hoof rattle, and only these ceremonies
feature sandpaintings and prayerstick offerings.

Each of the groups includes subgroups. Rather than discuss all
of these, a few examples will show how Wyman and Kluckhohn
conceived this level of their taxonomy. The subgroups are based on
connections between myths (which are the charters for each ceremony) and on similarities in etiological factors. Only one subgroup
(IIC) is expressed by a Navaho term: The phrase "those which
have supernatural impersonators" refers to the masked dancers ap-
pearing in the nine-night version of Night Way and in other chants
in that subcategory. The lack of native terminology makes the level
of subcategory somewhat suspect and suggests the possibility of an
alternative analysis.

The Shooting Chant group, for example, includes the following:

> IIA 1. Hail Way
> IIA 2. Water Way
> IIA 3. Shooting Way, Male Branch
> IIA 4. Shooting Way, Female Branch
> IIA 5. Red Ant Way
> IIA 6. Big Star Way

These chants have been grouped together because of common
incidents in the myths and their association with lightning or other
sky phenomena as etiological factors. Hail Way and Water Way are
both extinct and Red Ant Way and Big Star Way are rarely performed; Shooting Way, Male Branch, and Shooting Way, Female
Branch, thus emerge as the most important members of the subgroup. These chants can be differentiated in terms of the first
word of the label which we will designate as a "chant name." This
minimal referent for the chant may refer to an episode in the
accompanying myth or to an etiological factor against which the
chant is effective. For example, Red Ant Way takes its name from

an incident in the myth involving the Red Ant People. Shooting Way refers to "the shooting of objects that move in zigzags" and suggests lightning, snakes, and arrows, any of which are the presumed cause of the patient's illness. Hail Way and Water Way refer to hail and water as etiological factors.

Some pairs of ceremonies are differentiated only by a term for "male" and one for "female," e.g., Shooting Way, Male, and Shooting Way, Female, in Subgroup IIA. This distinguishes what Wyman and Kluckhohn call "branches" and refers to the mythology. In these cases, one branch recounts events which happen to the hero(s), and the second branch emphasizes other adventures, misfortunes, and positive outcomes which involve the same hero(s). For example, Newcomb and Reichard (1937:47) state that Shooting Chant, Female, emphasizes the birth and rearing of the twin heros, while the Male Branch recounts their dangerous exploits. Wyman and Kluckhohn report: "Although [male and female versions are] similar in underlying conception (and even in many details), the myth, sandpaintings, songs, certain medicines, and procedures differ to greater or lesser extent" (1938:24). They note that male and female branches of a ceremonial are often so similar that "as many singers have informed us, almost never does any one person try to learn both branches—'or they'd get mixed up'" (1938:23, fn. 68).

Wyman and Kluckhohn also present three additional sets of Navaho terms which they label "subritual," "phase," and "etiological factor" (1938:7–12). These further differentiate chants classed in Group II or Holy Way. Details of these terms will be discussed later, but the broad outlines are relevant here. First, their use of "subritual" refers to three Navaho terms which indicate whether or not anger (or weapon) of the supernatural is stressed as a causative factor. Second, terms listed as "phases" include those which describe various component ceremonies which can be combined to make up a Holy Way Chant (e.g., a sandpainting ceremony, a jewel-offering ceremony). Third, "etiological factors" refers to terms describing the disease-causing agent (such as thunder, snakes, lightning) which is to be emphasized. Presumably, in each of those chants which can be performed according to one of several etiological factors, different sandpaintings, songs, and medicines are used.

In summary, Wyman and Kluckhohn's presentation is a taxonomy of specific ceremonies (some with male and female branches) divided into groups and subgroups. The taxonomy is highly differentiated within the Holy Way group. There are more of these chants than in any of the other three groups, and many can be further distinguished in terms of subritual, phase, and etiological factor. This overdifferentiation suggests that placing ceremonies into four major categories may not be appropriate. Moreover, chant names or minimal referents in the Holy Way group (especially those of the Shooting Way) appear in the Evil Way and Life Way groups with one of these terms appended to the chant name. For example, Shooting Way, Male Branch, (IIA 3), occurs as Evil Way, Male Shooting Branch, (IVA 4), and Life Way, Male Shooting Branch, (IIIA 3). These terms may indicate variations of one ceremony rather than different ceremonies within three separate groups. Perhaps the name of the ceremony should be considered first and the terms Evil Way and Life Way treated as modifiers. Finally, there are no Navaho terms for most of the subgroups. Here Wyman and Kluckhohn have relied on relations between chant myths and etiological factors as a basis for the subcategories rather than statements by informants that "X is a kind of Y."

Some of these difficulties are eliminated in the scheme presented by Kluckhohn in "Navaho Categories" (1960e), which represents his later thinking on the topic and contains substantial revision of the 1938 monograph. Kluckhohn apparently adopted much of the viewpoint expressed by Father Berard Haile in his "Navaho Chantways and Ceremonials" (1938), in which he saw Navaho chants as a kind of ceremony or, literally, a "here and there (in a place) one person goes" or "something is going on." Since Blessing Way is not a chant or curing ceremony, it is excluded, although it is part of the broader designation "ceremony." Kluckhohn adopts this perspective: "The most sweeping and clear-cut distinction is that between 'chants' and all else" (1960e:68). In the "all else" category, he includes Blessing Way, prayer ceremonials, war ceremonials, hunting ceremonials, and rites of divination.

Kluckhohn also follows Father Berard in stating that ceremonies can be performed according to one of three rituals: Holy Way, Evil or Ugly Way, and Life Way:

Several chants provide for performance according to all three rituals; a much larger number for performance by Holy Way and Ugly Way only. The ritual is selected in accord with the assumed etiology of the disease of the patient being treated. If the illness is thought to be caused by angry supernaturals, Holy Way is appropriate. If the "cause" be the ghosts of fellow tribesmen or (sometimes) witches, Ugly Way is selected. The Life Way ceremonials are primarily for those suffering from injuries attributed to accidents, either recent or past. [1960e:69]

The four terms originally used to designate groups are now included in an all-encompassing class of ceremonies. Blessing Way ceremonies are grouped with other rituals which are not chants. Rather than being classed into three remaining groups, chants are seen as being performed in one of three manners which crosscut the list of chants (still listed in subgroups in the 1960 article). They correspond to different etiological factors (supernatural attack, ghosts, or injury) and are correlated with different arrangements of component ceremonies (see fig. 9 below).

Kluckhohn's second formulation seems to be a substantial improvement over the first. The puzzling overdifferentiation of the Holy Way group has been eliminated. Now there is only one list of chants, some of which can be performed in three ways. The new formulation also seems more consistent with Navaho word order. Shooting Way, Male Branch, indicates a ceremony performed according to Holy Way and the addition of either Evil Way or Life Way to this phrase indicates the ceremony is performed according to one of these two patterns or manners. Thus we would get, in literal translation: (1) Shooting Way (Holy Way group), Male Branch and Evil Way Manner, (2) Shooting Way (Holy Way group), Male Branch and Life Way Manner. This seems preferable to isolating each term under contrasting groups and stresses the importance of the chant name rather than the modifiers.

Although Kluckhohn had a standardized procedure for collecting data (the use of informants and careful cross-checking), it was not one which included a method for constructing the taxonomy

itself. The 1960 taxonomy seems to be a more consistent ordering
of the data, but Kluckhohn presented no method for validating this
taxonomy in terms of actual informant statements. Here is the
crucial difference between ethnographic methods of the 1930s and
1940s and those recently proposed by Frake (1962) and Metzger
and Williams (1962, 1963a and b, 1966). These authors have attempted to meet Conklin's criteria for an adequate ethnography
(1965). The method is one of discovering stable response frames
within a particular domain. The domain itself is also defined by
the eliciting procedure which is conducted in the native language.
As Frake states, "For every response, discover the set of inquiries
which appropriately evokes it; and for every inquiry, discover a set
of responses it appropriately evokes" (1964a:134).

Using response or substitution frames which are equivalent to
"What kind of X is it?" "What kinds of X are there?" "What kind
of Y is X?" and "What is X used for?" lexical items (segregates)
can be grouped together on the basis of class inclusion. The resulting
contrast sets can be linked together in a hierarchical relationship to
form a taxonomy (Frake 1962). Criterial attributes of dimensions
may also define a contrast set; the combination of such dimensions
or components results in a paradigm (Conklin 1965:27). The
influence of linguistics on the development of this method is apparent in the notions "substitution frame," "level of contrast,"
"contrast set," and "criterial attributes" or "components." As already
noted, Kluckhohn saw the relevance of linguistics for ethnography,
especially in Sapir's concept of pattern. However, a distributional
analysis based on the notions "substitution" and "contrast" is lacking as a guideline to his early ethnographic research; and it is in
the use of these concepts that some of the most recent advances
have taken place.

Reanalysis of Chant Terminology

The following distributional analysis will utilize the notion of
"contrast" to reexamine phrases referring to Navaho chants. It will
follow Kluckhohn's "Navaho Categories" (1960e), which is based
on a list of chants rather than groups of them. The attempt is to
combine Kluckhohn's carefully collected data and his more recent

insights with the assets of formal semantic analysis. The following modifications will be followed:

Wyman and Kluckhohn 1938	*Reanalysis*
groups or ritual	manner
subgroups	(eliminated)
chant names	chant names
branches	male/female distinction
(Holy Way distinctions)	
subritual	theme
phases	subceremonies
etiological factor	etiological factor

Some of Wyman and Kluckhohn's English terminology is indeed unfortunate. Both the terms "ritual" and "subritual" connote bounded segments of activity rather than systematic differences in various aspects of the ritual. Hence, "manner" has been substituted for "group" or "ritual" and "theme" has been substituted for "subritual." Subgroups have been eliminated since they are not reflected in Navaho terms. "Subceremony" has been substituted as a more appropriate rendering of "phase."

Since it has not been possible to use Navaho informants in eliciting queries and answers, basic contrasts have been reconstructed from phrases which appear in Wyman and Kluckhohn (1938) and other published material (Kluckhohn and Wyman 1940*b*; Haile 1938, 1947). English terms will be used throughout; phrases published in Navaho and those which have been reconstructed from English translations will be found in the Glossary at the end of this paper. Strings of terms will be analyzed in terms of Navaho word order. Thus, Shooting Way, Male Branch, Life Way Manner will be thought of as chant name + male + manner. In general, a chant (as indicated by a unique referent) can be discussed in terms of five distinctions: male/female + manner + theme + etiological factor + subceremony. However, there are limitations as to which elements of each distinction can co-occur, and there are relatively few chants which have all five possible distinctions. It is these patterns of co-occurrence which reveal the important contrasts at each level and also indicate important differences in ritual and causes of illness.

A brief discussion of the terms "theme" (subritual), "etiological factor," and "subceremony" (phase) will clarify their roles in signaling differences in ritual and causes of illness. Subritual (now called "theme") is used by Wyman and Kluckhohn to characterize three native terms: Fighting Side Theme, Angry Side Theme, Peaceful Side Theme (1938:7). They note that Father Berard says the first two terms are interchangeable, at least by certain practitioners (1938:8). Though the evidence is incomplete, this statement probably indicates that each term is associated with different chants, and hence they never contrast with each other. A Holy Way Chant which is performed according to Fighting Side Theme stresses either the weapon (such as an arrow or kind of wind) or the direct attack (by bear or snake); Angry Side Theme emphasizes the anger of the supernatural. Both terms concern driving out the evil, and both contrast with the Peaceful Side Theme since changes are made in the color symbolism so that reds, rather than blues, are placed on the outside of the sandpaintings.

Holy Way is performed Peaceful Side unless otherwise stated to be Angry Side or Fighting Side; it "is considered a restorative for the injuries and weaknesses resultant upon supernatural attack" (Wyman and Kluckhohn 1938:9). This use of the term (hereafter designated Peaceful Side II) is different from that of Peaceful Side I (the Blessing Way ceremony), and the two uses should not be confused.

Terminology dealt with by Wyman and Kluckhohn (1938:12) under the topic "etiological factors" includes the following:

Theme	Etiological Factor	Chant
Upper Regions Side or From Upper Regions Side	flash lightning	Shooting Ways
Thunderstruck Side	heavy lightning	Shooting Ways and Navaho Wind Way
From Under Plants Side	snakes	Mountain Top Way also others in Group IIB
Striped Side	striped wind	Navaho Wind Way

As figure 1 shows, Navaho recognize more than these four etiological factors; however, only these four are the object of special terminology. Clearly the above terms are euphemisms, oblique ways of indicating that a specific dangerous element is being counteracted in the chant. Not all Holy Way chants are designated by one or more of these terms. It may be that an etiological term is used to differentiate one from several other factors which are associated with that particular chant. For instance, Mountain Top Way, From Under Plants Side, may indicate a Mountain Top Way with special reference to snakes rather than bears or porcupines which are usually associated with the chant. Wyman and Kluckhohn's comments concerning the use of these terms are vague, and little is said about actual differences in the ritual which might be signaled by the use of one of them. In sum, these four terms occur with a restricted number of chants; although etiological factors are potentially specifiable for all illness and are always related to the selection of a particular chant, only this limited set of factors can be overtly specified in referring to a chant.

Terminology for subceremonies (phases) describing some of the component ceremonies of Holy Way is as follows (Wyman and Kluckhohn 1938:11):

A. Features
  1. Chant with Sandpaintings
  2. Chant with Offerings (i.e., prayersticks)
  3. Chant with Jewel Offerings
  4. Chant with Sun's House
  5. Chant with House
B. Public Exhibitions
  1. Dark Circle of Branches
  2. God-Impersonators (i.e., masked dancers)
  3. Interior Chant or Just Visiting Chant
     The above two subceremonies are known
     for ceremonials of the God-Impersonators
     (Subgroup IIC).

Not all these subceremonies are known for each Holy Way, although some of them may include several in a very elaborate performance. It is common for Holy Way to include a sandpainting subceremony. Other subceremonies are more specialized in occurrence, for example, the Corral Dance is usually only performed at a nine-night Mountain Top Way or Shooting Way, and the God-Impersonators at a nine-night Night Way. If only a five-night Night Way is performed, it is with Interior Chant, also called Just Visiting Chant.

The way in which several subceremonies can be combined into one chant is best illustrated by the five- and nine-night versions of Shooting Chant, Male. A performance of a five-night chant contains a Chant with (prayerstick) Offerings and a Chant with Sandpaintings. These may be conducted according to Angry Side or Peaceful Side themes. Both Angry Side and Peaceful Side may be combined into one to give a nine-night chant; prayersticks are cut on the first four mornings, sandpaintings are drawn on the last four mornings, and the Corral Dance may be added the last night (Haile 1947).

The subceremony terms do not include names for all the short rituals or component ceremonies which compose a chant. For example, the terms for the bath, final night, sweat and emetic, and unraveling are not included. The former two are expected parts of every chant, and the latter are performed in Ugly Way as well as in Holy Way. This suggests that subceremony terminology refers to those ritual sequences which are particularly part of a Holy Way form (e.g., sandpaintings, jewel or prayerstick offerings) and/or those which can be used for an elaborate performance (the Corral Dance, the Chant with Sun's House, and the Chant with House). These three are not necessary to a simplified two-night version but are part of the elaborations which the patient and his relatives may decide upon if planning a five- or nine-night chant.

With these additional three sets of terms, we can see that terminology referring to chants has the following structure:

(1) Each chant is labeled (often indirectly or by innuendo) by a chant name associated either with an incident in the corresponding myth or with a disease cause against which the chant is effective.

(2) Some chants have male and female branches, i.e., similar forms of the same ceremony but with the myth or some ritual practices differing.

(3) Most chants are considered Holy Way when directed against an etiological factor associated with the supernatural. If the chant is directed against ghosts or witches, it is considered Ugly Way; and if for an injury, it is considered Life Way; each of these versions has different component ceremonies, or the component ceremonies similar to those in the Holy Way version are arranged in a different order.

(4) When performed as Holy Way, a chant may be Angry Side or Fighting Side Theme, depending on whether the anger or weapon of the supernatural is stressed. Otherwise it is performed Peaceful Side Theme.

(5) If Angry Side or Fighting Side, a chant may be designated by one of four special terms referring to etiological factors.

(6) All Holy Way performances have some component ceremonies which are designated by the subceremony terminology. Different combinations of these subceremonies are used in five- and nine-night versions of various chants.

These relationships are shown in figure 3, which shows actual levels of contrast which Navahos distinguish as demonstrated by an analysis of how phrases concerning chants are used in Navaho discourse. The contrasts depicted refer to relations of classes of terms, not to individual members. Some, but not all, terms for Holy Way co-occur with some, but not all, the terms listed as themes, etiological factors, and subceremonies. Subceremony terminology is utilized for all Holy Way themes (both Peaceful Side and Angry Side/Fighting Side).

Father Berard Haile lists the following "popular query": "Which kind of ceremonial is it?" (1938:641). The pattern of answers to this query can be seen by examining phrases pertaining to Shooting Chant, Male. Any particular answer has one of the four forms shown in figure 4. In response to the query "Which kind of ceremonial is it?" a native may get an answer of Response Type 1; he finds out if the chant will be Holy Way, Life Way, or

3. ACTUAL LEVELS OF CONTRAST DISTINGUISHED BY NAVAHOS IN THEIR DISCOURSE CONCERNING CHANTS

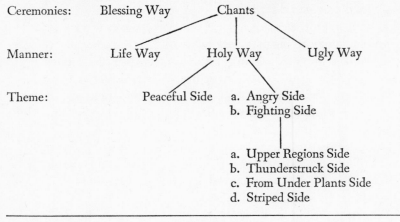

Ceremonies: Blessing Way   Chants

Manner: Life Way   Holy Way   Ugly Way

Theme: Peaceful Side   a. Angry Side
                                          b. Fighting Side

                                          a. Upper Regions Side
                                          b. Thunderstruck Side
                                          c. From Under Plants Side
                                          d. Striped Side

Subceremony: a. Chant with Prayersticks
                                b. Chant with Sandpaintings
                                c. Corral Dance
                                d. Chant with House
                                e. Chant with Sun's House

Ugly Way. The latter is indicated simply by the headword + male or female. If he wishes to know the theme, the etiological factor, or the particular subceremonies which are being performed, he will have to query further. There are, of course, constraints on the order of queries and responses, depending on which response is given to a particular query. If in response to "Which kind of ceremonial is it?" one hears Response Type 1, i.e., Shooting Chant, Male or Female, indicating Holy Way, then one may ask questions relevant to the information in Response Types 2, 3, and 4. Since only Holy Way has these three aspects, if one hears Shooting Chant, Male, Life Way or Shooting Chant, Male, Ugly Way, the questioning can go no further. Conversely, if one receives an answer to an initial inquiry which is of Response Types 2, 3, or 4, there is no need to make inquiry directed toward Response Type 1, since the chant is already known to be Holy Way. However, one can still ask for information in the other two categories.

Likewise, if one receives an initial answer of Shooting Chant,

4. RESPONSE PHRASES PERTAINING TO SHOOTING WAY, MALE BRANCH

Response Type	*Examples*
(1) (Chant name + male) + manner	Shooting Chant, Male, Holy Way Shooting Chant, Male, Life Way Shooting Chant, Male, Ugly Way
(2) (Chant name + male) + theme	Shooting Chant, Male, Fighting Side Shooting Chant, Male, Angry Side Shooting Chant, Male, Peaceful Side
(3) (Chant name + male) + etiological factor	Shooting Chant, Male, From Under Plants Side Shooting Chant, Male, Upper Regions Side Shooting Chant, Male, Thunderstruck Side
(4) (Chant name + male) + subceremony	Shooting Chant, Male, Chant with Prayer-sticks Shooting Chant, Male, Chant with Sand-paintings Shooting Chant, Male, Chant with Jewels Shooting Chant, Male, Chant with Sun's House Shooting Chant, Male, Chant with House Shooting Chant, Male, Chant with Corral Dance

Male, Thunderstruck Side, one knows immediately that it is Holy Way, performed Angry Side or Fighting Side Theme but not Peaceful Side Theme. These relationships have been indicated in figure 3, and appropriate questions or answers can be constructed by following any of the heavy black lines in the figure. Thus one can see that it would be inappropriate to ask about an etiological factor (Response Type 3) if one had learned that Shooting Chant, Male, Peaceful Side Theme was being performed. Also if one hears that Shooting Chant, Female, From Under Plants Side is taking place, it would be unnecessary to ask if it was Holy Way and inappropriate to ask if it was Ugly Way.

The relationship of terminology for subceremonies follows a different pattern since the same subceremonies can be given Peaceful Side Theme or Angry Side/Fighting Side Themes; if the latter,

they may be related to one of the etiological factors. Thus, if an
initial answer is one in Response Type 4, information contained in
Type 3 or 2 may be requested. However, only Holy Way has
subceremonies (i.e., component ceremonies noted in special terminology); so information in Response Type 1 is already assumed.

Thus far, ambiguous answers have not been considered. If in
response to the query "Which kind of ceremonial is it?" one hears
an answer without the chant name, such as just Ugly Way or Chant
with Sandpaintings, the answer is ambiguous. The Navaho does
not necessarily know which chant is being performed and further
questioning to elicit the chant name and the branch word, "male"
or "female," is necessary.

Figure 3 also reveals a structure which can be related to Navaho
ideas about the causes of illness. At the top level, chants which are
curative (i.e., to correct something which has gone wrong) are
distinguished from Blessing Way, which is performed to prevent
such disruption. Of the chants, those which are Holy Way and
Life Way are distinguished from those which are Ugly Way. The
former provide a cure for illness deriving from improper contacts
with dangerous natural phenomena, animals, and ceremonies; the
latter helps to cure illness due to the ugly things, namely witches
and ghosts. Within Holy Way, those chants which are performed
Peaceful Side emphasize immunity which is to be given to the
patient, while those performed Angry Side or Fighting Side emphasize the weapons or anger of the supernatural elements attacking the patient. The source of the weapon or anger is further
specified on the next level by reference to the etiological factor
(snakes, lightning, winds).

Thus the classification of dangerous elements which cause illness is congruent with the terminology for the cures for illnesses.
The relationship is shown in figure 5.

In addition to the close fit between etiology and appropriate
chant, ceremonial terminology also reflects the importance of two
key Navaho concepts: pleasant conditions and ugly conditions. At
each level of contrast in figure 3, these two concepts account for
important distinctions. Thus chants which are curative and correct
ugly conditions are contrasted with Blessing Way which is per-

5. RELATIONSHIPS BETWEEN NAVAHO CLASSIFICATION OF ELEMENTS CAUSING ILLNESS AND THE TERMINOLOGY OF CURES

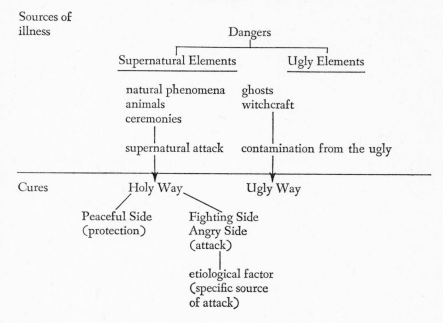

formed to prevent such disruption and preserve pleasant conditions. Of the chants, those which are Holy Way or Life Way emphasize return to pleasant conditions through immunity against the cause of illness, while Ugly Way chants remove the specific ugly conditions caused by ghosts and witchcraft. Of the ways of performing Holy Way, Peaceful Side Theme emphasizes return to pleasant conditions, while Angry Side or Fighting Side emphasizes something which is ugly, i.e., the anger or weapons of the supernatural which cause the illness. The source of the weapon or anger is further specified by reference to the etiological factor terminology. These relationships are shown in figure 6.

In reexamining the terminology presented by Wyman and Kluckhohn in 1938, the same six clusters of terms are encountered: (1) chant names, (2) ritual or manner, (3) branch or male-female distinction, (4) subritual or theme, (5) etiological factor, and (6)

6. RELATIONSHIPS BETWEEN NAVAHO CONCEPTS OF
PLEASANT AND UGLY CONDITIONS AND THEIR CEREMONIAL
TERMINOLOGY

Ceremony				
	Blessing Way and others	Chant name + branch		
Manner		Life Way	Holy Way	Ugly Way
Theme			Peaceful Side	Angry Side, Fighting Side
Etiological Factor				From Under Plants Side, Thunderstruck Side, etc.

 Ugly conditions

Pleasant conditions

phase or subceremony. These clusters of terms indicate changes in ritual procedure according to several levels of contrast as indicated in figure 3 and as substantiated by the reconstruction of queries and answers in the preceding pages. That these distinctions correspond to distinctions in disease causes is shown in figure 4. Figure 5 shows that, at each level, the important contrast is made in terms of the binary opposition between pleasant and ugly conditions. These might be thought of as criterial attributes or components which operate at each level of contrast.

Symbolism and Ritual Action

A distributional analysis using the notion of contrast is also relevant to the study of symbolism and ritual action. The material presented by Kluckhohn and Wyman in their 1940 monograph includes details on paraphernalia, medicines, and particular ritual actions, in addition to an outline of ways in which these are combined into component ceremonies and into chants. Descriptions of four chants are also provided. These data constitute rich source material for examining contrasts (1) between ritual and nonritual contexts and (2) among various symbols and action sequences within ritual scenes. In contrast to nonritual contexts, the chant setting and the arrangement of objects and persons in that setting correspond to the Navaho model or map of the universe. Navaho cosmology is replicated in each chant, and oppositions in this framework set the pattern within which ritual sequences take place. These sequences include transactions (or prestations) between the patient and the supernatural, again distinguishing ritual from nonritual contexts. Within sequences, the basic contrast is between those actions involving the patient's body, which identify him with the supernatural, and those which remove the conditions of sickness.

The Navaho model of the universe has been depicted (Haile 1943:71) as a circle which represents the point where the sky-horizon-edge meets the earth-horizon-edge. Various versions of the Navaho origin legend refer to the four light phenomena which were associated with each of the four directions when the ancestors of the Navaho emerged from the lower worlds. In the east is the dawn; in the south is horizontal blue; in the west is horizontal yellow; and in the north is darkness. Each of these four light phenomena has an inner form or "that which stands within" as follows: (1) Dawn Man (east), (2) Horizontal Blue Man (south), (3) Horizontal Yellow Woman (west), (4) Darkness Woman (north). Thus, a circular horizon is divided into light phenomena associated with four directions, and each of these in turn is given the human attribute of maleness or femaleness.

One of Haile's informants has depicted the relationships in figure 7. Here Dawn Man lies east to south, Horizontal Blue Man lies south to west, Evening Twilight Woman lies west to north, and Darkness Woman lies north to east. This basic fourfold scheme is repeated in the association of direction and color with the four sacred mountains, jewels, birds, types of corn, and various supernaturals

7. NAVAHO MODEL OF THE UNIVERSE: THE BASIC FOURFOLD SCHEME

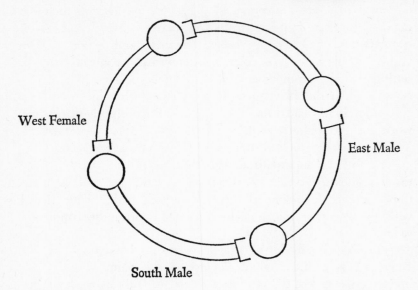

North Female

West Female

East Male

South Male

(Reichard 1945: table 2). Some of these are summarized as follows:

Direction	Color	Phenomenon	Mountain	Jewel	Bird
East	White	Dawn Man	Mt. Blanca	White Shell	Pigeon
South	Blue	Horizontal Blue Man	Mt. Taylor	Turquoise	Bluebird
West	Yellow	Horizontal Yellow Woman	San Francisco Peaks	Abalone	Yellow Warbler
North	Black	Darkness Woman	La Plata Peaks	Jet	Blackbird

The Navaho dwelling or hogan is used for a chant. It is made sacred or supernatural through the ritual rubbing of corn meal and the placing of oak sticks on the posts or wall beams in each of the four directions. This is done by the singer at the beginning of each chant (Kluckhohn and Wyman 1940b:7). The hogan is usually a five- to eight-sided dwelling of cribbed logs, the rounded appearance of which approximates the circle of sky horizon meeting earth horizon. The structure of the hogan itself and the placement of participants in the hogan during the chant replicates the Navaho model of the cosmos as in figure 8.

Men sit on the south side of the hogan; women sit on the north side. The singer sits on the southwest side, and the patient, when resting, sits on the northwest side. When participating in a bath or sandpainting or being sung over by the singer, the patient is always seated on the west side, directly opposite the door. Sandpaintings are always made in the area in front of the patient's position, that is, on the west side between the fire and the rear of the hogan.

The pairing of colors with directions is often seen in the sand-

8. NAVAHO HOGAN DURING A CHANT: PLACEMENT OF PARTICIPANTS REPLICATING THE NAVAHO MODEL OF THE COSMOS

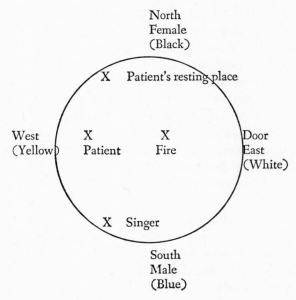

paintings and in the prayersticks. There are usually four of the latter, each painted one of the four directional colors. East is connected with whiteness, maleness (cf. Dawn Man), and sacred things. North, in contrast, is associated with black, darkness, femaleness (cf. Darkness Woman), and ugly things. Prayersticks and other offerings are deposited toward the east and the set-out of the chant fetishes faces in this direction. In contrast to these ritual objects presented to the supernaturals, objects which have been pressed against the patient in order to remove ugly things are deposited toward the north.

The hogan can be thought of as divided into two halves, the south and east versus the north and west. The singer or one who is able to cure through ritual knowledge is associated with maleness on the south and the supernaturals (and maleness) on the east. The patient, when resting, is associated with the female side of the hogan (the north) and hence with darkness, black, and the source of illness. When participating in the ritual, the patient sits to the west, halfway between the female north and male south (the contrast between sickness and health) and opposite the door on the east which is associated with the supernaturals.

Movement within the hogan during a chant is always clockwise and is expressed in Navaho by the term "sunward" or "in the direction of the sun." This contrasts with "against the sun" or counterclockwise. In northern latitudes, the sun has a southern orientation in the sky, i.e., it never advances north of the zenith. If the observer orients himself southward, as indicated by the Navaho term for south or "sunward," the sun is seen rising in the east and setting in the west. The direction of this motion is clockwise and provides the pattern for ritual movement during a chant. It is against this framework of four directions associated with four colors, male and female, and clockwise movement that events of the chant take place.

The pattern of ritual activities which brings the patient from sickness to health can be seen in terms of four important Navaho concepts. The contrast between pleasant conditions and ugly conditions has already been introduced. The term "ugly things" suggests anger, arrow, or other substances from a supernatural, witch, or ghost; these have entered the patient's body and must be removed if the patient is to attain again the pleasant conditions. Two other concepts are found in the verb stems "to sanctify" and "to do." The former stem is the basis for the term "supernatural" used in the phrase "supernatural (or 'holy') people." Other terms derived from the stem "to sanctify" not only connote the possession of superhuman abilities, but also immunity from sickness or other ugly conditions. One of these signifies that sanctifying or the process of making an object or person sacred is being done. The stem "to do" is the basis of the most common term for witchcraft, meaning literally "something is done terminatively" or "someone acts against him" (Kluckhohn 1944a). Another frequently used term for witchcraft (which Kluckhohn translates as "sorcery") means "evil wishing." Thus witchcraft is either action against or thinking against an individual by another Navaho. Significantly, the stem connoting "action against" is used in contexts other than those referring to witchcraft (action by humans). Haile (1938:644) cites the terms "Bear-Does-It-Way," "Thunder-Does-It-Way," "Big-Snake-Does-It-Way," which refer to etiological factors bringing about the patient's illness. These terms refer to causes rather than a particular chant which may cure the sickness, since more than one chant may be appropriate for bear, snake, or thunder illness.

The contrast between "to sanctify" and "to act against" is between two polar types of action: that which makes an individual immune to ugly conditions and hence brings about pleasant conditions and that which is against an individual and brings the former conditions and the absence of the latter. The relations between all four terms is seen in the following diagram:

	Positive	Negative
Condition	pleasant	ugly
Action	sanctify	act against him

The purpose of ritual action in a chant is thus (1) to produce immunity and make the patient supernatural or holy (the process of sanctifying) and (2) to counteract action against him and remove the ugly conditions.

One way in which ritual brings immunity has been outlined by Aberle in a recent article (1967). His analysis of ritual transactions provides the key to changes in the patient's relation to the supernatural. Various supernaturals (depending on the etiological factors involved and the chant being performed) must be petitioned. The petition is often called by a Navaho word also translated as "sacrifice" or "offering" and is usually in the form of a prayerstick; it is significant that prayersticks are used only in Holy Way and not in Evil Way where the emphasis is on removing the evil more than on the patient regaining a pleasant condition. The petition is a presentation to the supernatural which, if correctly made, compels them to aid the patient. Instances of a hero's offerings to a particular supernatural are recounted in most Navaho chant myths. In discussing an offering to Gila Monster in the Flintway Myth, Aberle says:

The *quantity* of goods offered to Gila Monster is not important; even four bundles do not move him. Only the *right* goods induce him to act. But this decision does not arise out of pleasure. On the contrary, he blames Big Fly Man for telling what his "proper" offering is. Quite evidently, this right offering compels him to act. For whatever reason, like many of the Holy People, he is not eager to help, but he is constrained when the right offering is made. [1967:17]

During a chant, the singer makes the same kind of offering as prescribed by the myth and presents it to the supernatural on behalf of the patient. Previous to the ceremony the patient has made a prestation to the singer in order to persuade him to perform. In sum, the initial ceremony recounted in the myth is performed because of an offering or prestation; validation of the right to perform the ceremony is presumably through a prestation (paid by the singer to his teacher); the singer receives a prestation for performing a ceremony; offerings are supplied on behalf of the patient to the supernaturals during a ceremony; and the patient's prayers request cure because of this offering (Aberle 1967:19). As Aberle suggests:

An unbroken chain of reciprocity binds the supernatural figure, the hero, the singer, and the patient together. Indeed the chain is a circle: In the

course of the ceremony the patient becomes one of the Holy Ones, a figure possessing temporary mana—not through trance or seizure, but
through ritual contact and identification. [1967:27]

   In addition to obtaining aid from the supernaturals through
presentation of offerings, much ritual symbolism associates the
patient's body with the supernaturals who are compelled to aid by
(1) applying objects externally and (2) by administering medicines
internally. This symbolism of "applying to" or "taking in" is contrasted with the symbolism of "removing" or "taking out" ugly
substances which are making the patient sick. These two themes of
"taking in" and "taking out" are found at all levels of complexity in
a chant. In terms of specific paraphernalia and medicines, the
following equations can be made:

	Application of holiness		Removal of ugly (evil) conditions
Medicine	*External*	*Internal*	
	body or "foot" lini-ment	"mouth put"	emetic or "vomit"
Objects	a. figures painted on body	pollen ball	unravelers
	b. token tied to patient		
	c. figures depicted in sand and applied to patient		
	d. fetishes pressed on patient		

These and other medicines and paraphernalia appear in component
ceremonies of a chant in such combinations that the emphasis of
the ceremony may be that of sanctification or removal of ugly
conditions. For instance, during the sweat and emetic ceremony
(Kluckhohn and Wyman 1940*b*:81), the participants sit in an
intensely heated hogan which causes profuse sweating and take the
liquid emetic which produces ritual vomiting. Participants also place

ashes on arrowheads and blow them northward, symbolizing the blowing away of evil (1940b:73).

As an example of emphasis on sanctification of the patient, figure 9 shows the main ritual actions which take place during a sandpainting subceremony during a five-night version of Shooting Chant, Male (Haile 1947:187–207). Here, the main symbols are the figures of the supernaturals (Holy Young Man, Holy Boy, Holy Young Woman, and Holy Girl), the sun, the moon, and darkness; these appear as figures on the wide boards, in the sandpainting, and in the body painting. Holy Young Man is the hero who in the central incident in the chant myth is taken by Thunder People into the sky to learn the ritual of Shooting Chant, Male (Spencer 1957:116; Haile 1947:66). All of these symbols are closely connected to the patient's body by painting them on the skin or by the action of "pressing" which Haile interprets as sanctification or making the patient holy (1947:53). Other objects and the medicines are first thrust toward the figures of the sandpainting and then administered to the patient. Thus a chant token, usually consisting of a feather or bit of turquoise or white shell, is tied to the patient's hair, the pollen ball is swallowed by the patient, and the "mouth put" medicine is drunk by the patient. The ritual thrusting signifies that the object or medicine is being transferred from the supernaturals to the patient; presumably this aid is in response to his offering (e.g., prayersticks) made at other times during the chant. Like the sandpainting subceremony, the prayerstick-cutting ceremony, the jewel-offering ceremony, and the ritual bath emphasize the sanctification of the patient. Other subceremonies such as the sweat and emetic (mentioned above), the hoop ceremony, and the unraveling ceremony emphasize the removal of evil.

The way in which such subceremonies are combined into an entire chant also shows a contrast between sanctification and removal of evil (the themes of "taking in" and "taking out"). This is the difference between Holy Way and Ugly Way. In comparison with the former, the latter lacks: (1) setting out of the contents of the medicine bundle (ritual presentation of contents to supernaturals), (2) offerings, (3) eating mush, (4) taking of mixed decoc-

9. SANDPAINTING CEREMONY

Events	Symbols	Meaning
1. Making of sand-painting by singer	*sandpainting:* Holy Young Man Holy Boy Holy Young Woman Holy Girl encircled by rainbow Two Big Flies at opening	Two male myth heroes and female counterparts. Holy Young Man is carried to the skies by Thunder and learns Shooting Way from the Hailway People there. Big Fly is the helper in the myth.
2. Singer places set-up (including wide boards and arrows) in back and south of sandpainting	*Wide Boards:* 1. Holy Young Man and Thunder; Big Fly and Otter (back) 2. Sun (front) Sky Man (back) 3. Moon (front) Earth (back) 4. Darkness and Dawn (front); Horizontal Blue and Evening Twilight (back)	Symbols on wide boards identify myth hero and key symbols in myth which are also mentioned in singing. The boards are placed around sandpainting so that "various supernaturals may look upon the painting and patient" (Haile 1947:74). Arrows represent offerings to the supernaturals.
3. Patient puts corn-meal on sandpainting figures		Sanctifies the sandpainting. (May represent power or means of travel which allows supernaturals to come to sand figures. Term for sandpainting is "they come.")
4. Body painting. Singer paints figures on the back and front of patient; he motions toward the sandpainting and sun with the paint before beginning.	Sun figure on chest (Blue) Moon figure on back (White)	Body painting is seen as offering of patient to the supernaturals. It also personifies the patient in terms of the supernaturals.
5. Chant token tying	Tying token to hair of patient	Identifies the patient with the supernaturals.

9. SANDPAINTING CEREMONY *continued*

Events	Symbols	Meaning
6. Singer swings the bull roarer, outside hogan	Noise represents the voice of the Flint People; these are identified with Thunder People and hence the voice of Thunder Man himself.	Drives away the evil influences around the hogan.
7. Patient sits on sandpainting while singer chants; sand is pressed against parts of patient's body	Symbols same as those listed in no. 1	The supernatural is pressed into the patient's body; evil removed.
8. Sand removed from hogan		Deposited in the north associated with evil.

Last day of five-night Shooting Way, Male Branch; from Haile 1947

tion (ceremonial stew), (5) sandpaintings (less frequent and may be at night). All of these involve either prestations to the supernaturals or ritual actions of taking in medicines or other symbolic food. On the other hand, Ugly Way may include: (1) spruce dress, (2) overshooting, (3) hoop ceremony, (4) out-of-door bath, (5) ritual blackening (which replaces body painting). These rituals all involve methods of extracting evil: the cutting and releasing of spruce branches covering the patient, the use of a hoop or arrows which also hold and release evil, and the association of the patient with black.

Songs and prayers which accompany ritual action also contain the contrast between the association of the patient with holiness and the removal of evil. Both have the structure outlined by Reichard (1944). They include, usually at the beginning of each section, the identification of the relevant supernatural and a characterization of his features and his place of origin. Succeeding phrases may mention the offering being transferred to the supernaturals; the supernatural is said to come to the patient, making him holy and calling him "my child" or "my grandchild." For example when the chant token is tied to the patient, the singer chants:

> Monster Slayer . . . at Sun's home
> One day having passed, he returned to me
> With a red head plume, he returned to me
> My child, you are sacred.
>
> [Adapted from Haile 1947:203]*

Songs and prayers for the purpose of removing evil mention both the identification of the supernatural with the patient and the removal of evil, as exemplified in the following lines from "Prayer of the First Night, Male Shooting Chant Evil" (Shooting Way, Male Branch, Ugly Way manner) analyzed by Reichard:

> Just as you are the sacred one, by means of these things
> So may I be sacred, by means of them
> There is one way by which we become sacred
> Ugly thing of evil-wishing, today far away, it has gone back. . . .
>
> [1944:60–61, lines 34–37; adaptation LL]*

Often the end of a prayer or song indicates that the patient has become holy and pleasant conditions have returned:

> before me, with pleasant conditions, I go about . . .
> These I have become again
> pleasant conditions have returned.
>
> [1944:92–93, lines 383, 392, 396; adaptation LL]*

It is this process of petition to the supernaturals, presentation of an offering, identification of the patient with the supernatural and/or removal of the evil, and the return of pleasant conditions that characterizes Navaho ritual. The process is repeated over and over again during an entire chant: in each subceremony, in each prayer, in each song set. Different aspects of the process may be emphasized at different times. For example, during the prayerstick ceremony, the offering is important; during an unraveling ceremony, the removal of evil is crucial; and during a sandpainting ceremony, the identification of the patient with supernatural is the focus of effort. The Dawn Songs (the final songs sung during the all-night singing on the last night) emphasize the return of pleasant conditions. This process always takes place within the context of color, sex, and directional symbolism which recall the Navaho

---

* Navaho texts of these chants will be found at end of Glossary.

model of the cosmos. Presumably, if such associations are used, the ceremony is proper and the aid of the supernaturals can be assured.

The basic themes of "taking in" the holiness and "taking out" the evil, which are so crucial for the change from sickness to health, are also those communicated in the elaborate ceremonial classification already discussed. At each level of terminological distinction, there is a contrast between the emphasis on holy/pleasant and witchcraft/evil; this is seen in such oppositions as (1) Peaceful Side Theme versus chant, (2) Holy Way versus Ugly Way, and (3) Fighting Side Theme versus Peaceful Side Theme. The terminology reflects the emphasis of the ritual to be performed and suggests to the native speaker the particular methods which might be used to achieve a cure. Since the nature of the cure is so closely connected to the etiological factors causing the illness, these too are suggested by the terminology used.

Conclusions

The basic thesis of this paper is that Clyde Kluckhohn's approach to Navaho ethnography as illustrated in his early publications (especially Wyman and Kluckhohn 1938; Kluckhohn and Wyman 1940b) shows an interest in native terminology and in the structure of ritual which anticipates the work of Metzger and Williams, Frake, and other ethnoscientists. Kluckhohn's theoretical concerns first focused on functionalism and then gradually turned to structuralism anticipating the work of Lévi-Strauss and others. Correlated with this shift in theoretical preoccupation was a decreasing interest in the details of Navaho ethnography and an increasing focus on more broadly conceived themes or values. In the last decade, recent developments in anthropology have emphasized a return to ethnographic detail in combination with more rigorous methods, both in the analysis of the structure of ritual and in various terminological domains.

Lamphere has attempted to show that, if the details of Kluckhohn's ethnography are combined with the structural approach, new regularities in the Navaho data emerge. It is now possible to see how the elaborate terminological classification and the symbolism of Navaho rituals are part of one system and reflect the opposition of pleasant (good) and ugly (evil). Kluckhohn himself observed some of these relationships but expressed them in terms of Navaho values, their desire for harmony and balance. The analysis suggested here has been able to validate Kluckhohn's tentative suggestions and hopefully to push further toward a more adequate understanding of Navaho culture.

GLOSSARY

Abalone: diichiłii

Act against (verb stem): −t'į́

Angry Side Theme: 'iidéelchįhjí

Apache Wind Way: chíshí bińłch-'ijí

Bad: hóch'ǫ

Bath: táá'agis

Bear-Does-It-Way: shash 'át'ííjí

Beauty Way: hozhónee

Big God Way: hasch'éétsohee

Big-Snake-Does-It-Way: tł'iistsoh 'at'į́į́jí

Big Star Way: sǫtsohjí

Blessing Way: hózhǫ́ǫ́jí

Ceremony: nahaghai

Chant (curing ceremony): hatáál

Chanter: hataałi

Chant token: siitł'óół

Chant with House: kin bee hatáál

Chant with Jewel Offerings: ntł'iz bee hatáál

Chant with Offerings (i.e., prayersticks): k'eetáán bee hatáál

Chant with Sandpaintings: 'iikááh bee hatáál

Chant with Sun's House: jóhonaa'ái baghan bee hatáál

Chant with Supernatural Impersonators ("those which have yéé'i"): yéé'i hołóonii

Chiricahua Wind Way: chíshí bińłch'ijí

Clockwise (sunward or in the direction of the sun): shábik'ehgo

Corral Dance: ił náshjin

Counterclockwise (against the sun): shada'jí

Coyote Way: ma'iijí

Curing ceremony (chant): hatáál

Dangerous: bahadzid

Dark Circle of Branches: 'ił náshjin

Darkness: chahałheeł

Darkness Woman (north): chahałheeł 'asdzán

Dawn: hayołkááł

Dawn Man (east): hayołkááł hastiin

Diagnostician: 'éé'deetihi

Do (verb stem): −t'į́

Dog Way: łééchąą'í
Eagle Way: 'atsájí
Earth horizon edge: ni'káshbąh
Earth-Surface People (Navaho):
   nahokáá din'é
East (Dawn Man): hayołkaał
   hastiin
East (round object comes up, a):
   ha'a'aah
Emetic: 'iikóóh
Evil (ugly conditions): hóch'ǫ
Evil Way: hóchǫ́ǫ́jí
Evil Way, Male Shooting Branch:
   na'at'oee bakǫ'jí hóchǫ́ǫ́jí
Evil wishing (verb stem): −zin
Excess Way: ajiłee
Fighting Side Theme: deezlááji
Final night: bitł'éé
From Under Plants Side: ch'ilya-
   adǫ́ǫ́
From Upper Regions Side: ghót'-
   ááhdǫ́ǫ́'
Ghosts: ch'iidí
God Impersonators (masked danc-
   ers): yée'i bichai
Hail Way: ńlóee
Hand trembling: ńdilnííh
Hand Trembling Way: ńdilniihjí
Holiness: diyin
Holy People: diyin or diyin dine'é'
Holy Way: diyink'ehjí
Holy Young Man: diyin diné
Horizontal blue: nahodeetł'iish
Horizontal Blue Man (south):
   nahodeetł'iish hastiin
Horizontal yellow: nahotsoi

Horizontal Yellow Woman (west):
   nahotsoi 'asdzán
Inner form: bii'gistiin
Interior Chant: wóne'é hatáál
Jet:. bashzhinii or yołizhin
Just Visiting Chant: t'óó naajé-
   hégo hatáál
La Plata Peaks: dibéntsah
Life Way: 'iinááji
Life Way, Male Shooting Branch:
   na'at'oee bakǫ'jí'iinááji
Liniment, body or foot: kétł'oh
Make sacred: 'oolghį́į́
Medicine: 'azee'
Mountain Top Way: dziłk'įjį́
Mount Blanca: sisnádjini
Mount Taylor: tsodził
"Mouth put": zaańił
Navaho (Earth-Surface People):
   nahokáá din'é
Navaho Wind Way: diné bińłch'iji
Night Way: tł'ééji
North (Darkness Woman): cha-
   hałheeł 'asdzán
Offering (stem): −gheel
Patient: bik'i hataałi
Peaceful Side Theme: hózhǫ́ǫ́ji
Petition (stem): −gheel
Pleasant conditions: hózhǫ́
Plume Way: 'atsosee
Pollen ball: 'ayeel
Power (for travel): 'agáál
Prayerstick: k'eet'áán
Pressing: 'ida'iilcood
Prestation (stem): −gheel
Red Ant Way: wóláchííji

Round object comes up, a (east): ha'a'aah

Round object goes down, a (west): e'e'aah

Sacred things: diyin

Sacrifice (stem): –gheel

Sanctify: 'oolghį́į́

Sanctify (verb stem): –ghį́į́ł

Sandpainting ("they come"): 'iikááh

San Francisco Peaks: doko'osłiid

Shooting Ways: na'at'oee

Shooting Way, Female Branch: na'at'oee ba'áájí

Shooting Way, Male Branch: na'at'oee baką'jí

Singer: hataałi

Sky horizon edge: yáskáshbah

Sorcery (witchcraft): 'anzin or 'iińzį́į́d

Source of illness: hóch'ǫ́

South (Horizontal Blue Man): nahodeeł'iish hastiin

South (sunward): shada'ááh

Spruce dress: chó 'éi

Star gazing: déez'į́į́

Striped Side: noodǫ́ǫ́zhjí

Sun, against the (counterclockwise): shada'jí

Sunward or in the direction of the sun (clockwise): shábik'ehgo

Supernatural: diyin, diyin dine'é'

Sweat and emetic: 'iiłkóóh

Thunder-Does-It-Way: 'iini' 'át'įįjí

Thunderstruck Side: 'ó'oosnii'jí

Turquoise: **dootl'izhi**

Ugly conditions (evil): hóch'ǫ́

Ugly things: hóch'ǫ́

Ugly Way: hóchǫ́ǫ́jí

Unravelers: gholtáád

Unraveling: gholtáád

Upper Regions Side: ghót'ááhjí

Vomit: 'iikóóh

Water Way: tóee

Werewolves: yeenaaldlooshi

West (Horizontal Yellow Woman): nahotsoi 'asdzán

West (round object goes down, a): e'e'aah

Which kind of ceremony is it?: ha'at'ééjí hatáál?

White shell: yołigai

Wide boards: tsin ńteel

Witchcraft ("something is done terminatively," "someone acts against him"): 'áńtį

Witchcraft (sorcery): 'anzin or 'iińzį́į́d

naaghéé' neezghání . . . jóhóna'ái bohoghandi

t'ááłá'í biiskaago shaanájá

bee'etsos łichíigo shaanájá

Shiyáázh diníighin

t'áá bee dinighinii

t'áá 'ái bee dinisin dooleeł.

t'ááłá'í bee diniidzin dooleeł

yáada nchó'ógíí be'eyoiinziin díís jí ńzaadgoo násdlį́į́'

sitsidji' hózhǫ́ǫ́go naasháadoo . . .

díí násisdlį́į́'

hózhó náhásdlį́į́'

LINGUISTIC MODELS AND
THE STUDY OF CULTURE:
CLYDE KLUCKHOHN'S APPROACH

John L. Fischer

CLYDE KLUCKHOHN'S published works dealing in substantial part with language in one way or another do not add up to a long list. There are about a dozen chapters, articles, and reviews which can be fairly considered to be works of major linguistic relevance, and not all of these deal primarily with language. Moreover, the works themselves leave a sense of incompleteness. For instance, the paper on Navaho value terms (1956h) gives the impression of being little more than a summary of field notes, while the four late papers on the study of values (1956e, 1958d, 1959e, 1961c), each more or less a different version of the same basic paper, are admittedly trial runs which are to serve as a stimulus for some larger work.

Nevertheless, Kluckhohn possessed a great and continuing interest in the area of language and culture and had considerable linguistic sophistication. Moreover, this was an interest which was particularly crucial to his view of anthropology. That this interest did not result in more publications or in more finished products may be due mainly to the relative lack of development of the aspects of the disciplines of anthropology and linguistics which were most relevant to Kluckhohn's interests, not to any doubts on his part about the importance of language and culture as an area of study.

To demonstrate the crucial position of the study of language and culture in Kluckhohn's thought requires exposition of some of his basic attitudes toward anthropology. This is not an easy task, since one basic characteristic was his seeking out of other people's views. He considered that the universe, society, culture, and personality were all complex and organized on various levels with relationships between levels and that it was difficult, though desirable, for one man to encompass all this. This led him accordingly to read widely and seek out a wide variety of people. When he wanted to be, which was often, he was a consummate academic statesman. He was a good listener and something of an ethnographer of his own society and academic circles. He used to threaten or promise to write a book on American culture, in which his many friends and acquaintances were to be informants. Like any good ethnographer, he was perceptive of his informant's views and would generally find something in them to praise. But again like a good ethnographer, he was often rather cautious about expressing his own views, in spite of a fondness for writing and talking, except in so far as they were relevant for a particular audience.

Thus, the view of Kluckhohn in this paper may run the danger, more than would be the case with most other men, of being a projection of the scholarly interests and anthropological postulates of the writer. This description of Kluckhohn's anthropological attitudes is probably not actually false in any important degree, but the selection and emphasis may be biased. That this precautionary prologue is necessary is a tribute to the breadth of his interests, to his sympathy as a conversationalist, and to his skill in encouraging originality in his students and colleagues.

Kluckhohn, with his eclectic interests, was quite aware of the possibility of conflict between different goals in science as in other areas of life. Much of his work may be understood as the product of a conflict of two anthropological goals or values: his synthetic concern to describe and understand overall patterning of cultures on the one hand and his conviction that anthropology should use rigorous scientific methods on the other. Kluckhohn recognized the contribution of an intuitive, humanistic approach and used to refer with approval to Kroeber's view that anthropology was a threefold discipline which combined humanities with natural and social science. But he seems in the long run to have given the humanities aspect of the discipline less weight than Kroeber did. Kluckhohn tended to regard an intuitive, humanistic approach as a primitive stage of anthropological work, necessary at this time in the historical development of the discipline and perhaps always necessary as a stage in thought or in the exploration of new frontiers, but not as the final goal. The final goal was to be a universal science.

Kluckhohn realized that the scientific method of contemporary anthropology was rather slight and feeble and could not deal with many problems of importance, including especially the nature of the overall patterns of cultures. Because of the need to develop scientific method in anthropology, he was likely to express admiration for works dealing with relatively minor questions which he considered to be important for their methodological contributions. At the same time, he did not wish to postpone the consideration of more global issues such as the overall patterning of cultures until these could be handled rigorously. He was a strong supporter of the configurational work of Ruth Benedict, for instance, and in the field of language and culture warmly advocated the intuitive works of Benjamin Whorf, some of the later works of Edward Sapir, and those of Dorothy Lee, although praising them more for their perceptiveness and boldness than for the rigor of their methods. However, in his own work along similar lines, such as the chapter on language in *The Navaho* (Kluckhohn and Leighton 1946a), a caution and restraint is evident which results in more modest—and probably less stimulating—conclusions than those of other authors. The source of this restraint seems to be his interest in scientific rigor and concern with developing explicit testing and verification.

Another manifestation of Kluckhohn's trends toward intellectual synthesis interacted with his interest in whole-culture patterns and in scientific rigor. This is his concern with human nature and cultural universals and near-universals. While he wanted to understand unique, whole-culture patterns, he also wanted to be able to compare these with each other and note similarities as well as differences. He seemed to be moving in the direction of defining all unique culture patterns as selections and combinations of basic universal (noncultural?) elements. His repeatedly expressed admiration for the distinctive feature analysis of phonemic systems by Roman Jakobson and his colleagues is an indication of this, as was also some of his collaboration with Talcott Parsons on general sociocultural theory.

The crucial importance of linguistics in Kluckhohn's thought stems from two propositions: (1) Language is an indispensable part of human culture and social life; (2) since cultures consist of complex systems of patterns, the successful scientific analysis of culture must depend upon the development of rigorous pattern analysis more than the quantification of simple variables, and it is in linguistics where the greatest progress has been made to date in pattern analysis. From the first proposition it follows that a thorough understanding of the language and speech of a people, with careful attention to meaning, would be a major step toward understanding their life and the rest of their culture. From the second proposition it follows that the analysis of language ought to provide a model for the analysis of other forms of culture. It has recently become popular to minimize the precision and rigor of linguistic analysis. Without questioning whether linguistics as a solid science may have been oversold, I believe that if Kluckhohn were alive today he would still be upholding linguistic analysis as a model for cultural anthropology. While his interest in language and culture was long-standing, if anything it increased toward the end of his life, and his most important publications in this field are late or posthumous (1956e, 1956h, 1958d, 1959e, 1960e, 1961c, 1961d).

There are in Kluckhohn's published work four distinct, major attempts to approach understanding of patterns of whole cultures through the use of language and linguistics. These have just been mentioned (1956e, 1958d, 1959e, 1961c are considered one approach); another attempt precedes these and is his discussion on language in *The Navaho* (Kluckhohn and Leighton 1946a), which is in part practically oriented toward the problems of government officials and others using interpreters in work with the Navaho and which, in so far as it deals with questions of language and culture, might be characterized as "cautious Whorf":

striking divergences in manner of thinking are crystallized in and perpetuated by the forms of Navaho grammar.

. . . . .

There is very little "give" in the language. It rather reminds one of a Bach fugue, in which everything is ordered in scrupulous symmetry.

. . . . .

The one fact that Navaho is a verb language, whereas English is mainly a noun-adjective language, of itself implies a different order of thought habits. [Kluckhohn and Leighton 1946a:198, 199, 208]

This particular work does not make striking theoretical innovations, although it is of interest and practical value to people working with the Navaho and also constitutes an additional ethnographic example of Whorf's type of analysis of relations between language and culture.

The Navaho value-terms paper (1956h) appeared ten years later—incidentally, in the same issue of *Language* with papers on componential analysis of kinship terminologies by Ward Goodenough (1956 on Trukese) and Floyd Lounsbury (1956 on Pawnee). In spite of a professed distaste for studies of kinship terminology, Kluckhohn repeatedly expressed his conviction of the importance of these particular articles, not necessarily so much for the light they threw on kinship, but as models of rigorous analysis of meaning by techniques analogous to those used in phonology and morphology. Kluckhohn's paper does not compare in methodic refinement to those of Goodenough and Lounsbury and, while as an example of lexicography, it is superior to the brief entries found in most dictionaries of exotic languages, the handling of each term is less thorough than in a good, large, unabridged dictionary of English. Of course, dictionaries of languages with substantial literature tend to prefer examples of uses taken from the works of reputable authors; Kluckhohn's emphasis on examples from speech is an inevitable result of dealing with a largely unwritten language. His frequent addition of the behavioral context is again a more or less natural consequence of the lack of an extensive body of Navaho written literature.

The main interest of this paper is not in its lexical method but in the fact that it is an attempt to get at the overall patterning of a particular culture, Navaho, by the use of selected linguistic materials. Kluckhohn tended to become impatient with studies of kinship terminology (and of many other subjects) because they did not seem to him to be of value in characterizing whole cultures uniquely. If we find, for instance, that Japanese kinship terminology is basically very similar to that of Central Eskimos, as well as that of Americans and English, we are led to conclude that analyses of kinship terminology alone will not lead to unique characterizations of cultures as wholes, even granting that there may be certain important similarities of family structure which all groups in this example share and many other groups do not.

However, Kluckhohn hoped that the value terminology of a culture might be a means of getting at a unique characterization of it: One way to approach an understanding of a culture as a whole would be to collect its value terms and analyze their meaning and use. In different languages, the terms used in particular contexts to translate such English words as "good," "bad," "kind," "wicked," etc., will have different extensions of meaning, different connotations, from their English counterparts. The particular structure and range of meaning of each value term is probably unique in each language; so a collection of the common value words for a culture would necessarily also be unique.

Of course, any term in any language may be regarded as semantically unique. This applies even to kinship terms if all the variant uses are taken into consideration and attention is also purposely restricted to their genealogical use. It is not, therefore, just the uniqueness of value terms which makes them of special importance in the characterization of whole-culture patterns; it is even more the central position of values in the whole-culture pattern. The terminology used to designate values might accordingly constitute a miniature model of the value system of the society. It would be a small and hopefully manageable system, moreover, which the speakers of the language had constructed themselves and which, therefore, if it could be analyzed and set forth objectively, might have special validity as compared to an analysis in which the observer worked from a wide range of materials: While working with a wide range of materials would provide behavioral and cultural observations for a broader base of generalization, it would also necessitate much greater selection and compression of materials in order to get an overall picture of the culture. Methodic rigor in such a process would be difficult to achieve, and the opportunity for subjective distortion of the culture by the ethnographer would be greater. Kluckhohn is by no means the first to suggest careful attention to the meaning of native terms for the understanding of a culture. The important contribution of the Navaho value-terms paper (1956h), however, is its calling attention to the special importance of value terms for study and its refusal to oversimplify the problem by considering these terms only in some very precise but narrow context. In view of this, Kluckhohn can certainly be excused for failing to come up with as elegant an analysis as those of Goodenough and Lounsbury. In fact, it may be only now that people are beginning to develop analytic techniques to deal with some rigor and elegance with the kind of semantic problems with which Kluckhohn was here concerned.

Yet another linguistically assisted approach to overall patterning of culture is represented by the series of papers on the study of values (1956e, 1958d, 1959e, 1961c). "Toward a Comparison of Value-Emphases In Different Cultures" (1956e) was published the same year as his paper on Navaho value terms, while the final one, "The Study of Values" (1961c), was published after his death. Comment upon these here will be relatively brief and limited to the relationship of these works to linguistics.

Judging from the number of pages involved and the repeated handling of similar material, Kluckhohn must have regarded this series of papers as a greater contribution to anthropology than his Navaho value-terms paper (1956h). In the latter he attempted to get at whole-culture patterns by selecting for special study the lexical items in the native language used to express value judgments. In the study-of-values series (cited above), he ignored the native language and used anthropological observers' evaluations of value emphases in the culture. Perhaps he was emboldened to do this, in spite of the risks of introducing observer bias, by the success which his wife, Florence Kluckhohn, and her associates had had in developing cross-cultural values questionnaires. Also, observer bias was eliminated as an independent factor in these papers by the fact that he was personally familiar with all the cultures involved. Bias might remain in the judgments on value emphases, but it would be the bias of a single observer working on five familiar cultures, not the biases of five different observers each working on a different culture. Certainly Kluckhohn was also motivated in these papers by the need to make cross-cultural comparisons and develop universal frames of reference, to isolate universal variables.

The linguistic relevance of the study-of-values papers does not lie in the data analyzed but in the analytical method used. Recent method in American linguistics has emphasized the analysis of single languages as self-contained systems, in which the elements are defined in terms of their contrast with other elements. However, these papers deal with the comparison of five distinct cultures (Navaho, Zuni, Mormon, Texan, and Spanish-American), so that the relevance of the methods of descriptive linguistics is not immediately apparent. To be sure, the five cultures are all in contact with each other and are located in the same general part of the country; this contact within a constant macroenvironment facilitated comparison. But judging from the last paper of the series at any rate (1961c), it was not Kluckhohn's intention to treat the five cultures as a single integrated system. They were chosen rather because they were sufficiently different from each other and could constitute a sample for a trial run of a method which was to be extended eventually to a worldwide sample of cultures, or to any group of cultures, and which would produce generalizations applicable to the entire body of value systems in human cultures.

With this goal in mind, Kluckhohn's preference for Roman Jakobson's phonological analyses as his prime linguistic model for the study of values takes on added meaning. For Jakobson does not stop at establishing the existence of phonemes in individual languages through contrastive distribution, as some other structural linguists did, but goes beyond this to say explicitly how the phonemes differ from each other in terms of distinctive features. These distinctive features are binary values of auditory or articulatory dimensions or variables in which the phonemes of a language differ but, since they are grounded in universal articulatory and auditory capacities of the human organism, most of them can be found in many different languages. A phoneme in this view consists of a bundle of these distinctive features, and it is these features which would appear to be the ultimate linguistic elements rather than the phonemes.

Jakobson's work inspired in Kluckhohn the hope that in studying whole-culture patterns one could go beyond developing configurational terms, such as Ruth Benedict's "Dionysian," "Appollonian," "paranoid," or "megolomanic," and analyze these configurations or patterns into a number of value dimensions, each of which would be applicable universally since each would have reference to universal problems of human animals living in societies. Just as Jakobson had found that a limited number of phonological dimensions would suffice to describe the phonemes of all known languages, so Kluckhohn hoped that a limited number of value dimensions would suffice to describe all known cultural configurations or whole-culture patterns.

We may question how far it is legitimate to push the analogy of phonological distinctive features and cultural values or the corresponding analogy of phonemes composed of distinctive features and value configurations composed of cultural values. With sounds, it is possible to say that the distinctive features uniting in a single phonemic bundle go together because they all co-occur at about the same point in time: Thus if English k is defined as (1) a consonant which is (2) a voiceless, (3) oral, (4) back, (5) stop, all of these distinctive features apply to a short stretch of the utterance of the same instant. Kluckhohn's value dimensions can also co-occur in the same bit of behavior, but there does not appear to be any limit to the number of them which could occur simultaneously in a single act. For instance, it is conceivable that a single act might be (1) individualistic, (2) present-oriented, (3) involving an assumption of determinacy, (4) of pluralism, etc.; or again, any number of these might be irrelevant to a particular act. It is, thus, not difficult to conceive of acts which would represent many different combinations of the values characteristic of a culture, although for purposes of constructing a value questionnaire one would choose minimal pairs of acts, that is, acts which differed from each other on only one value dimension at a time. While it does not seem to be a question which Kluckhohn raised, it may well be that, given the commutability of different value dimensions within the behavior of members of a single culture, there are no fixed combinations of elemental values analogous to phonological distinctive features and comprising a limited number of value configurations analogous to the phonemes of a language.

Moreover, if the analogy of Jakobson's phonological analysis holds and such phonemelike value configurations do exist within a single culture, one might expect pairs of them to contrast on basic value dimensions. Phonologically, a dimension such as voicing is considered irrelevant unless there are certain phonemes which are regularly voiced while there are others, comparable in all other relevant phonological dimensions to some of the voiced series, which are regularly voiceless. While Clyde Kluckhohn recognized Florence Kluckhohn's assertion that no culture could use exclusively a single value orientation out of a set belonging to a single dimension, he did not take advantage of this principle of alternate value orientations in his search for phonemic analogues in value systems and appears to have regarded it as useful mainly for eventually dealing with the problem of change in dominant values. In brief, Kluckhohn drew from Jakobson's phonological analysis mainly the idea of analysis into universal binary dimensions whose existence would be independent of particular cultures. While Kluckhohn also had the idea that it should be possible to combine the elemental values into bundles which would be analogues of phonemes, he did not follow the Jakobson phonological model closely in this respect. Due to differences in the nature of the materials of phonology and values, it is doubtful that it would have been profitable to try to do so.

Kluckhohn nevertheless retained the idea of developing some kind of bundles of basic values into phoneme analogues and turned to another linguistic model for this purpose, that of Bernard Bloch for grouping allophones into phonemes as presented in his "Contrast" (1953). The phoneme in this brief paper appears as a bundle of allophones, collected and grouped by the listener's reactions, not as a concrete bundle of phonetic features which can occur at one time. Note that at this point there is a shift from regarding the basic values as analogues of the distinctive features of phonemes to regarding pairs of values from different dimensions as analogues of allophones of a single phoneme, e.g., if the values "good" and

"discipline" always go together in any culture, they are said to have
identical distributions and are treated as free vairants of each other.
Bloch's note to which Kluckhohn refers (1956e:128) is subject to
the interpretation that the precise nature of the contrast between
two phonemes is irrelevant as long as the informants regularly
recognize and reproduce it, although Bloch himself does not state
this view and in other earlier work extensively discusses components
of phonemes. But in any case, Bloch's "Contrast" discusses only
distribution; so the shift between these two models is one from
phonological content to distribution. In terms of value analogues,
this may be interpreted as a shift from semantic content to distribution. The particular combination of the two approaches and the
shifting of levels from distinctive feature analogue to allophone
analogue are somewhat confusing but, since after all values are not
the same as phonemes, there would seem to be some merit in trying
out different combinations of analogies between values and language.

A further and more daring shift occurred along with the one
discussed above. Kluckhohn was inspired by the fact that Jakobson's
phonological dimensions were sufficiently basic to be applicable both
within particular languages and in comparisons of any number of
different languages. Bloch's distributional analysis, as Kluckhohn
recognized, was intended by its author to be applicable within single
languages, but Kluckhohn quite consciously decided to apply it in
cross-cultural comparison of value systems. In a footnote to his
article on value emphases he stated:

In my adaptation of Bloch to cross-cultural analysis it may be objected
that his technique is designed to investigate distributions and environments *within* single languages. I do not see why in principle it is not applicable comparatively. This may be methodologically wrong. If so, I
wait to be shown wherein. [1956e:128, fn. 16]

Evidently he never received any definite, satisfactory criticism of the
technique, since he continued to try to refine it in successive papers.

However, even in the study-of-values paper (1961c) five years
later, Kluckhohn does not claim to have made much progress.
Progress had indeed been made in defining the basic value dimensions, but questions remain about the usefulness of applying

Bloch's distributional criteria in a cross-cultural comparison in order to get at value bundles which will be analogues of phonemes considered as groups of different allophones. For a strong suspicion can be raised, as Kluckhohn himself realized, that it might be possible for either value on any binary dimension to co-occur with either value on any other dimension in one culture or another. Florence Kluckhohn's position, that in any culture alternate value orientations always coexist with the dominant value orientations and can replace the latter as demanded by circumstances, would imply considerable freedom in the combination of dichotomies of the various value dimensions. If such freedom should exist, then the addition of enough other cultures to the sample of five New Mexico cultures should provide exceptions to all of the consistent covariation of value emphases on different dimensions which held in the smaller sample.

However, Kluckhohn noted that investigation of covariation of value variables (dimensions) might still be useful on a statistical basis. As he wrote in his final study-of-values paper, "A central problem in value-theory is: what combinations are likely and unlikely . . . in a value-matrix?" (1961c:38). I would infer that in a study covering many cultures the combinations would be almost entirely matters of probability. It would be very interesting to find out about this, but it would modify or even destroy the analogy to Bloch's allophone sorting procedure, which depends upon all-or-none judgments about the relations of environment ranges of pairs of allophones. In terms of the analogy, this would mean that all the supposed allophones would really be in mutual contrast in one environment or another and would therefore be distinct phonemes. If so, there would be little point in applying the procedure, since doing so would not simplify the data.

Another weakness of the analogy is in the definition of environment in the two cases. For Bloch, the environment of a phone is most often the immediately preceding and following phones, if any, in a word, while the range of environments for a phone consists of all the other phones in adjacent positions in words of the dialect in question. For Kluckhohn, the elemental values are not associated in any definite order; so an environment of one value is considered to be simultaneously all the other dominant values co-occurring with it in a single culture, while the range of environments for the value is a cross-cultural matter involving the co-occurrence of that value with all other possible values in all cultures being considered. Ideally one would consider a large sample of the world's cultures. In sum, it seems that the linguistic model of distributional analysis in the study-of-values papers was not followed very closely and served mainly as a stimulus for thought. Perhaps progress was being made as the linguistic model was superseded.

A last published attempt at characterizing a whole-culture pattern, or some aspect of one, through the use of linguistic materials was the article on Navaho categories for the Paul Radin *Festschrift*. Kluckhohn described the purpose of this paper as examining "in some detail standard Navaho categories in various spheres, trying to discover the criteria, explicit and implicit, applied in each area and seeing the extent to which some criteria tend to pervade all or many areas" (1960e:66). Kluckhohn was searching for characteristics of what might be called "lexical style," asking not so much "What concepts do the Navahos distinguish?" as "How do the Navahos distinguish concepts?"

Perhaps the simplest thing which he did in this paper was to look at the use of certain morphemes as widespread qualifiers. He noted, for instance, that the Navaho often specified things as male or female which we and most other people would not normally specify as such. An example would be the Navaho idiom of calling a heavy rain "male" and a light one "female." This might be regarded as a kind of investigation of metaphor, since presumably the Navaho themselves recognize in some sense that rain does not literally have sex and that the basic meaning of sex is biological. Kluckhohn makes no attempt at an exhaustive or rigorous sampling treatment of Navaho categorical metaphors. In fact, the selection of all ethnographic material in this paper is impressionistic or intuitive. It would, however, be wrong to dismiss Kluckhohn's conclusions in this article by citing anecdotal counterexamples (e.g., a case where English speakers use sex in making a distinction but the Navaho do not, if one could be found), since these are impressions based on long-standing familiarity with Navaho language and culture.

In addition to the metaphorical use of categorical qualifiers, Kluckhohn tried to develop some more general characterizations of what might be called the "logical style" of Navaho categories. The frequency of dual categories would be one characteristic of Navaho logical style, and the widespread use of male/female would be merely one example of this. Of course, dual-opposed categories can be found in any language or culture. Kluckhohn was not merely asserting their presence in Navaho; he was asserting that they are appreciably more prominent than in many other cultures. Some sort of rigorous comparison of Navaho with another language and culture would have been of value in demonstrating this point, but we may take it as a probably valid intuition without the demonstration.

Perhaps the most interesting proposition in this paper is that Navaho categories are characterized by what he variously called "inclusiveness" or "syncretism," expanding on earlier comments by Gladys Reichard. A number of observations are related under the term "syncretism." For one thing, this involves what might be called an established use of synechdoche, where parts and wholes are called by the same term: e.g., a single word used for "medicine bundle with all its contents," "contents of medicine bundle," or "any separate item of these contents" (1960e:84). A second instance of syncretism might be described as the equation of morphological and functional criteria, e.g., the classing of bats with insects because, although of different form, the bat had allegedly been a partisan of the insects in a myth. A third instance of syncretism would be the arbitrary association of objects which were formally and functionally irrelevant, e.g., the symbolism in connection with religious chants of particular color, animal, directional, sex, numerical, and sound symbolism. Perhaps examples of this are concentrated in ritual categories. A fourth instance is that of overlapping categories, where some phenomena apparently belong to each of two different categories, at times contrasted, on the same taxonomic level, although I cannot find any good illustrations of this.

Kluckhohn does not discuss the lexical style of other simple, nonliterate societies. Perhaps, if the characteristic of syncretism could be established, it could be regarded as an example of a general pattern of concrete thought which seems to be widely characteristic of peoples of nonliterate societies. One characteristic of concrete thought would be to think of things inseparably from their context and in terms of their use or activity. The equation of morphological and functional criteria could be taken as one manifestation of concrete thought, and the synechdoche in calling an item in a medicine bundle by the same term as the entire bundle would be another instance, involving inseparability of the item from its context. Kluckhohn and Reichard speak as if Navaho categorization is distinct from the categorization of other cultures, but we are not told whether there is possibly a scale of concreteness of thought along which societies might be ordered. If so, this would be an interesting cultural-linguistic variable, but perhaps too simple to serve as a characterization of a whole-culture pattern, which Kluckhohn was hoping to find.

In reviewing the published works of Clyde Kluckhohn in language and culture, well-established conclusions are rare. However, since the greatest contribution of these works is in suggesting lines of further investigation, we may evaluate Kluckhohn's achievements by asking where these papers were pointing, what further intellectual developments would have been required for progress to be made toward his long-standing goal of a rigorous scientific description of patterns of whole cultures through the use of language and linguistics. Before developing briefly the implications of these papers, we may note one further idea which Kluckhohn had on this question but which did not result in any publication or even, as far as I have been able to tell, in any organized draft of an article. In his value-emphases paper, he stated in a footnote:

My attempts to combine this technique [Bloch's distributional analysis, as discussed above] with some of those used by Harris on "discourse analysis" . . . have thus far proved unsatisfactory. . . . I still feel that some combination of these two approaches may prove extremely fruitful toward supplying a system for objective analysis of core value elements in cultures. [1956e:128, fn. 16]

From personal conversation with Kluckhohn, I believe he considered that a combination of the contributions of these two lines of thought ought to enable an objective analysis of the structure and content of myth, and he states in various places that he used myths as data for his characterization of the values of the five New Mexico cultures. The implication of all this together is that Kluckhohn considered that it should be possible by objective linguistic techniques, not yet entirely developed, to reduce or condense myths to statements of values which would constitute the cores of the myths.

Whether or not such an objective conversion of myth narratives into values statements can be achieved has not yet been demonstrated. But the use of myths as sources of values suggests further leads as well as problems. One problem is that any dramatic narrative, to retain suspense and interest, must have the possibility of turning out two different ways at certain points. In actual mythologies, this implies that one should expect to find, as one does, that basically similar plots in two different myths, even in two variant versions of the same myth, can have opposite endings. Drama in myth or elsewhere, like values, depends on the existence of dilemmas, either horn of which is possible. There would be no drama if there were no opposing forces each tending to a different outcome, just as there would be no problem in value choice if decisions about serious alternatives were unnecessary. It would seem to follow from this that the values exemplified in myth would most likely be those about which there is the most conflict in the society, i.e., those on which the society makes no automatic choice. If myths are to yield data on values, then, perhaps what they would best yield would be information on which value variables or dilemmas are most prominent in a culture, i.e., which dilemmas people find difficult and important, not information on which answer to the dilemma is characteristic of the culture. For if a myth deals with a value dilemma in one way, it could also have turned out in the opposite way and probably has done so in another narrator's telling.

This is not to deny the usefulness of comparing different cultures as to their relative emphasis on alternate poles of particular value dimensions. But such a comparison is not primarily a matter of internal structure in the usual sense of descriptive linguistics. To use a linguistic example, one might compare two languages and find that both had the same number of voiced and voiceless consonant phonemes but that the frequency of voiced phonemes in the lexicon of one language was markedly greater than in the other. The latter finding would not affect the structural description of the phonemic system. However, if over time one of these alternatives should become so common as entirely to displace the other, e.g., if all consonants in one of the languages became voiceless, then the variable of voicing would lose its relevance as a distinctive feature in the phonology of that language. Only such an extreme result could affect (and simplify) the structural description. But in the case of values, if they are chosen to constitute alternatives in universal dilemmas which are inherent in the nature of human social life, then such an elimination of a value dimension by an extreme weighting of one horn of the dilemma cannot be expected to occur, and one is left with a need for a quantitative statement of some sort. Moreover, there would seem to be no need for society members to use myth to represent dimensions which are heavily weighted toward one pole, since the choice here would generally be easy. In brief, if one wants to characterize a culture in terms of the values contained in its myths, the result of a finished investigation would most likely turn out to be a list of value dilemmas in order of difficulty, with value variables not listed or with some sort of low ranking where the choice is one-sided, rather than what Kluckhohn was emphasizing, which was a list of value variables where the choice was unambiguous and one-sided. Such a description could itself result in a unique characterization of the value configuration of a whole culture, since even discounting the possibility of ties, the possible number of distinct ways of ordering ten value dimensions according to prominence or priority would be 10 factorial or 3,628,800, considerably more than the number of recorded human cultures. Kluckhohn does raise the possibility that not all value variables are equally prominent in all cultures (e.g., 1961c:35) but does not seem to have come around to this particular position. In addition, if we take into account the preference for or emphasis on one or the other pole of each dimension, as Kluckhohn was doing, the total number of unique value configurations of ten value dimensions noted above becomes multiplied much further, by 2^{10} or 1,024.

Conclusions

In discussing Kluckhohn's work in language and culture, four major approaches to the problem of characterizing configurations of whole cultures with the aid of linguistics have been noted. The first of these is a method used by Whorf, emphasizing the cultural implications of various obligatory grammatical categories, such as verb aspect, numerical classifiers, etc. The second is the investigation of the semantics of value terms. The third is the attempt to apply a combination of componential and distributional analysis to a universal values matrix. The last is the attempt to characterize the logical style of categorization in a culture. Probably none of these lines of approach was exhausted by Kluckhohn's work, but the second and third seem more promising than the first and last. The first method runs into the extreme conservatism of language: The fact that a given grammatical process or form has become obligatory probably has some value implications at the time it arises, but the linguistic phenomenon may take a long time to develop after the appropriate extralinguistic conditions have been created and then persist for a long time after the appropriate extralinguistic conditions have disappeared. The last approach is satisfactory as far as it goes and offers some room for further refinement, but the result might not be a unique characterization of whole-culture patterns but a single continuum of concreteness/abstractness of thought on which a culture might be placed.

The semantic analysis of the value terms of a culture was difficult at the time that Kluckhohn attempted it. Two views about the meaning of words were then popular, either of which rendered a rigorous approach to meaning practically impossible. On the one hand was the view represented by Bloomfield, who stated "each linguistic form has a constant and specific meaning," which, however, "the linguist cannot define" (1933:145). On the other hand was the view, represented by the general semanticists among others, that no form ever has the same meaning twice, since the meaning is dependent on context, linguistic and extralinguistic, and the context is never the same from one moment or person to the next. This again in effect leads to an ignoring of meaning for analytical purposes, since it is assumed that the analysis will be always incomplete. It is only recently that some of the following views have gained ground among linguists and anthropologists: that most lexical items may be characterized by limited or structured polysemy, i.e., that they have in fact different definable meanings in different contexts; that the multiple meanings of a single term have relationships to each other in terms of the overlapping of semantic components; that the number of common uses or meanings is not infinite; that a distinction must be made between intended or public meaning and private meaning, i.e., between the meaning which the speaker expects the listener to understand, which is on the whole the same as the meaning which the listener infers the speaker wishes to convey, and the special associations which are the result of the unique experience of a participant in a conversation and which he neither expects nor, perhaps, wishes others to understand; that even within intended or shared meaning there is a further distinction possible between frequently recurrent standard meanings (what some have called "allosemes") and added meaning specific to a particular text and situation.

Different readers might see a variety of amplifications of Kluckhohn's work in the papers discussed. If we agree that one of his major goals in this work was to devise a way of uniquely characterizing whole-culture patterns by objective and rigorous methods which would facilitate cross-cultural comparisons and contrast, then one promising development seems to the writer to be to combine some of the features of the Navaho value-terms paper (1956h) and the study-of-values series. Such a combination should frankly seek to explore the structured polysemy of value terms. The investigator would have to begin with the collection of many examples of each term in context and sort these into different uses, as Martin Joos has done with the English word "code" (1958: esp. 59 ff.). A semantic componential analysis of its several principal uses could be made for each term, more or less along the lines used by Nida in comparing the different but semantically related words for the anthropological term "shaman" in Mayan (1958: esp. 287–88). Some of the semantic components for some of the uses would undoubtedly be universal components of value terms which require expression in all cultures. The presence of these components is in fact necessary for the investigator to translate a term in another language by an English value term or to classify a term in another language as a value term. At the same time, there would be other semantic components of some uses of these value terms, which would not be directly relevant to values at all. Perhaps it is in these extensions and additions to the value terms that a possibility lies of developing an analysis of whole-culture patterns which would be both unique and reasonably comprehensive.

For example, Kluckhohn cites a Navaho term which may be translated as either "lazy" (a negative value term: "he does not work as hard as he should") or "drowsy" (a descriptive term: "he wants to go to sleep; it is hard for him to stay awake now") (1956h:144). These are distinct though overlapping meanings. The results in overt behavior would be rather similar, but in the sense of "lazy" the implication is that even when the person is most wide awake he will not want to work, while in the case of "drowsy" we impute some physiological grounds for the relative inactivity. Presumably the Navaho term has both meanings in different contexts, and the context generally makes clear which meaning is intended when the distinction is necessary. At the same time, representing both of these concepts with a single term must make for ambiguity at times. Conceivably this ambiguity persists because it is frequently functional in the culture. Without more information it would be pointless to discuss at length what this function might be, but we might guess for one thing that it is a way of blunting criticism of people for lack of hard work; this again might be a sign that the Navaho are especially sensitive to this particular criticism. The argument will certainly occur to some readers: How do we know that the Navaho term translated into English as both "lazy" and "drowsy" really has two distinguishable meanings for the Navaho speakers? Is this not a projection on Navaho by English speakers who do distinguish the two concepts, as is shown by the two different words? Might not the Navahos have only one concept which involves only the overt behavior and ignores the question as to whether the inactivity is physiological or volitional? A priori, this possibility is very improbable, but even if it should prove true for this one word it is surely unlikely that Navaho, in contrast to English and many other languages, should fail to have many other words, including value terms, with several distinguishable standard uses. Probably the key to demonstrating the existence of these variant meanings of words lies in analysis of actual occurrences in large numbers of contexts, especially in utterances but not excluding extralinguistic contexts when profitable. This, of course, is one thing which Kluckhohn was urging us to do in his Navaho value-terms paper (1956*h*). This could lead to some form of distributional analysis, not of linguistic forms as such, but of semantic components associated with these forms. Linguistic models from phonology or morphology should be useful here.

It was Clyde Kluckhohn's belief that anthropologists should be able to develop means of handling scientifically and objectively the whole-culture patterns of cultures of any degree of complexity. He suspected that language and linguistics were crucial in achieving this goal and made several attempts to so use them, although he was not very satisfied with any of these attempts. The general problem which he was attacking was a crucial one for the future of anthropology. As primitive, nonliterate cultures vanish, anthropologists must turn to the study of the major world societies if they are to continue field-work. There are already many specialists studying these societies, who know much more about particular aspects of them than we anthropologists do. Some of us have claimed that the unique contribution of anthropology in studying modern life is to provide an analysis of the overall patterns of cultures. Kluckhohn himself held this view. If it is not true that we can do this in some form or other, whether with the aid of linguistics or otherwise, then anthropologists will be forced to abandon their claim that they are scientists who can usefully investigate whole-culture patterns of societies of any size. They must then either abandon science for pure humanism or restrict their attention to the few expiring primitive cultures which are simple and still isolated enough for a single investigator to comprehend objectively in a sort of catalogue fashion.

THE ANTHROPOLOGY OF VALUES

Munro S. Edmonson

To me it is clear that the answer to these questions must be given not in an "either-or" but in a "both-and" form.

Clyde Kluckhohn 1952b:101

THE TWENTIETH century has been confronted from the outset with a variety of successful scientific syntheses, each relevant to a particular and limited range of the phenomenal world. It was already apparent by 1900, in fact, that the sciences were tending to grow by fission and that new syntheses would tend to subdivide the old, shattering the ecumenical pretensions of science in a welter of ever more specific generalizations. The need for a more comprehensive view of both the methods and results of science was acutely felt and has been a fundamental motif of the thought of our times.

The problem posed by this trend of scientific thought has also been experienced as a moral one, and it is in the range of the moral sciences that this problem has proved most crippling. Indeed, it is not too much to say that the sharp delineation of separate sciences and subsciences has had at least the latent function of shielding society from the corrosive effects of science upon the moral order. In this fashion, we have been able to preserve the impeccable amorality of the natural sciences in one sphere, leaving the social sciences in another as a buffer zone of accommodation to the moral (and extrascientific) pressures of the contemporary world. Even the natural sciences, however, suffered from their isolation, and a compartmental system of science has proved unworkable. Increasingly,

the frontiers between adjacent sciences have been breached by the
necessities of scientific growth, until the remaining boundaries are
primarily historical, social, and heuristic conventions rather than
divisions between truly discrete concept systems. It was inevitable
that the taboo line of morality should also be assaulted, and scientific
pressure has in fact built up markedly on that front for many years.
If man is not the measure of all things and morality is not a self
regulatory mechanism, it has also become increasingly awkward to
pretend that the universe is a living thing, a structured and functioning organism (Pepper 1942). Its parts and processes no longer
appear sufficiently compartmental to be captured by such a metaphor.
In short, the organic synthesis of the nineteenth and early twentieth
centuries has faltered, and science has grown beyond it. It is the
purpose of the present paper to explore this growth in the area of
twentieth century anthropology. The issues have centered more and
more on the problem of values, a phrasing predominantly attributable
to Clyde Kluckhohn.

Limitations of time, space, and preparation preclude my attempting any comprehensive view of this enormously ramifying
subject. Arbitrarily, therefore, I should like to focus upon three
particularly salient problems of the epistemology of anthropology as
convenient points from which to view the anthropology of values:
(1) the problem of determinism, (2) cultural relativism, and (3)
objectivity.

Determinism

One of the most tenacious of all scientific ideas is that of cause
and effect. A set of conditions both logically separable from, and
empirically antecedent to, another set of conditions has been assumed to be a cause, predictably and inevitably producing its effect
with exceptionless regularity. The formulation of precise statements
in causal logic of this type has been the professed aim of many, perhaps of most scientists, and the most successful of such formulations
are accorded the status of scientific laws. The effect is said to be explained by such laws (although the cause is not), and causality is
thus conceived as linear and determined. It follows that there must

be causes for the causes and consequently, ultimately, a first cause, which not uncommonly is a theological one.

This conception of causality has come to bear an ever more ambiguous relationship to the method of particular sciences. If a given set of circumstances will inevitably produce a given effect, it will do so only when all the components are brought together spatially and temporally in the right proportions and organization. Hydrogen and oxygen produce water, but much of the world's supply of the two gases is unaffected by this possibility at any one time. Modern science has become increasingly preoccupied with the problems of organization—of the structure that is required to get the hydrogen and oxygen together in the particular relationship we call water.

Structural relations have been explored more and more through measurement, and they bear a novel relationship to time. In causal terms, a resulting structure emerges slowly out of a causative proto-structure by gradations as fine as our measurements permit us to perceive. Thus we can isolate causes from effects in time—antecedent from subsequent structures—only in terms of the probabilities of measurement. Condition A does not give way categorically and abruptly to condition B; a little of each is inextricably part of the other. We can still speak of cause and effect, but only within the limitations of our measurement systems. The old categoric certainty is gone.

In the old logic of linear time, we could legitimately suppose that what was *post hoc* might, at least sometimes, be *propter hoc*. In structural time, sequence has lost this significance. The subsequent is merely another dimension of the antecedent, a dimension that must be measured if the phenomenon is to be scientifically described, but no longer the decisive element in the logic of prediction. The point may be illustrated with a biological example. Evolutionary change in living forms is presumed to be consequent upon random alteration in the gene plus the differential reproduction probability of different genes as members of the genetic community comprising the organism in question. We cannot usually predict the nature of a mutation. Even if we could, a forecast of its selection potential would be contingent upon environmental considerations not yet visible at the moment of mutation, including the helpful or deleterious effects of mutation of other genes in the community. Contingent probabilities describe the correlations among these elements with some elegance and precision, but they are not causes. The survival potential of a gene may be just as effectively altered by conditions arising subsequent to its appearance as by those that are antecedent.

By the beginning of the twentieth century, the inadequacy of a linear conception of cause and effect had come to be rather generally recognized. In most fields of science, attention began to shift to other phrasings of causation. The new phrasings were relational rather than linear and emphasized the covariation of factors within an organized system of relationships. The term *structure* has found its way into the theory of all of the sciences in this connection. Events are still interpreted as determined, but the causation is a matter of the configurational organization—the structure—of many factors rather than their sequence. In this construal, too, determinism takes place within compartmentalized systems which cannot be reduced to or derived from one another. Each system is interpreted as functioning at its own level. Thus chemical events were sharply differentiated from physical ones; biology was said not to be reducible to chemistry; psychologists argued that human and animal behavior was more than the sum of physical, chemical, and biological factors. Such concepts as "dynamic equilibrium" or "homeostasis" exemplify the trend of scientific thought. Each science was viewed as exploring a separate and integrated system of causation.

In the range of human affairs, too, the twentieth century embarked on the construction of system theories, each system being construed as autonomous and structurally integrated. Freud's view of personality, Durkheim's of society, Boas's of culture, and Sapir's of language illustrate the parallel character of this development over the whole range of social and psychological studies. An indefinite number of other systems could be invoked as the loci of particular problems of structure and function: the economic system, the political system, the kinship system, and so on and on.

The moral implications of this kind of system building have perhaps been most explicitly stated by Parsons (1937), who has characterized the position of Durkheim, Weber, Pareto, Marshall, and himself as "voluntaristic." The determinism characteristic of integrated systems is not absolute. In Parsons's terms, the "actor," confronted with a situation involving "means" and "ends," may be constrained to a measure of rationality and hence predictability in his choice of particular means toward a given end, but his choice of ends remains in some sense free. In another perspective, the existing system determines behavior, but the future system may be at least in part a consequence of real choice.

It is in this context that the modern anthropological interest in the value system has arisen. There are, to be sure, a number of other paths of inquiry which converge on the problem of values: the tradition of philosophical axiology, the specialized problematics of economic value, the apologetics of political philosophy, the dilemmas of comparative religion and modern theology. In social science, these interests have been represented also in studies of the philosophy of history and attempts at empirical characterization of the particular philosophies of various societies. The close connection between these problems and those of cultural psychology have long been recognized. Surely one of the most fundamental questions raised by the scientific attack in these areas is the question of the determinism of values. On the one hand, the very conception of a value system would seem to imply an order of predictable causation; on the other, the character of organicist theorizing about systems leaves open the possibility of true (that is, free) moral choice. This paradox is basic to some of the most difficult problems of modern social science. Enough has perhaps been said to indicate the extraordinary range of the issues raised.

The eclectic and segmental view of causality common to anthropology in the 1930s springs from the multiple competing determinisms of the preceding period. Geographic determinism, biological determinism, economic determinism, psychological determinism, social and cultural determinism were all accepted and were interpreted as complementary perspectives on the human condition. At the same time, there was general agreement on the necessity for a broader integration of these dimensions which would preserve the structural method already established but improve on the theoretical construals of dynamics and process. There was little agreement in detail as to how this could be achieved, and the controversies of the period tended to center on these problems. A comprehensive and representative view of the state of social anthropological theory at this time can be obtained from Linton's *The Study of Man*, a work so smoothly written that its subtleties passed almost unnoticed into the common domain but, for all that, a book of enormous influence over the development of anthropology in the United States. Linton does full justice to the structural and functional synthesis of Durkheim, Malinowski, and others, but he also faces squarely the nagging problems that functionalism has not resolved. Why doesn't function predict form? How do structures relate to processes? Where is the border between systems, such as society and the individual?

Such questions as these point up the theoretical difficulties that have caused increasing pressure on the walls between the separate systems of earlier theory. In area after area of science, synthetic disciplines have grown up dedicated to the exploration of such interscience frontiers as physical chemistry, biochemistry, psychosomatic medicine, or social psychology. And in many cases the supposed disjunction between one order of causation and another has proved illusory. The sciences no longer appear as a hierarchy of autonomous levels but as a continuum of intergrading and partly synthesized theories closely related to one another in many dimensions.

During the last thirty years anthropology has moved with the other sciences in this respect. Three decades ago there was general agreement that the problem of man could only be attacked on multiple differentiated planes of theory, each with its own method and traditional problematics. The sharpest possible division was made between biological and cultural causation; sociocultural problems were divorced from psychological problems; the theory of linguistics essayed to be an exploration of pure form, unrelated to nonlinguistic structures. Slowly and, as it were, reluctantly, all this has changed. In all of these fields, theory has remained structurally deterministic, but the structural regularities have expanded beyond the artificial boundaries of the old systems and become thoroughly commingled with each other. A more comprehensive and integrated determinism has begun to replace the separate segmental determinisms of the earlier part of the century. The tracing of this development is beyond the scope of this paper, but the fact of its occurrence is an essential part of the background of the anthropological preoccupation with values.

Concurrently with these general changes in the tenor of anthropological (and general) science, a particular thread of concern with values has led scholars of a variety of sorts toward a more deterministic view of moral phenomena. By about thirty years ago, the highly diverse phrasings of this problem had become truly convergent, in the anthropological perspective at least, upon the induction that values were indeed structured, that, far from being isolated and autonomous expressions of free will, values expressed themselves in systems of considerable consistency and coherence. This sort of coherence has an immediate feel of determinancy to the anthropological mind. Boas once wrote:

It is not given to any of us to free himself from the spell into which life has forced us. We think, feel, and act faithfully within the tradition in which we live. The only way we can free ourselves is by immersion in a new life and appreciation of the thought, feeling and action that have not grown from the soil of our own civilization, but have their roots in other *Kulturschichten.* [In Kroeber et al. 1943:4; translation MSE]

Perhaps the most influential and persuasive presentation of this conclusion in anthropology was Benedict's *Patterns of Culture.* The detailed interpretations in this work have been challenged and must in some cases be corrected, but the basic premise won rapid and general acceptance. Building upon a long tradition of cultural immersions and appreciations, Benedict's work was seconded and extended (in some cases it was also anticipated) by that of other anthropologists, so that the systematic or structural character of values stands as a documented, if somewhat inexact, empirical generalization in anthropology.

The historical congruence of the recognition of value systems with the decreasing viability of system theories in general presents us with a paradox of fundamental order. The preservation of freedom of choice even in the attenuated form implied by Parsonian voluntarism is dependent upon the assumption of the functional autonomy of systems. But the functional autonomy of the value system would mean isolation of the phenomenon of choice from all other systems. Since the functional autonomy of many systems can be questioned on other grounds, we may alternatively accept the structural character of values but deny the isolation of the value system from other structures. In the first case, value choices become in a sense unreal, for they have to do with nothing but themselves. In the second case, they cease to be free.

It is my contention that the anthropological study of values during the last three decades has pushed us very far toward a determinism we have been unwilling to confront. It is time for us to confront it.

Cultural Relativism

Our growing awareness of structured choices in the values of different cultures has given us in anthropology a rather intimate and on the whole uncomfortable understanding of the relativity of morals. It is in this guise that, as a profession, we have most abruptly confronted the theoretical dilemma to which our conclusions have brought us. If moral choices are always relative to the particular cultural context in which they are made and if each culture is regarded as a separate system, then, truly, we are forced to question the possibility of a generic or absolute morality.

Again, the problem centers on functional autonomy. Cultural relativism has usually been phrased in terms of unit cultures, each culture being interpreted as a discrete segment of general human tradition. Thus a moral practice as reprehensible as human sacrifice can be seen as functional in the peculiar matrix of Aztec culture, where it had a certain theological rationale, without implying that we approve it generally. We can even condemn similar occurrences in Nazi Germany, where the rationale involved an inconsistent duplicity. The attractiveness of this segmental view of cultural systems is somewhat dimmed on closer inspection when we attempt to give boundaries to the moral universes we wish to call cultures. What of the jarring value conflicts among subcultures, such as the northern and southern United States? How do we choose the units of analysis in such a context as the Hopi villages—by tribe? by village? by faction? Where do we separate a particular culture from its successor in time? We have some professional agreement that values are relative—but relative to what?

The problem of cultural relativism has been further complicated by its involvement in matters of cultural psychology. For a time it seemed credible that neither good and evil nor psychic health and disease would be susceptible to defensible supracultural definition. Hindsight now enables us to see with some clarity that we were beguiled by systems. If each culture could be interpreted as truly an autonomous entity, there was nothing in principle to preclude a radically relativistic conclusion of this sort. In the heyday of an-historical functionalism such autonomy began to seem reasonable. Then the reaction set in.

Both values and personality may reasonably be considered as structured in relation to a particular cultural context. But the autonomy of each such context is itself only relative. The Smith Sound Eskimo are reported to have thought themselves the only men on earth until their discovery by Europeans. Such a degree of isolation from the rest of mankind is, as far as I am aware, unique. But even then the linguistic and cultural evidence makes it unlikely that the autonomy of this culture had endured for more than a few generations. The variations we encounter in values or in motives in different cultures may thus reasonably be called relative, but they are relative to a universe of cultural experience which even in extreme cases is partly shared. Cultural relativism is a relativism of partial differences only.

In another perspective, the relativity of morals involves us far more deeply in psychological issues. For even a partial relativism opens the door to a kind of reductionism which, though finite, ends by explaining culture away as a psychological problem. If two cultures have a measure of autonomy and hence of cultural relativity by virtue of some degree of historical separation, so must two sub-cultures, or two differentiated institutions within a culture, or two families. The limit is reached only in the culture of a single individual, who thus becomes the sole arbiter of his own morality over at least some narrow range of conduct.

Faced with dilemmas at once subversive to established moral

philosophy and to established science, anthropologists have recoiled from cultural relativism as much by "instinct" as by reason. But wriggle as we may, we cannot avoid the trap we have ourselves built. Indeed, it is precisely where we can sense the vested interests of the established systems of science and society that we must as scientists most scrupulously beware of ethnocentrism. The moral inconvenience of relativism is not a sufficient scientific refutation of it. As scientists, we are forced to be even more deeply concerned with what relativism does to our proud boast of objectivity: What it does is to destroy it.

Objectivity

Scientific thought has approached man only obliquely. Indirection and caution have undeniably been conditioned by awareness of the realistic historical consequences of heresy, but in modern times they have also been a result of the scientific value of objectivity. Only the most ingenious and devious subterfuges have made it possible for us to lay even the foundations for an objective science of our subjective selves, and it is not difficult to understand our preference for the sheer demonstrability of fossilized bones or linguistic sounds as against the slippery ideas and meanings so obviously central to our nature.

Anthropology has become increasingly self-conscious in its efforts at objectivity. A science charged with chronicling the stranger vicissitudes of human thought must perhaps inevitably come to view itself a little quizzically as a remarkably distinctive and structured activity. In a former age, it was possible to insist on the privileged character of anthropological observation. But the destruction of the mystique of race and the early twentieth century conception of the savage removes the possibility of any facile definition of the observer and causes us to question not only our present but also our past objectivity. In most parts of the world, the savages now go clothed, but we confront them naked. We are forced to see ourselves as both subject and object of our scientific efforts.

The juxtaposition of functionalist theory of both the sociological and psychological types adds poignancy to this problem but does nothing to resolve the difficulties. We can see ourselves and our native informants as the products of social or psychic forces or both together, but we have lost our grounds for believing in the saving rationality and objectivity of science. The ubiquitous irrationality and subjectivity are all too apparent. We have the advantage of observing the world from the standpoint of one unique cultural tradition— that of anthropology, but this tradition does not escape determinism, does not elude relativism, and, far from guaranteeing objectivity, is predictably biased.

Values

Against the background of these problems, the emergence of an explicit, anthropological assault on the problem of values can readily be seen to have genuine strategic significance. A number of scholars contributed importantly to this result during the 1930s and 1940s, but the most focused and sustained effort to study values as such was that organized by Kluckhohn in 1948–49. The diverse studies which Kluckhohn led, directed, or inspired in the ensuing years succeeded in bringing to bear upon the problem of values a very wide range of social science techniques and concepts. They succeeded also in breaking some new ground and in moving the anthropological profession some steps further toward the resolution of value problems. It is my belief that they failed to come to grips with the problems of determinism, relativism, and objectivity as outlined above and that this failure was itself a value phenomenon of the greatest moment for our science.

The concept "value" has an extraordinarily large number of synonyms or near-synonyms, many of which have been current for a considerable time. Heuristically, these may be grouped into three very broad categories: philosophical, psychological, and culturological. Together these concepts suggest something of the range and diffuseness of the background of modern value study.

Philosophically, the idea of values has often been identified even in anthropological literature with particular ranges of philosophic thought: metaphysics, ethics, aesthetics, cosmology, epistemology, eschatology, or ontology. The terms "philosophy of life" or "philosophy of history" have also been used with a particular value emphasis. Idealism has lent the vocabulary of values such terms as "idea," "ideal," "idea culture," "ideology," and even "thought" (*la pensée chinoise*). "Spirit" is an occasional cognate in English, commoner in French (*esprit*) and German (*Geist, Zeitgeist*). It is likely that we should consider Durkheim's "*representations collectives*" as a related concept. "Life" or "essence" are sometimes used in a related sense as in the "culture and life" (*kultura i byt*) studies in Russian. Spanish and Spanish American authors lend similar significance to the term "reality" (*la realidad nacional*). Some uses lie on the borders between philosophy and science, as in "cultural premises," "world hypotheses," "meta-anthropology," or "metalinguistics."

Psychological concepts with strong value overtones include "mind" (the mind of the South, *la mentalité primitive*), "personality" (particularly modal or basic personality, status personality, culture and personality, the personality of Britain), "character" (national character), "attitude" (*Weltanschauung*), "unconscious" (collective unconscious), "temper" (the Spanish temper), and even "temperament." The term "psychology" itself has often been used with value implications (national psychology, social psychology, ethnopsychology, *Völkerpsychologie*).

Among the terms culturologically employed as near synonyms for value in various aspects are "pattern" and "configuration" (systemic pattern, institutional pattern, pattern variable), "theme" (motif, *Leitmotiv*), "focus" (climax, cynosure), "ethos," and "eidos." Ideas of form (structure, *Bild, Kulturbild*) and principle and even the concept of culture itself (e.g., covert culture) are often employed in senses closely linked to values. The concept is obviously one of the utmost complexity and scope.

Kluckhohn's concern with value problems is reflected in earlier papers (particularly 1941*a*, 1943*b*), but the most convenient starting point for our purposes is his dialogue on the concept of culture published in 1945 (Kluckhohn and Kelly 1945*b*). The form of this essay makes it somewhat difficult to be sure how closely Kluckhohn wished to associate himself with various of the views expressed, but this form is probably far from accidental and is thoroughly representative of the man: In many of his papers composed in a more standard format, Kluckhohn cites numbers of diverse views on a topic without identifying himself exclusively with any one of them. For present purposes, we may take this 1945 essay to exemplify his concerns, if not his commitments. At critical points these concerns are psychological, antifunctionalist, and normative. It is significant that Tylor's definition of culture is criticized for its lack of psychological involvement: "the definition is too intellectualistic. One gets no hint that people are other than affectively neutral toward their culture" (Kluckhohn and Kelly 1945*b*:82). Equally significant and pointed is the criticism of functionalism: "This is why all 'functional' definitions of culture tend to be unsatisfactory: they disregard the fact that cultures create needs as well as provide a means of fulfilling them" (Kluckhohn and Kelly 1945*b*:81). No such cogent criticisms are leveled against the definition that sounds like Kluckhohn's own: "By 'culture' we mean all those historically created designs for living, explicit and implicit, rational, irrational, and non-rational, which exist at any given time as potential guides for the behavior of men" (Kluckhohn and Kelly 1945*b*:97). That the "designs for living" in this definition are pretty close to being values seems obvious. Another definition in the same essay moves even farther in that direction and emphasizes selectivity in a framework even more explicitly psychological: "By 'culture' we mean those historically created selective processes which channel men's reactions both to internal and to external stimuli" (Kluckhohn and Kelly 1945*b*:84). The term "value" appears to be used only once in this discussion, in a context suggesting that it was borrowed from Dorothy Lee (Kluckhohn and Kelly 1945*b*:100). The mention is too casual to be significant. Nonetheless, it is clear that Kluckhohn already had in mind the considerations which led to the Comparative Study of Values Project three years later:

> Tribes like the Pueblo and Navaho, living in substantially identical natural and biological environments, still manifest very different ways of life.
>
> . . . . .
>
> The inhabitants of two not widely separated villages in New Mexico, Ramah and Fence Lake, are both of the so-called "Old American" physical

stock. Almost certainly a physical anthropologist would say they represented random samples from the same physical population. The rocky tablelands, the annual rainfall and its distribution, the flora and fauna surrounding the two villages hardly show perceptible variations. The density of population and the distance from a main highway is almost exactly the same in the two cases. Nevertheless, even the casual visitor immediately notices distinctions. . . . They have slightly different cultures. [Kluckhohn and Kelly 1945*b*:93]

That values were coming to be focal in Kluckhohn's thought at this time is suggested by his explicit concern with the problems of determinism, relativism, and objectivity. The problem of choice is explicitly confronted and an ambiguously deterministic answer is proposed:

While many patterned ways of reacting unquestionably represent almost inevitable responses to an external environment in which the group lives or once lived, there are certainly also many cases where the inexorable conditions of action merely limit the possibility of response rather than eventually compelling one and only one mode of adaptation. These "choices" are probably themselves determined—if we make our theoretical system wide enough to encompass all possible types of factors. But, within the more usual frame of reference, they are the "accidents of history." [Kluckhohn and Kelly 1945*b*:86]

Relativism is equally firmly confronted and resolved, as Kluckhohn continued to resolve it, through a qualitative contrast of cultural universals and particulars:

Every people not only has a sentiment structure which is to some degree unique but also a more or less coherent body of distinctive presuppositions about the world. This last is really a borderland between reason and feeling. Perhaps in a certain ultimate sense the "logic" of all peoples is the same. But their premises are certainly different. [Kluckhohn and Kelly 1945*b*:100]

Objectivity is not explicitly discussed in this essay, which is principally concerned with definition, but in another work published the same year Kluckhohn says: "The anthropological mode must become more objective both as regards gathering and analyzing data" (in Gottschalk et al. 1945:163). And he suggests a pragmatic way of doing this: "Multiple techniques, carried out by multiple observers and analysts, are the key to the problem of subjectivity" (1945:162).

The concern with value problems that Kluckhohn manifested in 1945 was explicit but still diffuse. Most of the elements are present, but they are nowhere drawn together and related to one another. Eventually, the linked problems of epistemology (determinism), theory (relativism), and method (objectivity) are neatly summarized by Kluckhohn and Murray:

Students of personality and culture are themselves victims of their own personalities and products of their culture. Only recently has a cross-cultural perspective provided some emancipation from those values that are not broadly "human" but merely local, in both space and time. Only gradually is our culture altering so as to permit social scientists to work and think with something approaching objectivity. [1948a:5]

This is a remarkably comprehensive statement of Kluckhohn's view of values.

His crystallization of several theoretical issues around the idea of values between 1945 and 1948 was importantly influenced by Kluckhohn's collaboration with his wife, which resulted in a joint formulation of American values (Kluckhohn and Kluckhohn 1947b). Florence Kluckhohn's interest in values was long-standing and parallel to his. Her doctoral dissertation in 1941 was on Spanish-American values ("patterns and configurations"), and her work on value orientations continued along these lines during the 1950s. Her interest grew into an approach to values emphasizing measurement of variation along preselected dimensions in a manner rather more congenial to sociological than to anthropological thinking, as was natural, but it is clear that she contributed importantly to her husband's view of values, as he to hers. The aprioristic categories of her analysis later formed the basis for his most important effort to solve the methodological riddles of cultural relativism, and he remained sensitive to the sociological viewpoint that she continued to represent.

A major influence on the thinking of both Kluckhohns about value problems was their close contact with Parsons, who was also at this time working on the analytic scheme of "pattern variables" which led him to an explicit interest in values. Parsons explains that much of the synthesis which was incorporated into *Toward a General Theory of Action* was the result of two informal seminars, one including the contributors to that volume (of whom Kluckhohn was one), and the other comprising all members of the Department of Social Relations at Harvard. He relates:

In November [1948] we reached agreement that the general theoretical scheme in which we were interested could be couched within what we agreed (in the smaller group) to call the "action" frame of reference. Shortly after that, stimulated especially by Clyde Kluckhohn's presentation, before the smaller group, of his approach to the analysis of values, the staff evolved a number of new theoretical insights and developments. [Parsons and Shils 1951:vi]

It is probably impossible at this point to factor out the individual contributions that different people made to Clyde Kluckhohn's formulation of value problems, but it is possible to differentiate certain matters of emphasis in which he tended to differ from colleagues with whom he was working closely. Like Florence Kluckhohn, Parsons conceptualized values as the choices made by particular individuals and groups in relation to certain salient general questions. These questions were in a very broad sense functional, that is they were interpreted as unavoidable problems that every society must face. This phrasing of the matter frames the serious dilemmas of determinism and objectivity, but it tends to underplay the significance of cultural relativism: The observer feels that he knows what the significant questions are before he looks at the specific culture.

As an anthropologist, Clyde Kluckhohn was more concerned with the dilemma of relativism than were his sociological associates and, while he accepted the approach to values implied by the functional schema, he was clearly uneasy about it and continually sought to better it. His restlessness with functionalism is apparent in *Navaho Witchcraft* (1944*a*) and in the criticism he leveled against it in 1945 (in Gottschalk et al. 1945). Nonetheless, his description of American values (Kluckhohn and Kluckhohn 1947*b*) and later formulations of Navaho values (Kluckhohn 1949*d*, 1956*c*; Kluckhohn and Romney 1961*b*) followed the method favored by Florence Kluckhohn, Parsons, and others.

It seems apparent that by 1948 Kluckhohn's fundamental theoretical interests had come to focus on the problem of choice and that he saw in this problem some serious difficulties for the structural-functional synthesis then in vogue. He conceptualized this as a matter of values and proposed to study them in the Ramah area of western New Mexico, where five differentiated cultures or sub-cultures provided an opportunity for close and intensive investigation, longitudinal as well as cross-sectional, descriptive and comparative, individual and sociocultural. He felt that the "multiple techniques carried out by multiple observers," on which he had already pinned his methodological faith, would make possible theoretical conclusions of crucial importance. With this very broad mandate, the Comparative Study of Values Project was established. It was designed to provide an answer to the general question: "Why do different value systems continue to exist in five cultures all having to meet similar problems of adjustment and survival in the same ecological area, all having been exposed by actual contact and by stimulus diffusion to each other's value ideas and practices?" (Kluckhohn 1951*k*:viii). The continuity with Kluckhohn's previous thought seems particularly clear here. If, as he had argued in *Navaho Witchcraft* (1944*a*), adaptation and adjustment are the essence of the functional interpretation of culture, how can cultures differ when the adaptive and adjustive conditions are essentially identical? Some extrafunctional factor must be invoked, and "value" was the clearest name Kluckhohn could give it. He explicitly criticized *Navaho Witchcraft* in these terms (1949*b*).

The Values Project was placed under the directorship of John M. Roberts and Evon Z. Vogt, and it was at this time (1949) that Kluckhohn undertook the directorship of the Russian Research Center at Harvard. His subsequent work on values was largely theoretical, and he did not again have the opportunity to devote himself to sustained fieldwork in the Ramah area. He did, however, continue to provide intellectual leadership to the Values Project through a series of papers and discussion of value problems and through consultation and advising of the large number of colleagues

and students who were working on these problems during the ensuing years. Most of his published work on values has something of
the character of working papers. Thorough, comprehensive, polished,
often brilliant, but almost always somehow provisional, these papers
chronicle with a certain precision the moving center of his views
on the matter as they were influenced year by year by research results, omnivorous reading, and the serendipity of his other interests.
Slowly and carefully Kluckhohn's value ideas moved toward a
synthesis which never came and which may have been forestalled
by his untimely death.

This work begins in 1949–50 with his attempt to define values.
Given the background of this endeavor, it seems apparent that two
main concerns preoccupied him: (1) the grave epistemological issues
raised by the idea of a scientific study of values, and (2) the troubled
question of culture and personality. Kluckhohn moved cautiously
on both these fronts, but his first (unpublished) attempt at a definition was bold and programmatic; he characterized value as: "A
selective orientation toward experience, characteristic of an individual
and/or of a group, which influences the choice between possible
alternatives in behavior" (draft ms of 1951f mimeographed:53). In
rejecting this definition later the same year, Kluckhohn comments
that it does not differentiate value from culture. The initial definition
remains perhaps the clearest indication of the degree to which he
felt values to be the central problem of anthropological theory. He
recoiled, however, from the broad simplification suggested by this
definition and amended it (before publication) to an intricate compromise: "A value is a conception, explicit or implicit, distinctive of
an individual or characteristic of a group, of the desirable which
influences the selection from available modes, means, and ends of
action" (1951f:395).

Like his earlier definition, this one may legitimately be para-
phrased as asserting that a value is a pattern of culture or personality,
but here only those patterns are included which involve the desirable. This was a neat bow toward norms in one direction and
needs in another. The crux of the matter is that this qualification
facilitates dodging the epistemological issues at the cultural level and
continues a certain orthodoxy about the relation of culture to moti-

vation (the emphasis on the desirable differentiates value from all other motivational concepts). The implications are nominalistic, antireductionistic, and nondeterministic. The conceptions influence but do not determine selection. The individual is still thoroughly distinguishable from the group. The status of the concept is like that of any category of implicit culture: It is a logical construct in the mind of the observer and sometimes of the informant as well. In one respect, however, the definition is at odds with Parsonian voluntarism: Whatever determinism is implied bears equally on means and ends.

This definition omits a considerable part of what Kluckhohn had previously defined as relevant to values, particularly psychological and cultural factors of a strictly cognitive character—science, for example. These other elements were included in his definition of value-orientation: "a generalized and organized conception, influencing behavior, of nature, of man's place in it, of man's relation to man, and of the desirable and nondesirable as they may relate to man-environment and interhuman relations" (1951f:411). A less technical phrasing appears in "The Philosophy of the Navaho Indians":

Each different way of life makes its own assumptions about the ends and purposes of human existence, about ways by which knowledge may be obtained, about the organization of the pigeonholes in which each sense datum is filed, about what human beings have a right to expect from each other and the gods, about what constitutes fulfillment and frustration. [1949d:358–59]

This bifurcation of the problem of values into values and value-orientations becomes comprehensible in the light of Kluckhohn's view of cultural relativism and the quite different views of Florence Kluckhohn and Talcott Parsons. In brief, Kluckhohn was not willing to become a complete relativist and hence felt continuing attraction to the generally functionalist position of his wife and Parsons, among others. He therefore defined values in a mutually acceptable but confining fashion and left the problematic areas in the limbo of value-orientations. It is significant that both Parsons and Florence Kluckhohn made extensive use of the latter concept, but Kluckhohn himself rarely mentioned it again. Value-orientations were an epistemological concession to voluntarism explicitly contradicted by the contemporaneous definition of values. Satisfactory in a sociological framework, the conception was too enumeratively explicit about the dimensions of conceptualization to fit comfortably with anthropological relativism. This question was therefore postponed, but it was not solved.

His own hesitations are illustrated by Kluckhohn's dissenting footnote to the introductory General Statement in *Toward a General Theory of Action*, which reads: "With the institutionalization of culture patterns, especially value-orientation patterns, in the social structure, the threefold reciprocal integration of personality, social system, and culture comes full circle" (Parsons et al. 1951:26). From this Kluckhohn dissents as follows:

Although—as must almost inevitably be the case with each individual signer—there are some things I should prefer to see said somewhat differently, there is only one point on which I remain slightly uncomfortable. This is the relation of social structure, social system, role, and culture. Many anthropologists (and certainly the undersigned) will agree today that there is an element of the social (i.e., interactive) process which is not culturally patterned, which is in some sense autonomous from culture. Nevertheless, one whose training, experiences, and prejudices are anthropological tends to feel that the present statement does not give full weight to the extent to which roles are culturally defined, social structure is part of the cultural map, the social system is built upon girders supplied by explicit and implicit culture. [In Parsons et al. 1951:26–27, fn.]

No such complication affected the problem in psychological terms, and here in an auxiliary definition, Kluckhohn returns to his original comprehensiveness: "value may be defined as that aspect of motivation which is referable to standards, personal or cultural, that do not arise solely out of immediate tensions or immediate situation" (1951f:425). It seems obvious here that an important aspect of Kluckhohn's interest in value was his hunch that the concept might provide unity to the problems of culture and personality in which he had long been interested. But at the time he wrote this essay (1949–50), he was not prepared to break with functionalistic sociology, and sociology had always had a strange and strained relationship to the psychoanthropological rapprochement. "Values and Value-Orientations" (1951f) was an impressive beginning on these problems, but it was far from a satisfactory synthesis.

Kluckhohn's own dissatisfaction is clear from the fact that he later returned to the comprehensive definition at the sociocultural level as well. Speaking "more loosely" in 1958, he said: "A value is a selective orientation toward experience, implying deep commitment or repudiation, which influences the 'choice' between possible alternatives in action" (1959e:25–26). It seems obvious that he was never completely convinced by the value-orientation approach. Two years later he repeated this last definition verbatim, without apology and in a context which clearly implies that he meant it both seriously and technically (1961c:18). That he continued to be disenchanted with functionalism even in 1949 may be illustrated from his remark that

every group's way of life, then, is a structure—not a haphazard collection of all the different physically possible *and functionally effective* patterns of belief and action but an interdependent system based upon linked premises and categories whose influence is greater rather than less because they are seldom brought out into explicit discussion. [1949d:358; italics MSE]

It seems strange in view of the explicit structuralism of this statement that the concept "value system" figures so little in Kluckhohn's writing.

Kluckhohn's view of the problem of determinism also remained equivocal. Thus, in *Mirror for Man* he notes:

From the short-range point of view man is still more or less at the mercy of irreversible trends he did not wilfully create. Nevertheless, in longer range, social science offers the possibility of understanding and of prediction, of speeding up desired trends, of greatly increased opportunities for successful adjustment if not of control. [1949a:289]

In sum, as he initiated his study of values, Kluckhohn appears to have had a considerable ambivalence about the major issues and problems in which he was enmeshed. He was convinced that the study of society "must include the objective investigation of human values" (1949a:284) and that "values are social facts of a certain type which can be discovered and described as neutrally as a linguistic structure or the technique of salmon fishing" (1949a:285). At the same time, he avoided direct confrontation of the issue of determinism, and he continued to be uneasy about relativism. These ghosts returned.

In 1951–52, Kluckhohn found time to edit (with Kroeber) a compendium of definitions of culture. This activity and the association with Kroeber may have had something to do with redirecting his attention to some of the more specifically anthropological aspects of the values problem, and it is noteworthy that the synthetic and summary definition of culture in that work includes values:

Culture consists of patterns, explicit and implicit, of and for behavior acquired and transmitted by symbols, constituting the distinctive achievement of human groups, including their embodiments in artifacts; the essential core of culture consists of traditional (i.e., historically derived and selected) ideas *and especially their attached values*; culture systems may, on the one hand, be considered as products of action, on the other as conditioning elements of further action. [Kroeber and Kluckhohn 1952: 181; italics MSE]

It is notable how much more comfortably values snuggle into this anthropological setting than into the thornbushes of interdisciplinary controversy.

In an essay on "Universal Values and Anthropological Relativism" published the same year, Kluckhohn maintains and expands this perspective, beginning with the forthright observation: "The matter of values is certainly the prime intellectual issue of the present day" (1952b:87). He is no less direct about relativism:

Cultural relativity has been completely established and there must be no attempt to explain it away or to deprecate its importance because it is inconvenient, hard to take, or hard to live with. Some values are almost purely cultural and draw their significance only from the matrix of that [sic] culture. Even the universal values have their special phrasings and emphases in accord with each distinct culture. And when a culture pattern, such as slavery, is derogated on the ground that it transgresses one of the more universal norms which in some sense and degree transcend cultural differences, one must still examine it not within a putatively absolutistic frame but in the light of cultural relativism. [1952b:106–7]

But limitations of relativism exist in the things that all men share. There is a new emphasis in Kluckhohn's phrasing of this as he continues: "At the same time one must never forget that cultural differences, real and important though they are, are still so many variations on themas supplied by raw human nature. . . . Anthropology's facts attest that the phrase a common humanity is in no sense meaningless" (1952*b*:107). And elsewhere: "The inescapable fact of cultural relativism does not justify the conclusion that cultures are in *all* respects utterly disparate and hence strictly incomparable entities" (1952*b*:102). Perhaps the crucial novelty in these assertions is the phrase "raw human nature." The idea of universal values had long served as a counterweight to radical relativism, both for anthropology in general and for Kluckhohn in particular, but universal values are cultural phenomena, and in traditional anthropological thinking they are remote from "raw human nature." It is striking that the examples of universal values proposed in this essay are vaguer and less satisfying than the general propositions quoted.

They were, in fact, less satisfying to Kluckhohn, for he turned next to a general review of the "Universal Categories of Culture." After discussing various views of the problem of cultural universals, he concluded with an emphasis that perhaps protests too much: "*biological, psychological, and sociosituational universals afford the possibility of comparison of cultures in terms which are not ethnocentric, which depart from givens, begging no needless questions*" (1953*b*:517).

An extraordinarily subtle shift in anthropological thinking was going on here. It is epitomized by the increasing need to fall back on reductionist explanations. Human nature had to be pressed into service to explain what could no longer be convincingly ascribed to function. Thus Kroeber concluded: "the universal categories of culture are unquestionably there, but they are not culture. . . . they exist essentially on the subcultural level and that is why they are constant" (in Tax et al. 1953:119). Kluckhohn did not agree, but it is apparent that he was hard put to avoid a more radical relativism, a more radical reductionism, and a more radical determinism than he found congenial, and he conceded the need for increasing recourse to "raw human nature."

By the following year, Kluckhohn was clarifying his views on determinism:

At the cultural level there are not many analogies to the determination of behavior by single gene substitutions. Perhaps the only unarguable one is language. . . . Some features of etiquette (such as the forms of greeting), the wearing of particular kinds of clothes, and food habits might also be rather generally accepted as exclusively determined by culture, but in the latter two cases environmental and indeed biological factors also play a role in at least some concrete instances. In general, "culturally influenced" is a much safer phrase than "culturally determined." [1954b:922–23]

He was not yet convinced of Kroeber's point about cultural universals. He conceded that: "It is not too important whether these likenesses be regarded as part of culture or as biological, psychological, and social preconditions or determinants of culture as some anthropologists would prefer" (1954b:954). But he clings to his conviction that: "Nevertheless these universals are ingredients of cultures in the sense that each culture takes account of and expresses them—and in many instances in highly similar ways" (1954b:954). This was a position he never entirely abandoned, but he found it troublesome, and he continually returned to reexamine it.

By the following year, he had moved still farther toward determinism and relativism: "The thesis of this paper will be that recent developments in the behavioral sciences have tended to narrow the areas of indeterminacy while still affirming the necessity of ethical relativity in certain contexts" (1955b:663). He reaffirms that "No anthropologist . . . doubts that the theory of cultural relativity is in some sense forced by the facts and meaningful" (1955b:669). But he also reaffirms, again a little defensively, that "*both* within and between cultures moral behavior in specific instances and in all its details must be judged within a wide context *but with reference to principles which are not relative*" (1955b:674). This was about as far as he found it possible to go, and his subsequent papers cling to the general theoretical stance he had assumed by this time. He continued to press this view vigorously, and he remained receptive to new data and fresh perspectives, but his basic ideas about values show little further movement. Nonetheless, his most significant specific innovation was still to come.

Kluckhohn's empirical work on values dealt principally with the Navaho and the Americans (the Russians and the Greeks were perhaps the next most prominent of his "tribes"). His treatment of the values of particular peoples may be rather sharply differentiated into two broad classes, each representative of a horn of the methodological dilemma of value study. The dominant mode was the functionalistic one implied by his continuing insistence on universals: each culture was profiled by description of its attitudes towards certain "universal" questions, selected intuitively, arbitrarily, or theoretically. The second mode, which became explicit in 1956, was structuralist and was based on a linguistic mode.

The papers on Navaho values cover a broad range of value problems with an experimental diversity of conceptualizations. Thus, "The Philosophy of the Navaho Indians" (1949*d*) summarizes separately the premises, the laws of thought, the categories, and the ethics of Navaho philosophy. "Navaho Morals" (1956*c*) reexamines Navaho ethics in terms of prescriptions and prohibitions, while "The Rimrock Navaho" (Kluckhohn and Romney 1961*b*) differentiates relational, time, man-nature, and activity values. Problems of value conflict in Navaho acculturation are a repeated theme, closely related to his waxing concern over relativism (see particularly 1949*d* and 1955*b*).

American value problems are very differently treated, both because of their heterogeneity, extensively discussed in "American Culture" (Kluckhohn and Kluckhohn 1947*b*), and because of their relatively rapid change, which is the primary focus of the later articles (1950*a*, 1958*a*, 1959*h*, 1960*d*). While the crisis in Navaho values led to reflections on universal values as a possible solution, they were rather pessimistically phrased. The crisis in American values led Kluckhohn to the same conclusions, but the general mood of his beliefs was avowedly optimistic. Over and over he rejected the idea that American or Western culture was in decline, and he saw in their contradictions and frustrations the growing pains of a new value system. He quotes Rapoport with approval: "it is incorrect to say that the scientific outlook is simply a by-product of a particular culture. It is rather the essence of a culture which has not yet been established—a *culture-studying* culture" (1954*f*:214). Methodologically these papers, whether Navaho or American, involve no fundamental departure from the customary treatment of values by social scientists. They are cogent, careful, and often fantastically broadly informed, but they are not theoretically innovative.

In 1956, however, Kluckhohn began to think seriously about the relevance of linguistic method for values. The first result was a brief but very stimulating paper on "Some Navaho Value Terms in Behavioral Context" (1956*h*), which is at least a step toward breaking out of Western and into Navaho concepts of evaluation. The same year saw the publication of the first of three papers (1956*c*, 1959*e*, 1961*c*) chronicling a brilliant attempt at a structural analysis of values, incomparably the most original of Kluckhohn's contributions to value theory. "Value-analysis," as he called this approach, does not rest on new descriptive categories, but upon a distinctive treatment of existing ones. These descriptive dimensions are treated in a manner conceptually similar to the linguist's handling of phonetic descriptions, that is, they are distributionally analyzed. Whereas the linguist compares phonetic features by environment, Kluckhohn compares value-orientations by culture, in order to arrive at a limited number of binary value-emphases (roughly comparable to phonemic principles) descriptive of the contrastive distributions within a given array of cultures. Whereas the systematics of the linguist's results usually refer to the system of *a* language, the systematics of value-analysis refer to one cultural, subcultural, or supercultural system made up of the cultures sampled. The value phonemes or value emphases in Kluckhohn's analysis describe the structure of the "Ramah system," the superculture to which his distributions refer, although he was never entirely clear on this point.

In the most usual linguistic method, a distributional analysis of this sort would begin with the assumption that two features with identical distributions but different meanings are to be considered as different phonemes, while two features in complementary distribution are to be considered allophones. Kluckhohn, however, followed rather a method proposed by Bloch (1953) for avoiding the component of meaning altogether. In Bloch's method, both complementary and identical distributions are taken to signify noncontrastive (i.e., allophonic) relationships, while overlapping or incorporating distributions betoken contrastive (i.e., phonemic) distinctiveness.

Bloch, in short, proposes that a really extensive exploration of contexts will reveal some unique distributional features for every true phoneme. It seems strange that Kluckhohn should have chosen to apply this undemonstrated and positivistic idea to values, but it is congruent with the structuralist tendency of his thought that he did so.

There was, further, a certain confusion in Kluckhohn's mind about the level at which he intended to apply the linguistic analogy. Thus, in the first paper, he notes:

In my adaptation of Bloch to cross-cultural analysis it may be objected that his technique is designed to investigate distributions and environments *within* single languages. I do not see why in principle it is not applicable comparatively. This may be methodologically wrong. If so, I wait to be shown wherein. [1956e:128, fn. 16]

Yet his only use of the term "allo-values" occurs in relation to intracultural variation. In a footnote on the scoring of the Texans as fulfillment-relaxed, he remarks: "There are strong variants here: disciplined-tense. Following the linguistic analogy, these could be called 'allo-values'" (1961c:38, fn. 11).

The method is tested on the materials from the Values Project, using thirteen value-orientations as descriptive dimensions (table 1).

1. DISTRIBUTION OF VALUE-ORIENTATIONS IN THE RAMAH AREA

	Mormon	Navaho	Spanish-American	Texan	Zuni
1. *Determinate* (Indeterminate)	+	+	−	−	+
2. *Unitary* (Pluralistic)	+	−	−	−	+
3. *Evil* (Good)	−	+	+	+	−
4. *Individual* (Group)	−	+	+	+	−
5. *Self* (Other)	−	−	−	−	+
6. *Autonomy* (Dependence)	−	−	−	+	−
7. *Active* (Acceptant)	+	+	−	+	+
8. *Discipline* (Fulfillment)	+	−	−	−	+
9. *Physical* (Mental)	+	+	−	+	−
10. *Tense* (Relaxed)	+	+	−	−	−
11. *Now* (Then)	−	+	+	−	+
12. *Quality* (Quantity)	−	+	+	−	+
13. *Unique* (General)	−	+	+	−	+

These dimensions are selected for comprehensiveness and scorability within the framework of Florence Kluckhohn's fivefold scheme of value-orientations, and ratings are then made of each of the five cultures of the Ramah area. When this array is searched for contrastive distributions, the results may be summarized in linguistic notation somewhat as follows:

/1/:	[1]	/5/:	[7]
/2/:	[2, 3, 4, 8]	/6/:	[9]
/3/:	[5]	/7/:	[10]
/4/:	[6]	/8/:	[11, 12, 13]

The thirteen "phonetic" value-orientations are thus reduced to eight "phonemic" value-emphases. The orientations grouped in brackets are, of course, allo-values within the Ramah system.

The pairs of value-orientations in the table have been defined as opposites. Hence, if any particular orientation is in complementary distribution with another, the converse naming of either one will change this to a distributional identity. It is, of course, arbitrary which term is named first. In generally accepted linguistic method, such a shift would be crucial; in Bloch's method it is irrelevant. Kluckhohn was uncertain at this point and contented himself with describing the distributions in Bloch's terms without drawing any conclusions. Toward the end, he was prepared to draw the conclusion for at least one part of the matrix: "Two previous trial runs with these data gave *identical* distributions for the pairs: now-quantity (then-quality), now-general (then-unique), quality-general (quantity-unique). This suggests that these are all reducible to a single value-contrast which I shall call general-unique" (1961c: 36; italics MSE). This corresponds to my notation /8/: [11, 12, 13]. Kluckhohn also dropped 9 (Physical/Mental) at this time, principally because it was hard to define and score. He remained uncertain about how to treat /2/: [2, 3, 4, 8]. As originally listed 2 and 8, 3 and 4 are in identical distribution, but the two pairs are in complementary distribution to one another (see table 1). In his 1961 publication, he unaccountably inverted the order of listing of 3, 4, 5, 6, and 13, thus bringing 2, 3, 4 and 8 into identical distribution, but he still hesitated to derive my "phoneme" /2/, by now completely analogous with "phoneme" /8/, which he had accepted.

The issue here is intricate but crucial. In his first two papers, Kluckhohn had compared the orientations italicized in table 1 with their opposites (unitalicized), thus giving a matrix showing the coincidence of each orientation with all its opposites, and it was from this doubled matrix that he drew his conclusions. But in response to a criticism from Wallace and Atkins, in the third paper he redoubled the matrix and compared both poles of each orientation with both poles of all the others. The implication of this procedure was to deny the need for distinguishing the directionality of the value-orientations: Each pole of each orientation was treated as a separate variable. The result is to blur the distinction between identical and complementary distributions (and between overlapping and incorporating ones), leaving only Bloch's dichotomy of noncontrastive (the former two) and contrastive (the latter two).

Kluckhohn was understandably ambivalent about pushing Bloch's method to its conclusion. Logically, however, I do not see that he had any choice. Lacking any analogy in his procedure for the use of semantic criteria in orthodox phonemics, he could only have employed a linguistic model that did not depend upon such criteria. It seems dubious that this method, which so rigorously excludes meaning, can be validated in either linguistics or values study without returning to semantics. Kluckhohn, in any case, did not attempt it. But it is strange that a man of his persuasion could be pushed so far toward pure structuralism—toward a concept of values excluding meaning. He hesitated and, rather than draw the conclusions indicated, he reexamined his data for a possible solution to the problem of directionality: That he was thinking along these lines is indicated by his inversion of some of the orientations.

The important difference in conceptual status between value-orientations and phonemic principles comes down in practice to the fact that the former have two heads and the latter only one. For example, the "self" orientation is clearly the negative of the "other" orientation—it is defined to be. But neither one is positive or negative in any absolute sense. On the other hand, there is general agreement among linguists that aspiration differs from nonaspiration in much the same way that the presence of an apple differs from its absence. There is little question about which term refers to a positive and which to a negative attribute. "Phonemic principle" is a directional concept; "value-orientation" is nondirectional. In sum, Kluckhohn's dilemma was either to solve the problem of directionality or to accept Bloch's positivistic solution. He found himself unable to do either.

It is worthy of remark that the extrapolation of Bloch's method to a universal sample—including all cultures—yields a conclusion which Kluckhohn clearly did not accept, namely the impossibility of universal values. In Bloch's scheme, each phonemic character must have at least one distributional uniqueness, hence there can be only one phoneme defined by distributional universality. Since we are denied access to its meaning, it seems doubtful that it would help us much to be able to assert the existence of such a structure.

Despite these difficulties, it remains clear that Kluckhohn's primary intention was to generate a structural approach to values comparable to that in linguistics. The distributional analysis he proposes could be equally well applied to subcultural as to cultural units. Disregarding the problem of directionality and accepting Bloch's proposals provisionally, what Kluckhohn achieved was a phonemic analysis of value-oppositions for the Ramah area, considered as a supracultural system. He remained dissatisfied and, while he continued to work toward a grammar of values applicable to particular cultures, he nonetheless felt that he had failed. "I was guilty of *hybris*," he remarked in the third lecture of his Brown University series on "Anthropology and the Classics" (1961a:43).

It was an inspired failure. The contradiction that made it impossible to differentiate identical from complementary distributions in value phenomena was not an error of method; it was the test of a whole theory. Kluckhohn's belief in structure had driven him, almost despite himself, to an experiment which had to succeed if the carefully constructed underlying theory was correct, but the theory was wrong. It is my belief, but it was not Kluckhohn's, that these brilliant papers conduce necessarily to a single, unavoidable conclusion: The crucial character of values to the functionalist theory (that caused him to select value problems for study to begin with) implies that either they must be structured in the manner he attempted to demonstrate or they do not exist at all.

Kluckhohn continued to work on this front and became increasingly aware that values had to have an objective anchoring point (the missing directionality in his design). In 1957 he observed:

In our world where varied peoples and cultures now find themselves in uncomfortably close contact, it is the primary intellectual function of anthropology to supply, on a smaller scale and in a scientific manner, the perspective which philosophy has traditionally attempted in a global and unscientific manner. [1957c:777; also cf. 1957j:xiv]

And he now recognized that objectivity could be attained only through the establishment of universals.

Most anthropologists agree today that if distinctiveness of cultures rests upon their principles of selectivity, in terms of which certain "paths" are consistently selected from the many that are "objectively" open, one can hope to understand these principles only insofar as one grasps the key values of each culture and sees these in the context of those broad pan-human values that are universals or near-universals. [1957i:xii]

His view of values continued to expand and generalize in the direction of an almost pure concept of structure: "To speak of values is one way of saying that human behavior is neither random nor solely instinctual" (1958d:474). But he was not ready to surrender real freedom of choice:

On the basis of what is now known to me, I suspect that one would conclude that both instrumental and intrinsic values may turn out to be either: (*a*) "free"—i.e., "taste" values, or (*b*) cultural values that are local in time and space, or (*c*) universal values embodied in all cultures. [1958d:474]

A sense of the degree and direction of movement in Kluckhohn's views may be gained by comparing the revised and expanded version of the Kluckhohn and Kelly essay on "The Concept of Culture" (1962c) with the original essay (Kluckhohn and Kelly 1945b) with which we began. The novelties in the revised version indicate a greater commitment to determinism, for example: "It is usually wise to think of a specified factor as *influencing* (rather than as *deter-*

mining) an outcome. There are no 'determinants' as palpable, dissectable elements; there are only processes that result in determination" (Kluckhohn and Kelly 1962c:34). There is also a new phrasing of the epistemology of objectivity.

The human mind can know "reality" only as sieved through an a priori net. Correspondence, however, between logical constructs and nature is not surprising, since the mind is itself a product of nature.

The main differences between nineteenth-century science and contemporary science is that scientists realize today that they cannot, in any literal sense, "describe reality." They can construct models that bear a relation to "objective fact." The scientist is more inventor than discoverer. [1962c:46–47]

But the problem which continued to be at the center of Kluckhohn's concern was that of cultural relativity, and his own final summary of that problem closes his third paper on value-analysis, published, like the above revision, after his death:

This is the end, for the moment, of this small exploration. I would argue only that schemas of this general order need to be further worked out theoretically and tried out empirically with many assemblages of data if cross-cultural comparison of values is to become comprehensive, parsimonious, and fruitful. I believe that a more formal and rigorous use of componential analysis will then become possible and will be the most likely avenue for attaining conceptual equivalences across cultural boundaries. And this is essential if we are to move beyond the empirical *description* of values. [1961c:45]

Culture

In retrospect, Kluckhohn's interest in values can be seen to be almost congruent with his interest in culture, and in this he spoke for the profession of anthropology. In appraising his contribution to anthropology in this connection we may therefore ask: What has the study of values done to the study of culture? In my opinion it has changed it greatly. Not all of this change is to be attributed to Kluckhohn for, while he was certainly a leading student of values, he was by no means the only one. Nonetheless, he stayed close to the fundamental issues, and his views stand as representative of the major developments in culture theory during the last two decades whether or not they were in specific instances the first enunciations of new principles. Often they were.

The first and perhaps the most fundamental innovation implied by the study of values in anthropology is the trend toward reductionism. This is manifest in the very definition of values as patterns of individual as well as group behavior. Increasingly we are pushed toward the view that it is not values alone which have this scope, but all of culture. "Culture and personality" is a poor phrasing of the matter because it implies two entities where we are more and more forced to recognize a single underlying process—of cultural communication. But the reductionism is not alone psychological. We have increasingly and pressingly returned to the biological roots of culture in search of the universal features which alone can give coherence to a science of the species *sapiens*. And even there we find no entities but merely another structure-creating process, itself increasingly explicable in terms of the structure and dynamics of all matter and energy.

Coordinate with this change is the overthrow of the concept of integration. Systems exist, but they do not exist for the fulfillment of homeostatic functions, guaranteeing stability and satisfaction. It is clear that culture is a structure-creating process in which we can find layer upon layer of unsuspected order and regularity, but this structure building has not always gone to the same point in every example of culture. Cultures are structured in varying degrees, not in proportion to their needs, but in proportion to the operation of the cultural process under given conditions. No real cultures have the symmetrical consistency of the ideal cultures depicted by Benedict. They do tend to be highly structured, but complete integration would be possible only to a system that had ceased to change. There has never been such a culture.

Jointly, these conclusions destroy the possibility of a categoric theory of man. Man did not emerge in a sudden mutational or inspirational leap from animal savagery; he evolved through the slow construction of a new level of structure—culture—differing in degree but not in kind from the protocultural communicative systems of other animals. The search for categoric universals is therefore vain; we shall find only the shifting facets of an orderly but protean process, the communicative process that is culture. It does not matter whether we describe the structure and process of culture in qualitative or in quantitative language—either way we are forced to define and employ our concepts, not in terms of categoric logic, but in terms of probability.

Categoric distinctions of specific cultures is another casualty. We cannot differentiate specific traditions as though they were discrete and autonomous entities, for they are always in greater or lesser degree a product of some order of cultural relationship to other segments of human communicative history. The structure of differing cultures is differentiable but not categorically so. They are more or less alike, more or less different; they can never be utterly distinct. To be so, a culture group would have to secede from the species and break with the communicative nexus that binds it to human history.

Cultures are not entities; they bear almost no relation to organisms, and their structure is not a product of functioning. The parts do not bear to the whole that subtle integrative relationship that lends integrity to an autonomous isolate, for the whole cannot be defined with such splendid precision of boundaries. This is not to deny that cultures are structured, definable, real phenomena, but they are probabilistic emergents from the historical matrix of communication, clearly defined or very loosely so, and they do not function.

The final and most paradoxical conclusion to which we are led by the scientific scrutiny of values is that values do not and cannot exist—at least in the sense in which Kluckhohn and others have defined them. They are an ethnocentric projection of our ancient Western preoccupation with freedom and can therefore be accorded a certain nominalistic and ethnographic reality in that connection. But the freedom of choice upon which values must be assumed to rest cannot be made scientifically compatible with the documentable determinism of choice in any value area we can study with sufficient intensity. What, then, is the meaning of the order of regularity we have discovered in the pursuit of values?

By concentrating our attention in a systematic way upon choice situations, we have in effect undertaken the study of that class of cultural phenomena which is by definition the least determinate. By demonstrating that individual and group reactions in these situations are not disorderly but selective, not random but structured, we have proved that they are not free but determined. By eliminating from consideration those cases in which apparent choice was conditioned by noncultural factors, we have showed that the determining factor in values is cultural. The study of values has thus sweepingly extended the purview of cultural causation.

The demonstration that values are structured has the additional effect of focusing our attention upon the segmental cultural traditions within which the structuring of choices is largely carried on. In a sense we may say that what has been proved is that the relativity of values is total. Similarity of values is only possible where there is similarity of culture. But this does not imply the utter incomparability or untranslatability of values. Values are determinate, cultural, and real. They are therefore completely bound to the cultural process that produces them. But by the same token they are completely accessible to the human intelligence through the selfsame process—culture. Like any other dimension of culture, explicit or implicit, values are communicable, and it is through communications that as scientists we can perceive and study them.

The intervention of the anthropologist is in itself a denial of the puncture-proof skins with which organic and functional theory surrounded cultures. The observational and analytic success of anthropologists is in itself a demonstration of the relativity of cultural autonomy and the provisionality of cultural isolation. The cultural process has guaranteed that there will be diverse cultures, but it has also guaranteed that there will be anthropologists to study them and that their study will be objective.

The responsibility for objectivity in science has usually been phrased as a moral imperative. It is a value. It is nonetheless my contention that scientists are objective not because they are moral, but because they have no choice. Science is a cultural activity involving the communication of highly schematized information to a specifically prepared community. Objectivity is an attribute of this information that greatly enhances its communicability. The scientist who fails to communicate successfully through lack of objectivity ceases to be part of science by virtue of and in proportion to that failure. Whatever our subjective impression of the matter may be, objectivity is created in science, not by an act of will on our part, but by the nature of the cultural process. Subjective observations are simply less communicable than objective ones, and that is why the scientific enterprise has developed (under favorable communicative circumstances) to begin with. Our ability, over the long haul, to weed out error and cling to truth is not an instinct; it is an intrinsic feature of culture. The pursuit of elegance and parsimony in science is not aesthetic; both are fundamental characteristics of the communicative process.

Communication

Human beings share by virtue of their common humanity an ability to communicate. In itself this ability does not differentiate us from other animals, many or even most of which also have it in some measure. What does differentiate us is that our communication has far more scope and intensity than that of any other species. In degree, if not in kind, we stand alone on this attribute, and the distinctive character of human life is primarily to be ascribed to this fact. The particularly intensive type of communication that we share may be defined as culture.

The most fundamental result of culture is the creation of structure. This, too, is anticipated in other species, but in communicative terms structure is a function of redundancy, of what I have just described as the intensity of communication. Particularly intensive systems of communication give rise to particularly intensive degrees of structure, hence cultural communication produces cultural structure. The two things are empirical and theoretical correlates. The particularly elaborate communicative structures characteristic of man may thus also be defined as culture.

There are many kinds of cultural structure, but the most problematic kind is that which has led us into the study of values. In some ways this is a residual category. Many structures appear in culture in connections which link them with greater or lesser clarity to noncultural causes. They are ecologically conditioned and are traceable at least in part to the organization of environing reality—our biological makeup and its physical setting. We have long seen these structures as determined by these outside factors. Values are the remaining structures, which are orderly for reasons intrinsic to culture. We have long viewed them as manifestations of the freedom of the human spirit, and indeed they display a notable flexibility and variability. But they are not free. Values are simply those patterns in individuals and groups which are structured entirely or primarily by cultural communication—the historical development of noninstrumental ideas—rather than by subcultural, precultural, or extracultural conditions. They are, in a sense, the most purely cultural of cultural structures.

Culture is a structure-creating process. We communicate with one another not in proportion to whether we have something of importance to say, but in proportion to our communicative capacity. We may solemnly transmit to each other the most arrant nonsense, but we receive and perpetuate such messages, not because they are true but only because they are communicable. The redundancy capacity of the human communication system has always greatly exceeded the structural requirements of the messages with which we need to load it. Inevitably we transmit, along with some simple and necessary patterns, a great deal of near-noise, for even unstructured and random inputs become communicable if they are accidentally repeated in a circuit with the capacity to perpetuate them. Human culture has a communicative capacity in excess of its instrumental requirements, and it therefore creates and communicates new messages whether they are true or false, relevant or irrelevant, helpful or detrimental.

The generation of new structures is not an infinite capacity, but it does give us a continuous supply of innovative ideas which are therefore available for selection. They are selected in terms of their communicability. Let us differentiate three cases. In the first case, a randomly generated cultural innovation encounters a preexisting redundancy in various individuals conditioned by some highly repetitive environing experiences. In such a case, for example hungry Mesolithic hunters hearing that oysters are edible, the innovation should have a greatly enhanced probability of diffusion. In the second case, a randomly generated cultural innovation encounters a redundancy conditioned by ethnicity. In such a case, a new word that fits the morphophonemic pattern of a language for instance, the innovation will have an increased probability of perpetuation, but only within the group sharing the preexisting pattern. In the third case, a randomly generated cultural innovation finds no echo in the preconditioning of any individual other than the innovator, a schizophrenic fantasy for example; it will fail of communication because of its experiential irrelevancy: It does not sufficiently correspond to the existing structure in potential hearers.

A variety of circumstances may cause variations in the communicative matrix of culture, but at the broadest level they may be grouped in two general types: human and nonhuman. In other words, culture is a process determined by intrinsic and extrinsic factors. The principal task of the science of man—which can be defined as the science of culture (the only generally accepted definitional attribute of man)—is the recognition and differentiation of these two sets of factors. The extrinsic factors, broadly ecological in character, have a structure of their own which operates to introduce variability into the concrete manifestations of the cultural process. It is only when this variability is experimentally or analytically removed that the basic regularities of culture can be discovered. This is anthropology's mission.

One of the regularities of culture is its cumulative character in certain specific connections. Like all cultural facts, this is a fact about communications. It may be taken to mean that the simplest and most diffusable of human ideas tend to spread so easily throughout the web of culture that they build up a generalized structure-creating redundancy. Groups of individuals favorably located in time and space thus become overloaded with such ideas, which consequently interact to generate new ideas. These secondary products are guaranteed communication in the typical case by the fact that they will be just as congenial communicatively to the properly prepared recipient as to the individual so located as to be the inventor. Since our generally common experience of the natural world is a major source of communicative redundancy within individuals, it is

small wonder that the aspects of culture that evolve most rapidly
are the objective ones. Individual and tribal poetic insights, even
when they are simple, have no such extrinsic head start. The locus
and development of scientific progress in history is a major anthropological problem, but it is confused by the eccentricities of geog-
raphy and the generally tribal character imposed on man by his
diverse ethnic traditions.

The extrinsic or ecological aspect of culture encompasses our
ability to perceive and communicate our experience of nature. The
intrinsic aspect encompasses our ability to communicate as such—
our continual exchange of information devoid of environmental
relevance but nonetheless contagious by virtue of the inherent re-
dundancies of human social organization. It is this intrinsic dimension of culture that Kluckhohn, in his broader definitions, has called
"values." In the traditional theories of man, the selection of one
metaphor over another, the decision to sin or repent, the choice of an
old or a new style, or a preference for rigidity or flexibility have
been construed as reflections of the free exercise of will. In cultural
perspective, they no longer appear to be so: They are predictably
determined. But they are not environmentally or extrinsically determined.

The fundamental feature of human life upon which the capacity
for these orders of cultural communication rests is the redundancy
of the human social order, which guarantees at one and the same
time the continued communication of scientifically cumulative rationality on an ecumenical scale and the perpetuation of all manner
of more particular and irrational structures on a parochial one. This
redundancy is readily traceable to the ancient institutions of endog-
amy and exogamy that establish and maintain human family life.

Our ability to differentiate the aspects of culture corresponding
to what I have here called "extrinsic" and "intrinsic" structure is still
limited, and it is therefore appropriate that modern anthropologists
study culture intensively from both angles. To some, these approaches appear contradictory, but this view seems to me short-
sighted. The common denominator of all of culture is its communicative character: Both cultural ecology and cultural values reflect the
operation of a single communicative process. Cultural evolution and

ethnocentrism are the common products of cultural communication in two of its most salient dimensions.

Conclusions

In the 1940s, Kluckhohn used to characterize his theoretical stance in anthropology by identifying himself with the structural-functionalist school of thought. It is my belief that his study of values went very far toward converting him into a pure structuralist. No later than 1945, he began to be explicitly critical of functionalism, and by 1949 he had rejected his own earlier functional interpretations. The thinking of several prominent anthropologists underwent a parallel development at about the same time.

Functional theory explained cultural facts by pointing to the instrumental features of culture—the needs that culture fulfilled, the adaptive functions that it discharged in relation to our environment. But one class of cultural functions had to be interpreted as almost purely homeostatic—the integrative or adjustive functions that were assumed to operate to maintain the integrity of the system itself. This latter class of functions corresponds to the value functions, and they are the source of most of the problematics of functional theory. If such functions are accorded any causal value, the result is a completely static model of society and culture, for the adjustive functions always tend toward stability. Functional theory got around this by assuming values to be free, thus introducing a definitional unpredictability into the theory of culture.

Kluckhohn's achievement was to focus attention on an empirically answerable question in this connection: that of the predictability of values. The resulting literature is prolix, confused, and incomplete, but the major answer to the question is clear enough. Values can be predicted. It follows that we must reject the possibility that the exercise of free will accounts for the dynamic element otherwise lacking in the functionalist scheme, and this in turn calls the whole of functionalism into serious question.

It is very likely that the increasing tempo of culture change all over the world was an additional impetus to reconsidering this question of dynamics. Functional theory had simply gone on predicting stability and continuity where events confronted us with violent revolution. The awareness of the pressing need for a more dynamic theory was general, and functionalism has come under increasing attack for its inadequacies in this respect. Inevitably we have had to reject the functional explanation of cultural structure and construct a new one more in accord with observed fact. This change has been uneven and partial—more in some theorists than in others. Many continue to defend the functional synthesis unchanged. But an important group of thinkers has turned towards a new and more dynamic theory of structure.

I have tried to describe this theory as it appears to me—as a synthesis of existing structural method with a broad range of theories about communications. The result is not Kluckhohn, but it is Kluckhohnian. In one of his last published papers (1961*d*), in fact, Kluckhohn specifically surveyed the field of communications without seeing in it the implications I have here suggested. Nonetheless, a very vital part of what I have argued seems to me implicit in the pattern of development of Kluckhohn's ideas about values. Like him, I consider componential analysis and other modern techniques of structural analysis to be the most promising new development in descriptive anthropology. He believed that there was a process that explained cultural structure. I believe that process to be communications and that we are beginning to know a great deal about it.

Values are the rock on which functionalism founders. Value problems have a peculiar theoretical importance in this connection that they cannot have if we abandon the functionalist assumptions. It is thus imperative that we continue to study them. It is not too much to say that the crucial test of a better theory will be its ability to explain what we have already conceptualized just as adequately as functional theory has done, while simultaneously offering us a better comprehension of the elusive problems on which functionalism falters. It is my conviction that the structural analysis of culture as a communicative process offers this possibility and that we have virtually within our grasp a new and comprehensive understanding of the rigorously determined structures of intrinsic culture. If so, we shall owe it in large measure to Clyde Kluckhohn.

UNPATTERNING AND
REPATTERNING IN CULTURE:
A CRISIS THEORY

Robert N. Rapoport

THIS ESSAY, which is mainly limited to my own work, addresses the problem of a specific type of value-change: the substitution, by a significant sector of a community, of radically contrasting, even opposite values for the values previously held as dominant. This process has been referred to by Niebuhr as the "transvaluation of values" in relation to the development of sects. David Aberle, basing his formulation on the analysis of the Peyote Cult, developed a typology of social movements which takes into account the distinction between changes which are geared to individual values, "redemptive movements," and "transformative movements" which aim at fundamental change in the social value system (1966: 316 ff.). My own concern is less with the analysis and classification of social movements than with a specific process, hypothetically important in all types of social movement. The process—unpatterning and repatterning of cultural values—is one that I see as linked to personality on the one side and social structure on the other.

Though Kluckhohn's work was in many respects visionary, his emphasis, particularly in the last years of his work, centered on the consolidation of the values concept as a key element in the analysis of cultural patterning. In his Toronto lecture, he applied one of his favorite analogues in extending genetical concepts from their application in linguistics to the field of value theory:

in speaking of genetics, Anderson referred to a number of complementary categories ("forked" vs. "non-forked," etc.). Similarly, linguists in their elegant analyses of one aspect of culture have found it extremely useful to set up a series of distinctive contrasts or oppositions, usually binary, which serve to identify each separate phoneme. [1959e:42]

He notes that eleven distinctive binary contrasts suffice to define each Russian phoneme, seven each French phoneme, and so on. In this paper, Kluckhohn proposed thirteen binary contrasts in value orientation, against which he analyzed five New Mexican cultures. His aim was to refine the elements through examining their patterning of interrelationship so as to be able to extract a set of relatively pure elements with which he could perform a value analysis on specific cultures that would be comparable to the linguist's phonemic analysis.

Kluckhohn knew, of course, that dominant values were not the only values that people in a given culture held, that they are not held with the same degree of commitment by all, and that shifts in value patterns can occur in response to various kinds of stimuli. In his paper in the Romano volume, he noted:

We require a way of thinking which takes account of the pull of expectancies as well as the push of tensions, which recognizes that growth and creativity come as much or more from instability as from stability, which emphasizes culturally created values as well as the immediately observable external environment. . . . All cultures create problems for individuals as well as solve them. Only in part is culture an adaptive and adjustive instrument. [1949b:112–13]

His own work did not pursue these suggestive lines of thought, but he indicates in the Toronto lecture that the formulation by Florence Kluckhohn and Fred Strodtbeck does proceed along this path. They classify cultures not only according to dominant value-orientation, but according to their subordinate orientations as well. Kluckhohn says about this:

The systematic variation always contains the potentiality for change but remains dormant or latent until environmental events or intensified contacts with other cultures bring a second- or third-order position into dominance. [1959e:37]

It is precisely this process of transposition of low-order values into dominance with which we are here concerned. Two stages are postulated as operative in such a process: the unpatterning event which produces a crisis in the functioning of the social structure and the repatterning activities which are conducted by self-selected individuals in relation to the new structural situation.

In order to approach a better understanding of how this process may occur, three situations will be reexamined in this framework— the Navaho conversions to Christianity at Rimrock, the development of the therapeutic community movement within psychiatry, and the emergence of depressed communities in Stirling County, Nova Scotia, Canada. The three social structures involved are on a similar scale, i.e., a few hundred persons living in some sort of interdependent or community situation and sharing a culture. They are: a Navaho band, a mental hospital (or "total community," in Goffman's terms), and a small rural community. The cultures, in their steady states, were of course extremely different. Hence, the type of repatterning process, the rearticulation process of persons and social structures, is different. In addition, two other types of unpatterning/repatterning process will be mentioned in relation to large scale, complex society; these may be referred to in a shorthand way as "calculative" and "projective" forms of repatterning processes. The discussion to follow is, it hardly need be said, highly tentative and exploratory in nature, though in the first three sections it explores data long since laid to rest.

The Navaho and Christianity:
Traumatic Unpatterning/Reparative Repatterning

Many observers of Navaho culture, including Kluckhohn and Reichard, have been impressed with the degree to which Navaho beliefs and values were antithetical to those of Christianity. Christianity centers on a monotheistic cult, while Navaho religion is polytheistic; Christianity seeks to assure salvation in a life after death and celebrates the resurrection of Christ from the dead, while Navahos have no developed notion of an afterlife and fear and abhor creatures who are associated with death; Christianity is concerned with good

and evil, while Navaho religion is concerned with the maintenance
of harmony or a balance of power in the universe; and so on. Thus,
despite Navaho culture's historical incorporative tendencies, Navaho
Indians did not show much interest in Christianity until recently.

At the time of my own study of the Rimrock Navaho, in
1948–50, the success of Christian missionaries (Mormons and a
fundamentalist group that I termed, pseudonymically, "Galileans")
were strikingly successful, having attracted nearly one third of the
adult population to their membership. A number of psychological
variables and characteristics of individual social matrices differentiated the converts from the nonconverts. The converts, as individuals, were more dependent and more anxious than nonconverts; on
the other hand, they had a greater drive toward leadership, a higher
identification with whites, and a correspondingly higher negative
orientation toward traditional Navaho ways. They tended to come
from social matrices that contained aberrant or missing figures
where role models in the traditional patterns of Navaho behavior
might have been expected (e.g., father, mother's brother). Women
were more numerous than men among the converts, a finding that is
rather widespread in the literature on religious participation and
acculturation. However, in most of the situations described in the
literature, women's position is more clearly subordinate to men
than in Navaho society; women therefore experience a relative
deprivation against which the success of religious proselytising can
be readily understood. In the Navaho situation, by contrast, women
were relatively strong in their structural position, owning property
and participating equally with men in most areas of life. Their conversion cannot, therefore, be seen in terms of deprivation in relation
to the traditional situation, but only in relation to the contemporary
culture-contact situation. Another point of unexpected finding had
to do with the history of relationships with whites. Though the
strong converts had a high white identification, they also had a
greater degree of trouble in their past relationships with whites than
any group with the exception of the ceremonial practitioners. Furthermore, the converts, unlike those converted to the kinds of sects
which elsewhere show the transvaluation-of-values pattern, were not
drawn from the poorer members of the local band but, on the con-

trary, from the wealthier "outfits." Also unexpectedly, they came largely from backgrounds of traditional Navaho cultural experience, and not predominantly from backgrounds of early educational experiences in white schools.

In my original analysis, I tried to make sense of these findings, the anomalies as well as the expected ones, but I have never felt very satisfied with the analysis, partly because it required an implicit model which was too fragmented. The gist of the argument was that Navaho culture had been severely traumatized by the conquest experience and, as a consequence, had reproduced itself with a variety of social, cultural, and personal deficiencies which set up needs which the missionary satisfied: many kinds of individuals converted for many different reasons. I would like to try to reformulate what I observed, in the framework suggested here.

I believe that the unpatterning event, the trauma of conquest and subordination to an alien culture and social system, is an adequate formulation of the relevant sociocultural crisis. This precipitated a situation in which variant patterns increased extremely rapidly: Individuals were reared in families with absent role models, mechanisms for propagating Navaho culture were interrupted and alternative channels of education were imposed, ownership and inheritance of property were regulated by new laws, economic resources were acquired and distributed according to new and, to some degree, uncontrollable processes, the curing function of religious ceremonialism, at the core of the traditional cultural value system, was contested both by medical and religious systems of the white society, and so on. Overarching all of these sources of sociocultural disintegration was the power situation. It was important that the white society, from which acculturative influences emanated, was the conquering society, although not in terms of the imposed nature of the changes, which operated primarily in the area of property. Far more important, in terms of Navaho traditional logics, was the sense that power resided not in their own institutions but in those of the white society. It is this point that I feel is the key to the explanation of why so many conservatively oriented Navahos converted to a value system which would have been anathema to their forefathers.

An important locus of power was clearly operating externally to the Navaho cosmology and system of logics. Internal harmony was disturbed in a number of ways. Therefore, the restoration of harmony had to be accomplished, and different individuals attempted different methods. The joining of the Church was not, as the data demonstrated, a phenomenon exclusively for misfits, marginal and disgruntled types, though these were represented, to be sure. It was rather taken up by many of the more active, intelligent, well-off, and even traditionally reared types, who had, previously to this, clashed vigorously with their more powerful white conquerors. When the church was presented to them in this context, they adopted it actively, seeking to repair and reconstruct a culture which was shattered beyond the point of being able to incorporate the external elements. This, I term "reparative repatterning."

This, I feel, is a more adequate analysis than I provided in my original work, because the theoretical model I was using then was one that assigned a relatively passive role to man, responding rather mechanically to needs on the one hand and falling into sociocultural categories on the other. Man as a patterner of cultures is more active and creative than this.

The Therapeutic Community:
Martial Unpatterning/Antithetical Repatterning

The Renaissance reconceptualization of human nature led, in the eighteenth and nineteenth centuries, to the redefinition of psychiatric illness from its previous status as a form of bewitchment to the view still predominant in the Western world, namely, that it is a form of malady to come under the purview of medicine. The reforms in various countries by such figures as Phillippe Pinel, William Tuke, and Dorothea Dix led to the setting up of mental hospitals into which the mentally ill were sent for treatment. However, while the humanistic spirit and naturalistic outlook which prompted this development, which Zilboorg refers to as "the first revolution in psychiatry," was morally commendable, it was technically problematic. Scientific knowledge on which to base therapeutic programs was lacking, and there grew up a mental hospital subculture which was primarily custodial in orientation, classifying and studying their charges in secure settings apart from the larger community but having little by way of systematic or understandable therapeutic procedure. All sorts of therapies were tried empirically, among them a form of moral treatment which foreshadowed the later therapeutic community movement. Few of the forms of treatment were related to a scientific body of theory, and therefore most failed to persist or to develop. There grew up a separate structure of mental hospitals, somewhat apart not only from the larger society whose casualties they harbored, but from the other branches of medicine. They tended to be understaffed and dealt with the problems of social control by setting up a highly impersonal system of authoritarian management of patients. The sense of pessimism about the possibility of returning most of the patients to the outside society contributed still further to the tendency to treat the inmates as nonpersons or to desocialize them. The emotional distance that this created between staff and patients was functional, given the paucity of techniques for dealing with the disturbed and disturbing behavior of the patients. Recruitment was, in these situations, difficult, and there developed a tendency for individuals with authoritarian personalities to move into staff roles in such institutions and to have these tendencies confirmed in them. The recent research of Levinson, Belknap, Goffman, and others has delineated the custodial orientation and its associated types in the total communities of the old-fashioned mental hospital system.

At the same time, a subculture, or linked set of subcultures, was arising in the same societies, which was attuned to a set of principles antithetical to those being confirmed within the mental hospital system. The development of social science, psychoanalysis, and the general humane emphases in the sociopolitical culture brought about a situation where young men, trained in medicine, were enculturated to believe in the dignity and worth of every individual, in the doctrine that psychological disturbances were products of disturbed experiences in one's early social relationships and that these could be undone through appropriate psychological therapies. Young idealistic doctors, however, had to experience a radical discontinuity when they moved from their general and medical education in this

branch of psychiatric work. Their junior positions in a rigid, hierarchical system dampened their efforts, and the tendency was to
conform or leave. There did build up, however, a marked and widespread sense of discrepancy and tension between the cultural values
of modern social and psychological medicine and the social structural
system of the mental hospitals.

The crisis or critical unpatterning event that occurred to bring
about a state of flux and major repatterning was that of World
War II. British psychiatrists were leaders in this repatterning activity,
with a group of psychoanalytically oriented psychiatrists and psychologists, Thomas Main, Maxwell Jones, and Eric Trist most prominent among them. They developed, first, a series of what they called
"therapeutic communities" to deal with men suffering from frontline
stress complaints which were clearly of a functional nature and,
later, a series of transitional communities to deal with the resocializa-
tion of ex-prisoners of war who had become adjusted to the culture
and social structure of prison camps, making their functioning in
ordinary life difficult.

Bruno Bettelheim has pointed out that once more war was the
father of all things. He asks why do we need suffering and emer-
gency to make the right, the obvious steps. Ten years after the war,
the importance of therapeutic community methods was generally
recognized, and the walls of the mental hospitals were tumbling
down, figuratively and literally. The parallels between the tasks of
the wartime therapeutic and transitional communities and those of
the mental hospitals were drawn, and elements of organization,
which originally were expedients which functioned in crises, became
principles of treatment. For example, given the lack of trained nursing staff, young, wholesome, but untrained girls were recruited,
who interacted naturally and warmly (rather than remotely and
autocratically) with patients. This gave rise to the view that conventional nursing training, with its stiff and starchy products and its
emphasis on orderliness and discipline, was positively dysfunctional.
Opposite types were sought, foreigners (Scandinavian girls, who
were "democratic," where English were seen as "class-oriented,"
moralizing, and formal); they were taken only if they did not have
any formal training but were desirous of receiving the kind to be

provided within the community. In a subsequent study, a set of cultural value themes were delineated (Hughes et al. 1961), which had the clear characteristic of being antithetical to those of the old-fashioned mental hospital system: (1) The therapeutic community stressed democracy, while the old-fashioned mental hospital system was seen as autocratic; (2) the therapeutic community stressed permissiveness, while the mental hospital system was seen as restrictive; (3) the therapeutic community stressed communal sharing and free communications, where the old-fashioned mental hospital system was segregated and communication was limited and asymetrical; (4) the therapeutic community stressed rehabilitation (i.e., return of the patients to normal living, initially through making the hospital into a microcosm of the outside world in which role rehearsals could occur), while mental hospitals were custodial.

In our analysis of the functioning of Maxwell Jones's therapeutic community, my colleagues and I pointed out that the pattern which they had evolved, with its emphasis on antithetical principles, was inadequate. The extreme of democracy, for example, could not be realized without contravening other conditions in the system, such as the actual differences in responsibility associated with the formal role requirements of physicians as compared with patients. The idea of complete permissiveness might contravene the idea of rehabilitation, given the restrictions in the real environment outside the specific institutional structure. The conceptualization of this repatterning process, however, is something still to be worked out adequately. De-bureaucratization, as some sociologists have viewed the process, gives only part of the picture, particularly in the unpatterning phase. As the ideas of the therapeutic community have diffused, they have not always been absorbed as a complete culture-complex but have been disarticulated and selectively integrated into other patterns, all as part of the larger process of repatterning in relation to the mental hospital structure and system.

The process which I have described resembles, of course, the classical Hegelian dialectic. The challenge to the contemporary theorists of cultural dynamics is in the area of the precise principles governing the synthesis or repatterning phase. This seems to occur by the sifting and readaptation of the creative, antithetical pattern through the relevant parts of the larger structure and the emergence of a new pattern based less on protest than was the case in the original repatterning formulation, though arising out of it. The emphasis I wish to suggest here, to supplement classical analysis using the dialectical and/or diffusion models, is on the extent to which people repattern their cultures with a sense of actively searching for effective solutions to issues raised by the specific structural, cultural, and personality misalignments. They may learn to live with misalignments, e.g., between cultural values and structural possibilities for realising them. But when an unpatterning event occurs, they will actively seek a more efficient way of accomplishing the cultural goals, bringing about a good fit between social structural, cultural, and personal dimensions of their lives.

The Depressed Communities:
Technological Unpatterning/Anomic Repatterning

In the Canadian Maritimes at the end of the last century, there was a thriving complex of industries which made the small communities prosperous and well integrated. Two cultures flourished, the French and the English, each functioning around a different set of linguistic and religious cultural foci, but with similar ecological cores. Timber was cut and milled in the hinterlands, food was raised in an agricultural belt between forest and shore, fish were taken from the sea, and a rich trade was conducted via ships plying between Nova Scotia, New England, and the West Indies. These were the days of "wooden ships and iron men."

The advent of the steamship, together with a complex of other factors associated with the depletion of local timber resources, the erection of tariff barriers between Canada and the United States, and the growth of industry in other parts of Canada brought about a massive technological shift at the core of this culture complex. The particular situation that prevailed here was one of technological displacement. That is, the changes that occurred did not lead to an orderly superseding of simpler technological inventions by more complex ones or even the introduction of more advanced technology into a culture which had previously functioned with a different or simpler form. The changes were at a level of sociopolitical integration above that of the local community and made the activities of the local communities marginal and lagging in relation to new centers of trade and industry in other parts of Canada.

In the region as a whole, several processes emerged in response to the new technological situation. In some areas, new technology was taken on and adapted to new patterns of production and distribution of goods. In other areas, there was a shift to different processes and industries (e.g., deep-freezing of fish, the tourist industry). In still other areas, the economic decline was cushioned by a relatively productive agricultural base. Most areas suffered heavy losses through emigration of their young and vigorous members. The growth in importance of higher education reenforced this tendency, and the return rate of those who prepared for and eventually left to obtain higher educations was, inevitably, small. In the course of this extended and multiplex process, there emerged a locally well-recognized type of community that we have designated as a "depressed area." These were areas in which there prevailed a value system contrary to that of their developing technologically oriented neighbors. This is the sort of rural slum immortalized by Al Capp and more recently brought into social science research focus in such programs as that of Appalachia.

In addition to describing these depressed areas in terms of their demographic and major institutional patterns (e.g., religious participation, family life, etc.), we delineated a dozen patterns of sentiments which impressed us not only as describing the major value themes of people in these areas, but also in terms of their contrasting, antithetical character as compared with the themes prevailing in the major established subcultures, French and English, in their environment. Some examples are: (1) "People here are mentally and morally inferior" (contrasts with the proud self-esteem of the neighboring communities; (2) "It is good to be with people but you have to watch your step" (reflects an ambivalence about social interaction not present in the neighboring communities); (3) "People in authority should not be trusted, but you have to show them respect to their faces," and "Defying authority is a good way to gain prestige" (reflect their fundamental alienation from the authority structure which their neighboring communities support); (4) "Self-improvement is practically impossible" and "Work should be avoided wherever possible" (contrast sharply with the effort-optimism of their neighbors); (5) "The best thing to do in life is to escape from your problems as quickly as possible" (is usually expressed through the excessive use of alcohol).

In these and other respects, the people of the depressed areas had set up a cultural pattern which reflected their failure to adapt to changes in their environment, with the emergence of an anomic culture of distrust, lack of purpose, and the adoption of self-destructive defenses (e.g., drinking to excess and other ways of attempting to obliterate their problems). It also reflected a mutually antagonistic relationship with their neighboring communities which had managed to adapt better to the changes and to preserve the main outlines of their former cultures, even strengthening them at some points. For the neighbors, the people of the depressed areas presented negative cultural models, useful for bolstering their own self-esteem, scape-goating, and in some cases exploiting economically and in other ways. For the people of the depressed areas, their neighbors represented hated and distrusted figures to whom one had to accommodate because they controlled the resources. This pattern was remarkably stable and had the functional character of an ecological couple.

Additional Forms of Unpatterning/Repatterning

The two additional forms will be only cursorily mentioned, as the work in which I am involved in these areas is still underway. They have in common that they relate to an environmental situation of considerable complexity, that the future will be different from the past, and that as a consequence the culture patterns that will have to be developed will differ from those which are received. This environmental circumstance, then, is the unpatterning social structural condition. The two types of repatterning processes which will be briefly described are termed the "calculative" and the "projective" types. In the first instance, the unpatterning events are the major status transitions which punctuate the life cycle; in the second instance, it is a threat of unpatterning rather than an unpatterning event which stimulates the repatterning process.

The calculative repatterning process. Another type of crisis or turning point which confronts individuals systematically within a given society and which has neither the unexpected nor undesirable features of those described in previous sections is that occasioned by status transitions in the life cycle. Van Gennep, of course, first described the importance of ritual at these points but, in so doing, made it plain that in primitive societies the tasks of making these critical transitions were very similar from generation to generation and that, therefore, rituals could be shared and reciprocally enacted by elder and younger generations, helping to make the passage effective. It is not only secularization, but the establishment of an expectation of change, a dynamic condition of the milieu, that makes such rituals less effective in contemporary society. As Gluckman and others have pointed out, there may be continuing functions of ceremonials even in situations where they are clearly archaic, but in such instances they serve different functions than those for which they were developed and need to be supplemented if not supplanted by another kind of repatterning process.

This supplementary process, which may be dominant in some instances, is what I term (borrowing Etzioni's phrase) the "calculative approach." The same social and psychological functions toward which rituals had been directed in previous generations are increasingly dealt with as tasks to be accomplished rather than as functions which were automatically fulfilled by virtue or performing unquestioningly the same rituals on the same occasions as had one's forebears. The accomplishment of these tasks, e.g., of achieving a mutually satisfactory pattern of sexual relations in the process of getting married and establishing a family, is seen as a fresh challenge which could be responded to with fresh solutions. The emphasis, in contrast to traditional situations, is on the limits within which there is considerable freedom to form new cultural patterns, rather than on the modally prescribed patterns themselves. The calculative element in this sort of repatterning is expressed in the following observation by one of our research subjects on his own experiences with cultural repatterning associated with marriage and the establishment of a new family: "My mother has ideas on things, and her mother has ideas on the way she wants things, and usually we have ideas which are completely different from both of them. I usually skirmish a line which we can hit on that will satisfy all of us to some extent."

The projective repatterning process. It has become a widely held viewpoint in contemporary society that, given the tendency for radical social change to be the rule and for the past to be limited as a useful guide to what the future holds, one ought to engage in systematic activities of social forecasting. The Rand Corporation, the American Academy of Arts & Sciences, the British Social Science Research Council, and various other agencies in several American and European countries are actively involved in the attempt to project the future or several possible futures which might be anticipated.

A current project that has brought us into contact with the general field of social forecasting, "projective repatterning" of culture as we term it here, has been the attempt by the American Academy of Arts & Sciences, under a grant from National Aeronautical and Space Administration, to assess the impact of the space effort on American society (see Bauer and Rapoport in preparation; Mazlisch 1965; Bauer 1966). An earlier report by the Brookings Institution under the editorship of Donald Michael (1961) had indicated some of the topical areas that would be of likely relevance and a large number of possible consequences including potentially contradictory or incompatible potentialities. Michael proposed that research be mounted to determine actual implications. In the terms of the American Academy project, two sorts of information were desired, a feedback of information about what was actually happening as a consequence of the national backing of this major technological industry and some indications of what might be likely to happen in the future to aid in planning. These were seen as devices of anticipation.

In considering the projections made by informed speculation of experienced social scientists in conjunction with actual data that might indicate trends and contingencies or directive interventions, it seems clear that the study of projective patterning in culture, i.e., the predictions of future patterns, may provide a particularly powerful research approach. It may have once been assumed that the reason that men like Edison made such poor predictions about the social implications of technology ("I can see no future for the airplane except as a plaything for wealthy aristocrats") was their lack of social science sophistication. In fact, however, at this stage of knowledge, an assembly of top social scientists cannot do much better. Clearly the technological power will improve: for weather observation and forecasting, for communications broadcasting, for photographic and other surveillance of wide areas of the world's surface, etc. However, in relation to social factors, the matter is more problematic. The changes could lead to the stimulating or to the disruption of our system of higher education, to a drain on skilled and scientific manpower or to a gain to the economy, to an increase in cooperation with the rival powers or to a decrease in cooperation, to a further disintegrating influence for the family or to a new potential for maintaining and cementing contacts among dispersed kin, to a death knell for organized religion or to stimulating man's sense of awe in relation to the universe, etc. The process of adaptation to massive technological change in an affluent society seems to be one of continuous reorganization rather than a series of parallel or undulating trend lines. The contingencies that make for specific patterns of reorganization, including socially informed and purposeful intervention, become focal topics of study and may ultimately give rise to formulations that will affect theory pertaining to retrospective reconstructions of cultural dynamics, making study of cultural repatterning more useful to culture historians.

Recapitulation

In all of the cases presented here, the unpatterning/repatterning process was set in motion or catalyzed by a stimulus external to the cultural system in focus. In the case of the Navahos, the conquest by white Americans created not only a series of disrupted social networks and cultural practices, but also a new element of power in the environment of the Navahos themselves. Their traditional emphasis on the maintenance of harmony in a world which they had always construed in power terms would seem to have led to reparative efforts not exclusively by the marginal and deviant types, but by the resourceful and creative ones as well.

In the psychiatric case, the opposition from young, reformist psychiatrists toward the obsolescent establishment in the mental hospital system was brought into the open by the circumstances of war, with the enemy providing the challenge in relation to which the traditional sociocultural pattern of coping with psychiatric casualties was found to be inadequate, and new therapeutic community procedures were institutionalized. The early form of cultural repatterning in this case was antithetical to the old rather than reparative, because it was the first successful expression of the dissenting pattern which had hitherto been covert. Subsequent reformulations have been more varied to adapt to different situations.

The case of the depressed areas in Canada was one in which the external situation that unpatterned the social structural elements in the environment was one of rapid technological change. The depressed communities represented social structures which had failed to repattern their culture in adaptation to the new circumstances. They lived instead in an anomic pattern which placed them in a disparaged dependency relationship with their neighboring communities, who had adapted more successfully but at a great cost socially and psychologically. The presence of depressed areas served a scapegoating function for their own sense of anger at having to give up a valued previous pattern.

The calculative and projective repatternings of culture occur in the face of anticipated changes in structure: in the former case within the context of life-cycle status transitions in a changing society, in the latter within the context of a sense of continuous restructuring of the field of forces associated with the control of power, prestige, and resources in a world situation of political rivalry between major powers.

The situations described in the first three instances represent types of disruption and repatterning that occur in situations where an equilibrium has been established but where there emerge new cultural ideas and values which cannot find expression in the old structural framework. Under certain circumstances, conquest, war, rapid technological change, the old structure is disrupted and a state of flux ensues. In the repatterning that occurs, the new patterns are determined by elements present in the situation, including the presence or absence of charismatic leaders. These are illustrations of crisis unpatterning and repatterning sequences. In the last two instances, there is established an orientation that is more dynamic, and the conception of crisis is that it is periodic or even continuous. New challenges are raised in such a situation for students of cultural process, and new patterns will have to be devised for their study.

Bibliography

All citations of Kluckhohn's works follow the Wales bibliography in *Culture and Behavior* (Kluckhohn 1962a); the "AAA numbers" in parentheses following the date of each Kluckhohn citation refer to the bibliography published in connection with Kluckhohn's obituary by Parsons and Vogt (*American Anthropologist* 64:140–61).

Aberle, David F.
    1966   *The peyote religion among the Navaho.* Viking Fund Publications in Anthropology, no. 42. New York: Wenner-Gren Foundation.
    1967   The Navaho singer's "fee": payment or prestation? In *Studies in southwestern ethnolinguistics*, Dell H. Hymes, ed., pp. 15–32. Paris and The Hague: Mouton.

Adair, John
    1963   Physicians, medicine men and their Navaho patients. In *Man's image in medicine and anthropology*, Iago Galdston, ed., pp. 237–57. Monograph 4, Institute of Social and Historical Medicine, New York Academy of Medicine. New York: International Universities Press.

Bauer, Raymond A.
    1952   *The new man in Soviet psychology.* Cambridge: Harvard University Press.

Bauer, Raymond A., ed.
    1966   *Social indicators.* Cambridge: Massachusetts Institute of Technology Press.

Bauer, Raymond A.; Inkeles, Alex; and Kluckhohn, Clyde
    1956   (AAA 202) *How the Soviet system works.* Cambridge: Harvard University Press.

Bauer, Raymond A., and Rapoport, Robert N.
    n.d.   The space effort and social change. In preparation.

Benedict, Ruth F.
    1934   *Patterns of culture.* Boston: Houghton Mifflin.

Bloch, Bernard
    1953   Contrast. *Language* 29:59–61.
Bloomfield, Leonard
    1933   *Language.* New York: Henry Holt.
Brand, Donald D.; Hawley, Florence M.; Hibben, Frank C. et al.
    1937   *Tseh So, a small house ruin, Chaco Canyon, New Mexico.* University of New Mexico Bulletin 308, Anthropological Series 2, no. 2.
Conklin, Harold C.
    1965   Ethnogenealogical method. In *Explorations in cultural anthropology,* W. Goodenough, ed., pp. 25–55. New York: McGraw-Hill.
Dicks, Henry V.
    1952   Observations on contemporary Russian behaviour. *Human Relations* 5:111–75.
Frake, Charles
    1962   The ethnographic study of cognitive systems. In *Anthropology and human behavior,* T. Gladwin and W. C. Sturtevant, eds., pp. 72–93. Washington, D.C.: Anthropological Society of Washington.
    1964a   Notes on queries in ethnography. *In* Transcultural studies in cognition, A. K. Romney and R. G. D'Andrade, eds. *American Anthropologist* 66, 3, pt. 2:132–45.
    1964b   A structural description of Subanun "religious behavior." In *Explorations in cultural anthropology,* W. H. Goodenough, ed., pp. 111–29. New York: McGraw-Hill.
Gerard, Ralph W.; Kluckhohn, Clyde; and Rapoport, Anatol
    1956   (AAA 201) Biological and cultural evolution: some analogies and explorations. *Behavioral Science* 1:6–34.
Goldenweiser, A. A.
    1915   Les formes élémentaires de la vie religieuse. Review of *Le systéme totémique en Australie,* by Emile Durkheim. *American Anthropologist* 17:719–35.
Goodenough, Ward
    1956   Componential analysis and the study of meaning. *Language* 32:195–216.
Gottschalk, Louis; Kluckhohn, Clyde; and Angell, Robert
    1945   (AAA 70) *The personal document in history, anthropology, and sociology.* Social Science Research Council, Bulletin 53:79–174.
Haile, Berard
    1938   Navaho chantways and ceremonials. *American Anthropologist* 40:639–52.
    1943   Soul concepts of the Navaho. *Annali Lateranansi,* 7. Citta Del Vaticano: Tipografia Poliglotta Vaticana.
    1947   *Prayerstick cutting in a five-night Navaho ceremonial of the male branch of Shootingway.* Chicago: University of Chicago Press.

Hughes, C. C.; Trembley, M. A.; Rapoport, R. N.; Leighton, A. H.
1961   *People of cove and woodlot.* New York: Basic Books.
Inkeles, Alex, and Bauer, Raymond A.
1959   *The Soviet citizen: daily life in a totalitarian society.* Cambridge: Harvard University Press.
Inkeles, Alex; Hanfmann, Eugenia; and Beier, Helen
1958   Modal personality and adjustment to the Soviet socio-political system. *Human Relations* 11:3–12.
Jakobson, Roman; Fant, C. G. M.; and Halle, Morris A.
1952   *Preliminaries to speech analysis.* Massachusetts Institute of Technology, Acoustics Laboratory, Technical Report no. 13.
Jakobson, Roman, and Halle, Morris
1956   *Fundamentals of language.* The Hague: Mouton.
Joos, Martin
1958   Semology: a linguistic theory of meaning. University of Buffalo, *Studies in Linguistics* 13:53–70.
Kluckhohn, Clyde
1923   (AAA 1) The dance of Hasjelti. *El Palacio* 15:187–92.
1927   (AAA 2) *To the foot of the rainbow.* New York: Century.
1933*a*   (AAA 3) *Beyond the rainbow.* Boston: Christopher.
1933*b*   (AAA 4) The great chants of the Navaho. *Theatre Arts Monthly* 17:639–45.
1935*a*   (AAA 8) A note on the sources of the drawings in the Del Rio volume on Palenque. *Maya Research* 2:287–90.
1936*a*   (AAA 11) Some reflections on the method and theory of the Kulturkreislehre. *American Anthropologist* 38:157–96.
1937   (AAA 12) The field of higher education in the Southwest. *New Mexico Quarterly* 7:23–30.
1938*b*   (AAA 15) Navaho women's knowledge of their song ceremonials. *El Palacio* 45:87–92.
1938*c*   (AAA 16) Participation in ceremonials in a Navaho community. *American Anthropologist* 40:359–69.
1939*b*   (AAA 18) On certain recent applications of association coefficients to ethnological data. *American Anthropologist* 41:345–77.
1939*c*   (AAA 21) The place of theory in anthropological studies. *Philosophy of Science* 6:328–44.
1939*d*   (AAA 20) Some personal and social aspects of Navaho ceremonial practice. *Harvard Theological Review* 32:67–82.
1939*e*   (AAA 23) Theoretical bases for an empirical method of studying the acquisition of culture by individuals. *Man* 39:98–103.
1940*c*   (AAA 31) The conceptual structure in Middle American studies. In *The Maya and their neighbors*, C. L. Hay, R. L. Linton, S. K. Lothrop, H. L. Shapiro, G. C. Vaillant, eds., pp. 41–51. New York: D. Appleton-Century.

1941a (AAA 36) Patterning as exemplified in Navaho culture. In *Language, culture, and personality*, Leslie Spier, ed., pp. 109–30. Sapir Memorial Publication Fund: Menasha.

1942a (AAA 44) Myths and rituals: a general theory. *Harvard Theological Review* 35:45–79.

1942b (AAA 45) The Navahos in the machine age. *Technology Review* 44:2–6.

1943b (AAA 50) Covert culture and administrative problems. *American Anthropologist* 45:213–27.

1944a (AAA 62) *Navaho witchcraft*. Papers of the Peabody Museum of American Archaeology and Ethnology, vol. 22, no. 2. Cambridge: Harvard University.

1945c (AAA 67) Group tensions: analysis of a case history. In *Approaches to national unity*, Lyman Bryson, Louis Finkelstein, Robert M. MacIver, eds., pp. 222–31. New York: Harper and Bros.

1945e (AAA 69) A Navaho personal document with a brief paretian analysis. *Southwestern Journal of Anthropology* 1:260–83.

1945g (AAA 72) Comment on papers by H. Overstreet, P. Sorokin, W. Albright, T. Das, K. Shrindharani, and C. Friedrich. In *Approaches to national unity*, Lyman Bryson, L. Finkelstein, R. M. MacIver, eds., pp. 82–84, 215–17, 272–74, 297–300, 312–14, 628–34. New York: Harper and Bros.

1948d (AAA 91) Conceptions of death among the Southwestern Indians. (Ingersoll Lecture on the Immorality of Man, for the academic year 1947–48, Harvard University.) *Divinity School Bulletin* 66:5–19.

1949a (AAA 103) *Mirror for Man*. New York: McGraw-Hill.

1949b (AAA 102) The limitations of adaption and adjustment as concepts for understanding cultural behavior. In *Adaption*, John Romano, ed., pp. 97–113. Ithaca: Cornell University Press.

1949d (AAA 105) The philosophy of the Navaho Indians. In *Ideological differences and world order*, F. S. C. Northrop, ed., pp. 356–84. New Haven: Yale University Press.

1949f (AAA 107) Russian research at Harvard. *World Politics* 1:267–71.

1949j (AAA 106) The Ramah Project. In *Gregorio, the hand-trembler*, by A. H. and Dorothea Leighton. Papers of the Peabody Museum of American Archaeology and Ethnology, 40, no. 1, v–x. Cambridge: Harvard University.

1950a (AAA 114) Manners and morals: A.D. 1950. *New Republic* 122:10–14.

1951d (AAA 134) Student-Teacher. In *The People in your life*, Margaret M. Hughes, ed., pp. 158–81. New York: Alfred Knopf.

1951f (AAA 136) Values and value-orientations in the theory of action. In *Toward a general theory of action*, Talcott Parsons and Edward Shils, eds., pp. 388–433. Cambridge: Harvard University Press.

1951k (AAA 138) A comparative study of values in five cultures. Foreword in *Navaho veterans, a study of changing values*, by Evon Z. Vogt. Papers of the Peabody Museum of American Archaeology and Ethnology, 41, no. 1, vii–ix. Cambridge: Harvard University.

1952b (AAA 146) Universal values and anthropological relativism. In *Modern education and human values*, vol. 4, pp. 87–112. Pittsburgh: University of Pittsburgh Press.

1953b (AAA 156) Universal categories of culture. In *Anthropology today*, A. L. Kroeber, ed. ,pp. 507–23. Chicago: University of Chicago Press.

1954b (AAA 165) Culture and behavior. In *Handbook of social psychology*, Gardner Lindzey, ed., pp. 921–76. Cambridge: Addison-Wesley.

1954d (AAA 167) Methods of study at the Russian Research Center, Harvard University. *Civilizations* (Revue d'Institut International des Civilisations Différentes) 4:199–206.

1954f (AAA 169) Science as a possible source of new moral values. *Humanist* 14:211–14.

1955b (AAA 185) Ethical relativity: *sic et non*. *Journal of Philosophy* 52:663–77.

1955d (AAA 187) Indian Americans in a white man's world: a study of Indian American values and culture change. *Advance* (Congregational Christian Journal) 147:13–15.

1955g (AAA 190) Recent studies of the "national character" of Great Russians. *Human Development Bulletin*, papers presented at the Sixth Annual Symposium, February 5, 1955, pp. 39–60. Chicago.

1955h (AAA 193) Politics, history, and psychology. Review of *The appeals of communism*, by Gabriel Almond; *A study of bolshevism*, by Nathan Leites and Elsa Bernaut; *Ritual of liquidation: the case of the Moscow trials*, by Nathan Leites and Elsa Bernaut. *World Politics* 8:112–23.

1956c (AAA 204) Navaho morals. In *Encyclopedia of morals*, Vergilius Ferm, ed., pp. 383–90. New York: Philosophical Library.

1956e (AAA 208) Toward a comparison of value-emphases in different cultures. In *The state of the social sciences*, Leonard D. White, ed., pp. 116–32. Chicago: University of Chicago Press.

1956h (AAA 206) Some Navaho value terms in behavioral context. *Language* 32:140–45.

1957   Foreword in *Factory and manager in the U.S.S.R.*, by Joseph S. Berliner, pp. xiii–xv. Cambridge: Harvard University Press. (This reference not in Wales bibliography.)

1957c (AAA 220) Developments in the field of anthropology in the twentieth century. *Journal of World History* 3:754–77.

1957i (AAA 225) Foreword in *Cultural foundations of education, an interdisciplinary exploration*, by Theodore B. H. Brameld, pp. xi–xiii. New York: Harper and Bros.

1957j (AAA 226) Foreword in *The structure of a moral code: a philosophical analysis of ethical discourse applied to the ethics of the Navaho Indians*, by John Ladd, pp. xiii–xv. Cambridge: Harvard University Press.

1958a (AAA 233) Have there been discernible shifts in American values during the past generation? In *The American style*, Elting Morison, ed., pp. 145–217. New York: Harper and Bros.

1958d (AAA 235) The scientific study of values and contemporary civilization. *Proceedings of the American Philosophical Society* 102: 469–76.

1959e (AAA 246) The scientific study of values. In *Three lectures* (University of Toronto Installation Lectures, 1958), pp. 25–54. Toronto: University of Toronto Press.

1959h (AAA 257) Shifts in American values. Review of *America as a civilization: life and thought in the United States today*, by Max Lerner. *World Politics* 11:251–61.

1960d (AAA 263) The moral order in the expanding society. In *The city invincible*, Carl H. Kraeling and Robert M. Adams, eds., pp. 391–404. Chicago: University of Chicago Press.

1960e (AAA 264) Navaho categories. In *Culture in history: essays in honor of Paul Radin*, Stanley Diamond, ed., pp. 65–98. New York: published for Brandeis University by Columbia University Press.

1960f (AAA 265) A Navaho politician. In *In the company of man: twenty portraits by anthropologists*, Joseph B. Casagrande, ed., pp. 439–65. New York: Harper and Bros.

1961a (AAA 276) *Anthropology and the classics*. Brown University Clover Lectures, 1960. Providence: Brown University Press.

1961c (AAA 283) The study of values. In *Values in America*, Donald N. Barrett, ed., pp. 17–45. Notre Dame: University of Notre Dame Press.

1961d (AAA 281) Notes on some anthropological aspects of communication. *American Anthropologist* 63:895–910.

1961e (AAA 279) Navaho. In *Encyclopaedia Britannica*.

1962a *Culture and behavior: collected essays of Clyde Kluckhohn*, Richard Kluckhohn, ed. New York: The Free Press.

1966 *The Ramah Navaho*. Bureau of American Ethnology Bulletin 196, Anthropological Papers 79.

Kluckhohn, Clyde, and Hackenberg, Robert A.
1954c (AAA 170) Social science principles and the Indian Reorganization Act. In *Indian affairs and the Indian Reorganization Act,* W. H. Kelly, ed., pp. 29–34. Tucson: University of Arizona. Mimeographed.

Kluckhohn, Clyde; Inkeles, Alex; and Bauer, Raymond A.
1954s (AAA 172) Strategic, psychological, and sociological strength and vulnerabilities of the Soviet social system. Cambridge: Russian Research Center, Harvard University. Duplicated.

Kluckhohn, Clyde, and Kelly, William H.
1945b (AAA 66) The concept of culture. In *The science of man in the world crisis,* Ralph Linton, ed., pp. 78–106. New York: Columbia University Press.
1962c The concept of culture. In *Culture and behavior: collected essays of Clyde Kluckhohn,* Richard Kluckhohn, ed., pp. 19–73. New York: The Free Press. (Included in 1962a of the Wales bibliography.)

Kluckhohn, Clyde, and Kluckhohn, Florence R.
1947b (AAA 82) American culture: generalized orientations and class patterns. In *Conflicts of power in modern culture,* Lyman Bryson, Louis Finkelstein, and R. M. MacIver, eds., pp. 106–28. New York: Harper and Bros.

Kluckhohn, Clyde, and Leighton, Dorothea
1946a (AAA 76) *The Navaho.* Cambridge: Harvard University Press.

Kluckhohn, Clyde, and Murray, Henry A.
1948a (AAA 92) *Personality in nature, society, and culture.* New York: Alfred Knopf.

Kluckhohn, Clyde, and Reiter, Paul, eds.
1939a (AAA 22) *Preliminary report on the 1937 excavations, Bc 50–51, Chaco Canyon, New Mexico.* University of New Mexico Bulletin, Anthropological Series 3, no. 2.

Kluckhohn, Clyde, and Romney, A. Kimball
1961b (AAA 282) The Rimrock Navaho. In *Variations in value orientations,* Florence R. Kluckhohn and Fred Strodtbeck, eds., pp. 318–39. Evanston: Row, Peterson.

Kluckhohn, Clyde, and Spencer, Katherine
1940a (AAA 30) *A bibliography of the Navaho Indians.* New York: J. J. Augustin.

Kluckhohn, Clyde, and Vogt, Evon Z.
1955n (AAA 192) Obituary: The Son of Many Beads, 1866–1954. *American Anthropologist* 57:1036–37.

Kluckhohn, Clyde, and Wyman, Leland C.
1940b (AAA 32) *An introduction to Navaho chant practice with an ac-*

count of the behaviors observed in four chants. American Anthropological Association Memoir 53. Menasha.

Krader, Lawrence
   1954 Buryat religion and society. *Southwestern Journal of Anthropology* 10:332–51.

Kroeber, Alfred L.; Benedict, Ruth; Emeneau, M. B.; Herskovits, M. J.; Reichard, G. A.; and Mason, J. A.
   1943 *Franz Boas, 1858–1942.* American Anthropological Association Memoir 61. Menasha.

Kroeber, A. L., and Kluckhohn, Clyde
   1952 (AAA 143) *Culture: a critical review of concepts and definitions.* Papers of the Peabody Museum of American Archaeology and Ethnology, vol. 47, no. 1. Cambridge: Harvard University.

Leighton, Alexander H.
   1949 *Human relations in a changing world.* New York: E. P. Dutton.

Leighton, Dorothea, and Kluckhohn, Clyde
   1947 *Children of the people.* Cambridge: Harvard University Press.

Lévi-Strauss, Claude
   1963 *Structural anthropology.* New York: Basic Books.
   1964 *Mythologuiques I: le cru et le cuit.* Paris: Plon.

Linton, Ralph
   1936 *The study of man.* New York: D. Appleton-Century.

Lounsbury, Floyd
   1956 A semantic analysis of Pawnee kinship usage. *Language* 32:158–94.

Lowie, Robert
   1920 *Primitive society.* New York: Liveright.

McCombe, Leonard; Vogt, E. Z.; and Kluckhohn, Clyde
   1951 (AAA 131) *Navaho means people.* Cambridge: Harvard University Press.

Mazlisch, Bruce, ed.
   1965 *The railroad and the space program.* Cambridge: Massachusetts Institute of Technology Press.

Merton, Robert K.
   1949 *Social theory and social structure.* Glencoe: The Free Press.

Metzger, Duane, and Williams, Gerald E.
   1962 *Tenejapa medicine II: sources and harbingers of illness.* Anthropology Research Projects, Preliminary Report 14. Stanford: Stanford University Press.
   1963a A formal ethnographic analysis of Tenejapa ladino weddings. *American Anthropologist* 65:1076–1101.
   1963b Tenejapa medicine I: the curer. *Southwestern Journal of Anthropology* 19:216–34.
   1966 Some procedures and results in the study of native categories:

Tzeltal "firewood." *American Anthropologist* 68:389–407.
Michael, Donald N., ed.
1961   *Proposed studies on the implications on peaceful space activities for human affairs.* Washington: Brookings Institution.
Moore, Barrington
1950   *Soviet politics: the dilemma of power.* Cambridge: Harvard University Press.
1954   *Terror and progress USSR.* Cambridge: Harvard University Press.
Murdock, George Peter
1949   *Social structure.* New York: MacMillan.
Newcomb, Franc J., and Reichard, Gladys A.
1937   *Sandpaintings of the Navaho Shooting Chant.* New York: J. J. Augustin.
Nida, Eugene Albert
1958   Analysis of meaning and dictionary making. *International Journal of American Linguistics* 24:279–92.
Parsons, Talcott
1937   *The structure of social action.* New York: McGraw-Hill.
1949   *Essays in sociological theory.* Glencoe: The Free Press.
1960   Clyde Kluckhohn, 1905–1960. *American Sociological Review* 25:960–62.
1965a Evaluation and objectivity in social science: an interpretation of Max Weber's contribution. *UNESCO Journal of Social Sciences,* vol. 17, no. 1.
1965b Unity and diversity in the modern intellectual disciplines, pp. 39–69. In *Science and culture,* Gerald Holton, ed. Boston: Houghton Mifflin.
Parsons, Talcott; Dunlop, J. T.; Gilmore, M. P.; Kluckhohn, C.; and Taylor, O. H.
1941   (AAA 38) Toward a common language for the area of social science. Cambridge: Harvard University. Mimeographed.
Parsons, Talcott, and Kroeber, A. L.
1958   The concepts of culture and of social system. *American Sociological Review* 23:582–83.
Parsons, Talcott, and Shils, Edward A., eds.
1951   *Toward a general theory of action.* Cambridge: Harvard University Press.
Parsons, Talcott; Shils, E. A.; Allport, G. W.; Kluckhohn, C. et al.
1951   (AAA 132) Some fundamental categories of the theory of action: a general statement. In *Toward a general theory of action,* Talcott Parsons and Edward Shils, eds., pp. 3–29. Cambridge: Harvard University Press.
Parsons, Talcott, and Smelser, Neil J.
1956   *Economy and society.* Glencoe: The Free Press.

Parsons, Talcott, and Vogt, Evon Z.
 1962   Clyde Kay Maben Kluckhohn. *American Anthropologist* 64, 1,
        pt. 1:140–61.
Pepper, Stephen Coburn
 1942   World hypotheses. Berkeley: University of California Press.
Reichard, Gladys A.
 1928   *Social life of the Navaho Indians, with some attention to minor
        ceremonies.* Columbia University Contributions to Anthropology 7.
 1944   *Prayer: the compulsive word.* Monographs of the American Ethno-
        logical Society 7.
 1945   Distinctive features of Navaho religion. *Southwestern Journal of
        Anthropology* 1:199–220.
Sapir, Edward
 1927   The unconscious patterning of behavior in society. In *The un-
        conscious: a symposium,* E. S. Dummer, ed., pp. 114–42. New
        York: Alfred Knopf.
von Schelting, Alexander
 1934   *Max Weber's Wissenschaftslehre.* Tubingen: J. C. B. Mohr.
Selznick, Philip
 1949   *TVA and the grass roots.* University of California Publications in
        Culture and Society, vol. 3. Berkeley: University of California
        Press.
Sheldon, Richard
 1952   Socio-economic development in a Karelian village. Doctoral disser-
        tation, Harvard University.
Shimkin, Demitri
 1949   Recent trends in Soviet anthropology. *American Anthropologist*
        51:621–25.
Shimkin, Demitri, consulting ed.
 1954   *The new century cyclopedia of names,* C. L. Bernhart, ed. New
        York: Appleton-Century.
Shimkin, Demitri, and Sanjuan, Pedro
 1953   Culture and world view: a method of analysis applied to rural
        Russia. *American Anthropologist* 55:329–48.
Spencer, Katherine
 1957   *Mythology and values.* American Folklore Society Memoir 48.
Tax, Sol; Eiseley, L. C.; Rouse, Irving; and Voegelin, C. F., eds.
 1953   *An appraisal of anthropology today.* Chicago: University of Chi-
        cago Press.
Vogt, Evon Z., and Albert, Ethel M., eds.
 1966   *People of Rimrock.* Cambridge: Harvard University Press.
Woodbury, Richard B.
 1961   Clyde Kay Maben Kluckhohn, 1905–1960. *American Antiquity*
        26:407–9.

Wyman, Leland C.
  1957 *Beauty Way*. New York: Bollingen.
Wyman, Leland C., and Kluckhohn, Clyde
  1938 (AAA 14) *Navaho classification of their song ceremonials*. American Anthropological Association Memoir 50. Menasha.